Better Call Saul
and
Philosophy

Pop Culture and Philosophy®

General Editor: George A. Reisch

For full details of all Pop Culture and Philosophy® books, and all Open Universe® books, visit www.carusbooks.com

Pop Culture and Philosophy®

Better Call Saul and Philosophy

I Think Therefore I Scam

Edited by
JOSHUA HETER AND
BRETT COPPENGER

OPEN UNIVERSE
Chicago

Volume 8 in the series, Pop Culture and Philosophy®, edited by George A. Reisch

To find out more about Open Universe and Carus Books, visit our website at www.carusbooks.com.

Better Call Saul *and Philosophy: I Think Therefore I Scam*

ISBN: 978-1-63770-026-6

This book is also available as an e-book (978-1-63770-027-3).

Library of Congress Control Number: 2021941784

Contents

It's Showtime, Folks!

Better Call Saul started as somewhat of a joke. As legend has it, sometime during the run of *Breaking Bad*, the writers' room developed a tongue-in-cheek way of discarding potential subplots for Saul: "Ah, we'll save that one for the spin-off!", the writers quipped. This happened enough for the *Breaking Bad* crew to begin to wonder: maybe a spin-off following everyone's favorite *criminal* lawyer actually isn't such a bad idea after all. Eventual showrunners Peter Gould and Vince Gilligan then began brainstorming what a show based around Saul Goodman would be—what it *could* be. And of course, hindsight being what it is, we can now see that *Better Call Saul* was destined to be a more than worthy addition to the *Breaking Bad* canon, carving out its own place in the new golden age of television.

The story of how this book came to be is not entirely dissimilar. Initially, the idea of a book dedicated solely to the philosophical ideas found in an action-dramedy sounded like a fun but perhaps ultimately unrealistic idea. But, the more the idea was considered, the more it sounded like it wasn't so far-fetched.

Many of the philosophical ideas present in the show aren't tucked away in some small story or character detail; they are right there on the screen. Both Kim and Jimmy wrestle with moving on from what philosophers and economists call "sunk costs." In a character defining monologue, underworld fixer Mike Ehrmantraut delivers his personal manifesto; an ethical worldview he uses to justify (at least to his own satisfaction) his criminal activities. And of course, Chuck's electromagnetic hypersensitivity raises a host of fascinating philosophical questions. What control does Chuck have over his own mental states (what control do *any of us* have)? Is Chuck's condition real; what (in this case) does "real" even *mean*?

Other philosophical issues appear in the show more subtly, but they are just as much a part of the story and call for their own inquiry. What are the ethical implications of defending the guilty? What's the difference between a cartel and a government pursuing it (via the DEA) *really*? Is Nacho Varga a good man?

As the book started to come together, it became clear that the project (at least in its *aim*) is warranted to say the least; the intricacies and ideas found in *Better Call Saul* are more than deserving of having a handful of philosophers give them a good, thorough analysis. Is the final product worthy of being considered a part of the new golden age of the philosophical analysis of television? That, dear reader, is for you to decide. We certainly hope so.

Whether or not we've achieved that end, it's showtime, folks!

I

Slippin' Jimmy with a law degree is like a chimp with a machine gun

1
Scamming for Fun

PATRICK CLIPSHAM

Jimmy McGill doesn't shy away from deceiving people. He'll lie in the courtroom if it will help his client. He'll spin a yarn to get himself out of a sticky situation. But many of the times that Jimmy deceives people over the course of *Better Call Saul*, he is not motivated by the promise of some specific benefit. Jimmy and Kim often scam people simply because they find it fun.

There's clearly a difference between this 'scamming for fun' and the ways that most other characters on *Better Call Saul* use deception to manipulate others. Many main characters will weave elaborate lies in order to trick others. But when they do so, it's generally in order to acquire a specific benefit. Is this type of deception (which I refer to as 'scheming for benefits') morally better or morally worse than the scams run 'just for fun' by Jimmy and Kim?

Scamming for Fun: Jimmy and Kim

The audience's initial glimpse of Jimmy McGill is of him standing in front of a mirror, practicing a nonchalant laugh and attempting to find the words that would allow him to justify his clients' heinous act of necrophilia to a judge and jury. But the words just don't seem to be coming. With a frustrated sigh, Jimmy enters the courtroom and provides an account of his clients' behavior as nothing more than them "feeling their oats" and "going a little bananas" ("Uno").

While it's obvious that Jimmy is genuinely trying to give his clients the best defense he can, it's also clear that he's not enjoying it. Jimmy looks hesitant, uncertain, and deflated while articulating his defense. Given the unshakeable video evidence used by the prosecutor, Jimmy knows that there's no way for him to avoid, minimize, or hide the truth. But later in this same episode, the audience sees a very different side of Jimmy McGill. While talking to the two skaters Cal and Lars, Jimmy regales them with a story of "Slippin' Jimmy"—the con artist whom he used to be. Jimmy tells the story wistfully, pining for a time when he wasn't constrained by the truth.

It rapidly becomes apparent that Jimmy feels most comfortable and most at home when he's scamming. A scam, for the purposes of this chapter, is an attempt to convince someone to pursue a specific end through the use of manipulation and deception. This kind of scamming comes naturally to Jimmy, so much so that he even claims at one point that the muse "speaks through" him ("Cobbler").

And the muse works through Jimmy extremely well. His propensity for scamming becomes clear as he sets up a ruse in order to get the Kettlemans as clients ("Uno"). We also see Jimmy's comfort switching seamlessly between truth ("I'm a lawyer . . . I was running a scam") and lies ("I'm special Agent Jeffrey Steele, FBI") when he wakes up in the desert with Tuco ("Mijo"). Jimmy almost instinctively knows what to say to prevent his finger from being cut off, and he deceives Tuco with eloquence and poise.

Before long, Jimmy starts scamming consistently, almost as his default mode of interacting with the world. In "Hero," Jimmy decides to drum up business for his firm by staging the rescue of a worker who was removing his billboard. Those who know Jimmy well (like Kim and his brother Chuck) have no doubt that he set up this scene. Despite his insistence in "Mijo" that "I'm not backsliding. This isn't Slippin' Jimmy," Jimmy can't resist the allure of scamming.

For Jimmy, scamming is not merely a tool or a trick he can use to get what he wants out of people. It's not just a means to an end. Scamming, for Jimmy, is an activity that's challenging and fun. He almost sees it as a craft, or an art form. And it doesn't take much coaxing for others (most notably, Kim Wexler) to become seduced by the allure of scamming. While representing themselves as Giselle St. Clair and Viktor, Jimmy and Kim revel in the joy of manipulating a deserving mark ("Switch").

This is the feature of Jimmy and Kim's tendency to scam that I find most interesting. When Jimmy and Kim participate in their antics at a variety of bars, they don't do it with any clear objective in mind. In contrast to nearly every other character in the show, their deceptions are not carefully curated, or geared at some greater purpose. Rather, they take pleasure in the act of scamming itself. It is a pastime, a hobby, or an art that they enjoy mastering together. Even when the pair must refrain from scamming in order to protect Jimmy from further legal consequences, their preferred pastime is to fantasize about the cons they could be running. Once Jimmy gets carried away and proposes a scam that seems a little bit too realistic, Kim has to remind him that they are just pretending ("Expenses").

Like many of the other characters on the show, Jimmy and Kim are liars. But they're specific kinds of liars. They don't just lie to get what they want, and they don't lie out of a compulsion to do so. They lie in the context of scams because *scamming is fun*. And this feature makes them unique characters in the context of the show.

Scheming for Benefits: Mike, Gus, and Chuck

While the cast of *Better Call Saul* is peppered with a rogues' gallery of criminals willing to commit horrific acts, none of them share Jimmy and Kim's love of scamming.

Consider Mike Ehrmantrout. Unlike Jimmy, Mike does not have an immediate inclination towards scamming. In fact, Mike seems to actively avoid it. In "Five-O," Mike has a need to check on the progress made by the police from Philadelphia regarding the murders he committed in retaliation for his son Matt's death. Rather than simply developing a ruse he could pull off himself, he brings in Jimmy as his attorney and gives him clear instructions about how to spill coffee on the detective, thus giving Mike an opportunity to steal a notebook. Unlike Kim and Jimmy, Mike does not seem to take any enjoyment in the scam. He approaches it with severity and seriousness.

From Mike's perspective, this con was not fun. It was meant to help him accomplish a very specific goal—gather information about the status of the investigation into his crimes. For Mike, deceiving is something that is done in a calculated, cold, and effective way, but is in no way enjoyable or playful. Even when Mike develops a complex scheme to trick Tuco into being charged with severe crimes ("Gloves Off"), he does so only to find a solution to Nacho's problems that won't involve murder. Mike doesn't revel in the opportunity to trick Tuco, but approaches it with a dispassionate, cold, clinical perspective. In other words, Mike will lie, deceive, and scheme when doing so is the only way for him to get a specific benefit. But he does not scam for fun.

Similar points can be made about Gustavo Fring. In some ways, Gus's entire life is one big scam. He hides in plain sight by constantly misrepresenting who he is and what he has done and does not hesitate to lie when he will benefit from it. For example, after Hector Salamanca turns up at Los Pollos Hermanos, Gus tells his staff an elaborate fabrication about his history with these men in Michoacan ("Sabrosito"). But, unlike Jimmy, Gus deceives others with complete sobriety, and only when he has no other option. While Gus lies to nearly everyone all the time, he always does so in a cool, calculated, and purposeful way. He schemes in order to protect himself or to get something that he wants. But he never revels in these schemes. As Mike says to Gus in "Dedicado a Max:" "You don't do anything without a reason." Similarly, criminals like Nacho Varga lie and present falsehoods in careful ways to protect themselves and get what they want. Even Jimmy's own brother Chuck regularly uses deception to acquire certain benefits. For example, Chuck told an elaborate lie about the power going out in order to hide the symptoms of his disease from his then-wife. And in order to hurt Jimmy, Chuck claims that he "exaggerated his symptoms in order to extract the truth" ("Chicanery").

The overall conclusion to draw from this analysis is that Jimmy and—later in the series—Kim, have a unique perspective towards deception. For every other character in the show, scheming and lying are mere tools. They are something that can be used to achieve a specific goal, or to get one out of trouble when one's back is against the wall. Whereas Jimmy and Kim are *scammers* (people with a propensity for scamming others), the other characters above are *schemers* (people who develop complicated deceptions in order to receive specific benefits). This analysis raises the question: is it morally better to be a scammer or a schemer?

Does Scamming for Fun Cause Harm?

One of the most obvious things that might be wrong with scamming for fun is that doing so can often cause harm. After all, such deceptions frequently result in people being hurt.

For example, when Chuck tricks Jimmy into confessing that he changed the address on the Mesa Verde paperwork, he caused significant harm to both Jimmy and himself ("Klick"). This scheme not only led to Jimmy being suspended from practicing law for a year (and thus threatening the law office established by him and Kim), but also served to further fray the fraternal relationship between Jimmy and Chuck. This deception also led to Chuck being harmed in a number of ways. His lie set in motion a series of events that culminated in his mental illness being exposed in front of the Bar Association ("Chicanery"), conflicts between him and Howard, and his eventual suicide in "Lantern." There are, in other words, many examples of lies, deceptions, and schemes causing extensive harm in *Better Call Saul*.

Even schemes that initially seem to have positive overall consequences ultimately result in more harm than good. In "Gloves Off" Mike avoids assassinating Tuco with a scheme that involves convincing Tuco to attack Mike in front of the police. The consequence of this is that Tuco is imprisoned which, at first glance, seems to benefit everyone. Nacho can remain secure in the fact that he will not be one of Tuco's impulsive murder victims (as was their former confederate, Dog). The Salamanca cartel no longer has to worry about a methamphetamine-addled Tuco generating more attention and problems for them. And, of course, the people of Albuquerque will be safer with one fewer murdering lunatic on the streets. But, while this one lie by Mike was designed to generate only good consequences, we can easily see how his plan fell through. After Mike tricks Tuco, Hector Salamanca threatens his granddaughter ("Bali Ha'i"). This causes Mike to lie to the police and, more indirectly, leads to his involvement with Gus Fring and the cartels (after all, if Mike had not had reason to interact with the Salamancas, Gus would have never had to prevent him from attempting to assassinate Hector). Thus, even though this one deception by Mike had noble goals, it ultimately produced significantly more harm than good. The path created by this one scheme ultimately leads to Mike's demise at the hands of Walter White and the seizure of all the funds that he had secured in order to provide for his granddaughter Kaylee.

In sum, *Better Call Saul* provides us with ample evidence that even schemes that seem to be designed to have only good consequences can often lead to very negative results. But, while many of the lies depicted in the show wind up causing significantly more harm than good, there are a number of examples where Jimmy scams people in a way that produces almost entirely good consequences. Jimmy (or, later in the series, Saul) often seems to wield his ability to scam in order to produce generally good outcomes that benefit everyone involved.

When Kim is having difficulty convincing one of her *pro bono* clients to accept a plea bargain, Saul quickly develops and implements a plan to represent himself as a district attorney who has found more evidence against the client ("Magic Man"). This small scam allows Kim to convince the client to take the deal, thus minimizing the time that he would have to be away from his small children. And yet, despite the noble reasons for telling this lie, it makes Kim very uncomfortable and she is hesitant to participate.

There are plenty of other examples of Jimmy's scams resulting in overall positive consequences. By scamming the Kettlemans into revealing the location of their money, he manages to return millions to the county and convince them to take a deal which significantly benefits their family ("Bingo"). By tricking the residents of Sandpiper into thinking that their bus broke down, Jimmy manages to initiate a class-action lawsuit that was in everyone's best interest (except, of course, for the crooked retirement facilities) ("Amarillo"). Even Jimmy and Kim's first scam (against the reviled hedge fund employee Ken) seems as if it resulted in a form of justice for the immoral, crass, and manipulative stockbroker who was trying to bilk two ignorant heirs out of (at least a portion) of their newfound wealth ("Switch").

Thus, there are many examples of Jimmy scamming people in such a way that the scams do not result in morally significant harm, but rather in genuinely good consequences. There are, of course, exceptions to this general pattern. The first con we see Jimmy orchestrate in the show is his attempt to manipulate the Kettlemans, which directly leads to threats of murder and multiple broken bones for Jimmy's confederates ("Uno"). But keep in mind that this con was not developed just for fun, but rather in order to get new clients. Thus, this example seems more like Jimmy 'scheming for benefits' rather than 'scamming for fun'.

So Jimmy's fun scams are not generally as harmful as the schemes weaved by others in order to procure benefits. But what if harm is not what makes scamming wrong? What if it's wrong because it involves using, manipulating, or disrespecting people in a way that is inherently morally problematic?

Does Scamming for Fun Disrespect People?

Perhaps the wrongness of scamming for fun has nothing to do with whether those scams are harmful. Maybe all forms of deception are wrong because the deceiver treats other humans as tools or objects, rather than as individuals who should be afforded basic moral respect.

Plenty of philosophers have suggested that this is how we should think about the wrongness of deception. Immanuel Kant famously argued that it is always morally wrong to treat another person as a means to your own end, rather than as an 'end in themselves.' Lying to people, scamming them, or treating them as pawns in your scheme therefore *disrespects* those people by treating them as if they are little more than tools or objects of use.

But even if we accept this view of the wrongness of deception, we do not have to accept that all scams and schemes involve an equal level of disrespect. Certain forms of deception might be more or less disrespectful of others. Furthermore, there are good reasons for thinking that many of Jimmy's scams are less disrespectful than the schemes hatched by other characters. A closer look at two different examples of cons can illustrate this.

First, consider why Howard and Chuck lied to Jimmy in order to deprive him a job at HHM ("Pimento"). Chuck chose to deceive Jimmy in this situation so that he could achieve a very specific goal: ensure that Jimmy will not acquire the same kind of notoriety and prestige that Chuck did. In this case, Chuck was not only depriving Jimmy of knowing the truth, but was also manipulating Jimmy so that Chuck could benefit.

The second example is the scam run by Kim and Jimmy on the stockbroker Ken ("Switch"). While both Jimmy and Kim benefited from this exchange, it doesn't seem accurate to say that they were deceiving Ken in order to acquire a specific benefit. After all, what did they really get out of this scam? It's true that they had the opportunity to drink some very expensive and rare tequila, but neither of them had a particularly strong desire to try this beverage (or had even heard of it) earlier. They are manipulating and lying to Ken, to be sure, but they are not using him as a means to any specific end. Kim and Jimmy are just scamming because it's fun. Seeing what they can get away with is like a game to them. They treat Ken more like an unwitting participant in their game, rather than as a tool to be manipulated to their ends. They deprive him of true information about who they are and what they want, but don't exhibit the same level of disrespect that Chuck exhibited to Jimmy.

These examples suggest that there are at least two ways that scamming and scheming can disrespect people, and that one is more morally severe than the other.

One of the ways that lying can disrespect people is that it leads them to base their decisions on false information. This makes it difficult—if not impossible—for these people to be able to make their own, authentic, free, decisions (as Kant put it, this type of lying fails to treat people as "ends in themselves"). All forms of lying, scamming, and scheming (whether it's just for fun or in order to get some specific benefit) involve this kind of disrespect.

But sometimes, a lie can disrespect someone in a much deeper sense. Sometimes, lying to someone involves treating that person as a tool or an instrument that is being used to achieve a specific goal. In the terminology I used above, these types of schemes involve treating someone as a means to an end. When people like Jimmy and Kim scam for fun, it is not as clear that they are trying to use another individual as a tool, or an object. Thus, while scamming for fun does involve a degree of disrespect to other individuals, this disrespect is much more limited and less serious than the kinds of disrespect that is exhibited when one person hatches a scheme in order to manipulate another into giving them some specific benefit.

Does Scamming for Fun Make You a Worse Person?

A third and very plausible concern about scamming for fun is that doing so consistently would turn you into a dishonest person who was very inclined to lie to, deceive, and manipulate others. In other words, even if scamming for fun is not necessarily harmful, and even if it does not involve disrespect to the same extent as does lying to get some specific benefit, won't it eventually turn you into a morally worse, less virtuous, person?

This concern stems from the observation that, as people get used to scamming others, they tend to grow more comfortable with it and might become more likely to lie, deceive, or manipulate others as one of their natural, default behaviors. *Better Call Saul* actually presents a very interesting case study of this exact kind of character development. While Kim initially rejected and was firmly opposed to Jimmy's tendency towards scamming, participating in these scams (as her alternate persona Giselle St. Clair) rapidly becomes her favorite pastime. And this recreational scamming quickly leads her down a path that results in her being unambiguously "in the game" ("Bad Choice Road"). Kim is almost a perfect case study of how scamming for fun can change you for the worse and can result in significant moral corruption.

But is it inevitable that scamming for fun will result in this corruption and loss of virtue? *Better Call Saul* provides us with two reasons to doubt this.

First, it is clear that not everyone who scams for fun is made morally worse as a result. Jimmy, for example, didn't start off as someone who predominantly scams for fun. He honed his deceptive craft by conning people out of money at bars, or convincing business owners to pay him off after he "slipped" on their property. He only acknowledges and appreciates the sheer pleasure and fun of scamming after he's already moved on from this lifestyle and no longer needs to con people in order to earn money. While Jimmy and Marco used to deceive people in order to get the things they wanted, they later indulge in a literal montage of cons just for the fun of it ("Marco"). In other words, scamming for fun didn't make Jimmy a worse or more dishonest person. He was already dishonest, and this tendency towards dishonesty is what made him choose to scam for fun. Scamming for fun did not make Jimmy a dishonest person. Rather, being a dishonest person made Jimmy scam for fun.

Second, some of the most morally corrupt and dangerous people in the show—such as Gus Fring or Lalo Salamanca— are rarely, if ever, depicted as scamming for fun. Their violence, ruthlessness, and lack of moral compass does not seem to have stemmed from an impulse to lie to others for the sheet enjoyment of it. Rather, it comes from their upbringing and their past exposure to criminality and violence. This suggests that some of the worse moral vices don't have a particularly strong connection to scamming for fun. This may not amount to a complete vindication of scamming for fun, but it does problematize any attempt to claim that scamming for fun has a particularly worrisome impact on a person's moral character.

Not So Bad after All

Overall, Jimmy and Kim serve as a compelling case study regarding the motivations for deception. They are unique in *Better Call Saul* in the sense that they love scamming and often do it just for fun. But Jimmy and Kim's scams are rarely significantly harmful, and often have positive consequences. There are also plausible arguments in favor of the conclusion that it is more disrespectful to deceive someone in order to receive a benefit from them (scheme) than it is to lie to them just for fun (scam). And finally, there's no strong connection between a tendency to scam for fun and some of the most ethically significant character flaws depicted in *Better Call Saul*. Jimmy and Kim do love to scam, but this doesn't mean they're bad people.

2
Don't Go to Lawyers for Moral Guidance

SHANE J. RALSTON

I'm not a criminal. I'm a lawyer.

—JIMMY McGILL

If it were followed by "I'm a president," Richard Nixon's tele-vised denial ("I am not a crook") would be tantamount to Jimmy McGill's self-portrayal in *Better Call Saul*. Out of the crooked timber of humanity, an honest president or an ethical lawyer rarely emerges. They're like needles in a haystack. Nevertheless, it's worthwhile to search for these rare artifacts and, in the process, ask, "Why do so many lawyers (and presi-dents) fall from grace, transforming into morally bad or corrupt actors?"

The ability to be a good or ethical person can deteriorate over time. In their personal and professional lives, people can make consistently poor choices in their capacity as moral agents. In turn, they cultivate flawed habits or what are often referred to as *vices*. Jimmy McGill's trajectory is, without a doubt, a harrowing story of moral decline. In some ways, his transformation into Saul Goodman resembles a trite story about how a profession, lawyering, corrupts its practitioners. On a deeper level, McGill's journey involves a fundamental change in how he habitually interacts with his environment, a change of motivation and disposition that is, almost entirely, a change for the worse. To know the content of Jimmy's character is to be familiar with his story, a story of moral decline and eth-ical failure.

While moral philosophers (such as Immanuel Kant and John Stuart Mill) and developmental psychologists (such as Jean Piaget and Lawrence Kohlberg) have long discussed what it means to cultivate moral acuity, few have properly thought about moral decline. Thinkers who appeal to habit, such as John Dewey and Pierre Bourdieu, can help make sense of Jimmy's fall from grace and exactly why, ultimately, lawyers make poor ethicists. If you need advice about how you ought to act in any morally problematic situation (such as whether to lie to a murderer or steal to feed your family), better not call Saul—but why exactly?

Good Jimmy, Meet Evil Saul

A flashback to Jimmy's choice to give up a life of scamming and petty crime, a time long ago when he earned the nickname Slippin' Jimmy, foreshadows his decline ("Nacho"). Jimmy makes the monstrous decision to embark on the path of the law. The scene also foreshadows Jimmy's transformation into Saul Goodman, a man who's anything but good. After a period of incarceration in a Chicago prison (for an offense that could have easily landed him on a sex offenders' registry), Jimmy receives a visit from his elder brother and practicing lawyer, Chuck.

Chuck agrees to help Jimmy so long as Jimmy doesn't return to his old, criminal ways. "It's about time I made both of us proud," Jimmy promises his brother. Although a legal career awaits, Chuck will never see his younger brother as anything more than Slippin' Jimmy with a law degree, a likely factor catalyzing his moral decline.

Years later Jimmy learns that he's passed the State Bar Exam after years of taking correspondence courses at the University of American Samoa ("Rico"). Kim Wexler greets the news with joy and excitement, giving Jimmy a smacking kiss on the lips. When he asks Chuck if there'll be a job waiting for him at the HHM firm, after years of loyal service as a mail clerk, Chuck opines, "Of course, I cannot imagine why not." In the next scene, a party in the HHM mailroom, he finds out from his future nemesis, Howard, that there's no place for him at the firm. Jimmy's disappointment is palpable. The remainder of the episode chronicles the two-man legal crusade of Jimmy and Chuck to defend assisted living residents from economic exploitation by an unscrupulous corporation, Sandpiper. It's one of Jimmy's last noble deeds before going over to the dark side. Chuck convinces Jimmy to refer the case to HHM. Jimmy exclaims, "Finally out of the mailroom, huh?"

Jimmy's transformation from scammer to lawyer is similar to the origin stories of superheroes insofar as it offers valuable insight into the character's development. In this case, it's probably closer to the origin story of a villain or a villain-in-the-making, offering insight into the character's moral decline. The tale of Jimmy's ethical failure begins with him choosing to become a lawyer, proceeds to him helping the elderly fight a corporation and reaches its lowest point when he defends members of the drug cartel. It's not as if good Jimmy could meet evil Saul. Instead, the process of moral decline is steady and slow. To gain a deeper understanding of the process, it's important to keep the origin story in mind.

Hey Jimmy, You're Getting Worse!

Is Jimmy's transformation from a con-artist to a lawyer a movement towards redemption or decline? As the story progresses, we get the sense that lawyering has far worse consequences than Jimmy's petty cons. Indeed, as a lawyer, the line between right and wrong is always subject to interpretation and negotiation. Sometimes what is considered ethically wrong or morally repugnant can be recast as legally necessary (such as a plea deal that significantly reduces the prison sentence of a serial rapist).

In his early career as a public defender, Jimmy implores the state's prosecutor, "Say the words 'I accept the deal'." Plea bargaining is the metaphorical gateway to increasingly suspect moral behavior, including scams for quick cash, defending criminals in exchange for the proceeds of their crimes and, eventually, representing members of illegal drug manufacturing and distribution networks, helping them to escape prosecution for their crimes.

Most developmental psychologists and moral philosophers are more concerned with moral growth than decline. Jean Piaget conceived of moral development as a constructive process whereby ethical concepts result from the interplay of a child's actions and thoughts.

Following Piaget, Lawrence Kohlberg outlined six stages of moral development: 1. adhering to a set of strict rules; 2. evaluating actions relative to people's needs; 3. conformity for the sake of getting along or being nice; 4. respecting authority figures; 5. assessing actions relative to individual rights; and 6. appealing to ethical principles using abstract reasoning.

The English moral philosopher John Stuart Mill thought that good moral judgment was the outcome of choosing the alternative that maximized human happiness, especially happiness associated with the higher faculties.

The German philosopher Immanuel Kant theorized that moral reasoning involves following the categorical imperative, a procedure for determining the maxim or rule underlying your action, universalizing it and seeing whether it leads to a contradiction.

Choosing to maximize happiness or to follow the categorical imperative raises the question: Why do those who are perfectly capable of determining the right course of action instead consistently choose the wrong path? Moral decline or ethical failure is philosophically uninteresting to most psychologists and philosophers, yet utterly fascinating to the rest of us!

Writers who do consider moral decline are those who about the power of habit. The French sociologist Pierre Bourdieu sees habit (or what he refers to as 'habitus') as a disposition to action, both shaped by past events and channelled by future possibilities. The American philosopher John Dewey likewise thinks of habit as a tendency toward action cultivated over time, enabling growth or decline, and resulting from an organism's regular interaction with its environment.

Habit helps explain Jimmy's fall from grace. His moral decline involved mounting influences within his environment (such as intense relationships with criminal clients, a brother who believed he couldn't ever be a legitimate lawyer, rejection by his brother's legal firm, HHM) that slowly wore down his will to do good. In other words, Jimmy developed a habit of moving down morally questionable paths, even when the right or principled course of action was staring him right in the face!

Perhaps someone should have staged an intervention, saying to Jimmy, "Hey, you're getting worse!" Occasionally Kim Wexler reminds Jimmy that he has a choice to be "a colorful lawyer" or a respectable member of the legal profession. But aren't there rules to stop lawyers from choosing the path of immorality and vice?

Don't Lawyers Have Rules?

There are ethical rules governing members of the legal profession. Following the American Bar Association's (ABA) Model Rules of Professional Conduct, each state adopts its own version of the rules and sanction lawyers who break them.

But, not always. Unfortunately, many get away with violating the ABA rules because, as a profession, lawyers and judges dislike bad press and in-fighting. Both fuel the hatred of lawyering and inspire all those hilarious lawyer jokes Jimmy repeats during the dinner party with Chuck and his wife ("Rebecca"). "This is why people hate lawyers," Jimmy exclaims to Kim, responding to her concerns about incriminating her clients the Kettlemans, a family that enriched themselves by embezzling $1.5 million from the county treasury ("Nacho"). Jimmy decides to represent Nacho Varga, a criminal accused of kidnapping the Kettlemans, when the truth is that the Kettlemans kidnapped themselves after receiving an anonymous phone call from Jimmy, who had become privy to Nacho's plans to steal their embezzled money. Criminals stealing from criminals, a drama made even more interesting when lawyers are involved!

Jimmy confesses to Kim that lawyer-client confidentiality prevented him from disclosing Nacho's plans to the police. Jimmy says to Kim . . .

> I was worried my guy Varga [Nacho] was going after their money— and he was. He was gonna rip them off. I deduced it from a conversation that we had. It was lawyer to client, so there was confidentiality issues. But, I called the Kettlemans anonymously. ("Hero")

However, practically all codes of legal ethics exclude plans to commit crimes from protection under attorney-client confidentiality. The reason Jimmy didn't disclose his suspicions to authorities (instead choosing to do the bare minimum by alerting the Kettlemans with an anonymous phone call) is that he didn't want his criminal client to kill him.

After he discovers the Kettlemans camping in the woods, they offer Jimmy a bribe to stay quiet. Jimmy counters, offering to take the money as a retainer for his legal services, but they decline. When he pushes the Kettlemans for a reason, they frankly reply: "You're the kind of lawyer guilty people hire." Later, Jimmy confides in Mike Ehrmantraut (who helped him steal the embezzled funds back from the Kettlemans), "I know what stopped me" [from taking off with over a million dollars in embezzled funds] "and it's never stopping me again" ("Marco"). Without a conscience, good Jimmy's transition to evil Saul is nearly complete.

So, is Saul Goodman the kind of person you'd call for advice? What kind of advice? According to the Kettlemans, you should only call Saul for legal advice if you're guilty. For his many guilty clients, Saul offers advice that often frees them from criminal responsibility for their misdeeds. For those looking to do the right thing, perhaps it would be better to call an ethicist, not a lawyer like Saul Goodman.

Moral Flexibility and Doing the Right Thing

Mike Ehrmantraut calls Saul and asks, "Are you still morally flexible?" ("Cobbler"). Theirs is a relationship based on strong loyalty and tolerance of immorality. Jimmy has a way of defending his client's interests by wilfully bending the rules, especially when those interests are entangled with illegal activities.

In legal jargon, we say that a lawyer must be a genuine advocate for his client's cause, which means that there cannot be conflicting loyalties (conflicts of interest) or the sharing of the client's communications with others outside the relationship (attorney-client privilege). Of course, knowledge that a client is engaged in illegal activities defeats any presumption of privilege. Sometimes the end, though, justifies the choice of illicit means.

The proceeding to disbar Jimmy, instigated by his brother Chuck, is an excellent example of how Jimmy chooses unethical means to achieve his ends ("Chicanery"). Jimmy changed an address on documents for one of HHM's key clients, Mesa Verde, in order to gift the account to his partner, Kim Wexler. Jimmy's brother, Chuck, was blamed for the mistake. Suspecting Jimmy's scheme, Chuck faked depression and suicidal tendencies to stealthily extract a taped confession from Jimmy. On the tape, Jimmy concedes that he altered evidence and that doing so is a felony, which could lead to his disbarment. In the disbarment proceedings, Jimmy lies, claiming that he falsely confessed to save his brother from killing himself. Exposing Chuck's psychological condition as if it were an entirely feigned physical ailment (Electromagnetic Sensitivity), Jimmy causes his brother's breakdown. Consequently, Chuck divulges the real reason for embarking on a crusade to derail his brother's legal career: jealousy.

Jimmy could have lain down and taken it, accepting the consequences of his brother's vindictive plot to have him disbarred. Instead, he fought back, not with the truth, but with lies. Was it prudent for Jimmy to fight fire with fire, to achieve victory by undermining his brother's mental state? Yes, if the point was to avoid being disbarred no matter what the moral costs. The strategy of unhinging his brother was not ethical; indeed, it reflected poorly on Jimmy's moral character. It was another disappointing step in the direction of Jimmy's moral decline, down the slippery slope to his full conversion into Saul Goodman, friend and lawyer of criminals everywhere.

The Perfect Is the Enemy of the Good

Jimmy and Kim interview a candidate, Francesca, to serve as a legal secretary for their two new solo practices ("Witness"). When Kim objects to Jimmy's quick decision to hire the first person they interview, Jimmy responds: "Kim, you're looking for perfection, and perfection is the enemy of the perfectly adequate."

This response suggests a defense against the claim that Jimmy's experience is one of moral decline. It's possible that he's just trying to do what's needed to get by, and struggling to live up to some high-minded moral ideal won't cut it. Plainly, he's an ethical pragmatist, not a moral perfectionist.

In Immanuel Kant's moral theory, the tension between perfectionism and pragmatism is best illustrated by reference to his distinction between a categorical imperative and an imperative of prudence. A categorical imperative is a moral rule that if made universal would motivate someone to do good unconditionally (possess a good will) and respect every affected person's autonomy (treat other rational agents as ends-in-themselves, not means for the satisfaction of one's personal ends). An imperative of prudence is a rule of thumb or skill, recommending certain means to effectively achieve a preferred end, regardless of the morality of the action.

'To be a good terrorist, make good bombs' is an imperative of prudence. 'Treat others as you would expect to be treated' is a categorical imperative. Jimmy McGill consistently chooses to follow imperatives of prudence; to choose any means whatsoever in order to achieve his ends; and to show little or no concern for the morality or immorality of his choices. This is, itself, a form of moral decline. Arguably, the same insensitivity to moral matters that Saul Goodman displays is exactly what is required to be a diligent advocate for criminal clients. So, if you commit a crime and need some advice about how to bend the rules and achieve a legal victory (imperative of prudence), better call Saul. But if you wish to choose the right course of action in a morally problematic situation (categorical or moral imperative), it's better to avoid lawyers like Jimmy altogether. In these instances, an ethicist or moral philosopher would be a better choice.

Better Not Call Saul—But Why Exactly?

So, why is an ethicist better than a lawyer when it comes to selecting the right course of action? In his separability thesis, the legal philosopher H.L.A. Hart claims that "it is in no sense a necessary truth that laws reproduce or satisfy certain demands of morality, though in fact they have often done so" (*The Concept of the Law*, pp. 181–82). In other words, to say some action is legal does not make it moral, even though many claims about what is moral have, as a matter of historical record, become codified in law. Sometimes our moral obligations far outstrip our legal obligations (such as the duty to be a Good Samaritan, though Good Samaritan laws often protect someone who attempts to do good from being successfully sued for unintended consequences). Following Hart's thesis, it's best to distinguish ethical advice from legal advice. The two are separable.

Princeton University philosopher Peter Singer outlines three advantages that ethicists have over ordinary untrained individuals, including lawyers. First, the ethicist's prior training in argumentation and critical thinking equip her to make valid inferences in a way the ordinary person cannot. Second, her understanding of moral concepts and how to deploy them in specific scenarios prepares the moral philosopher for the task of ethical analysis better than others. Lastly, the ethicist can devote more time than the average person to exploring moral issues.

While they may be well trained in crafting legal arguments, lawyers rarely deploy moral concepts. Outside of their busy law practices, they typically have little time to delve deeply into complex ethical issues (unless they're legal academics). Perhaps legal ethics is an oxymoron. Appealing to the rules that govern the legal profession can amount to saying "I'm not a crook" or "I'm not a criminal" while justifying a tolerable level of immorality. Too often good lawyering means invoking imperatives of prudence, not categorical or moral imperatives.

Truth be told, the ethical rules of lawyering do little to stop the Saul Goodmans of the world from achieving success for their clients at any moral cost. Too frequently lawyers display the habit of doling out poor ethical advice, either by falsely claiming to have expertise in moral philosophy or by conflating ethical and legal subject-matter. As Hart reminds us, moral and legal advice are separable. Lawyers make poor ethicists. So, do we really want lawyers giving us ethical advice? Not unless we value the judgment of those who make moral decline look like on-the-job training.

3
Can It Be Right to Defend the Guilty?

DANIEL COOK

Is it right for a lawyer to defend someone they know is guilty? And, if so, should there be any limitations on how guilty clients are defended? *Better Call Saul* forces us to confront these difficult legal and ethical questions through the rogue practices of Jimmy McGill and his alter ego, Saul Goodman, as they relapse into defending guilty clients time and again.

Jimmy having been cast as a marginal figure within both his family and society, we often find ourselves sympathizing with his decisions to represent guilty clients, as they symbolize his defense of nonconformism and ultimately himself. We even admire or praise Jimmy's conduct in certain cases. But there are also moments when our admiration turns to disapproval. Our intuitive moral judgments therefore seem to be leading us to say that it can be both morally right and morally wrong for lawyers to defend clients they know are guilty. How, if at all, can this conflict be resolved?

Answering this question requires us to look beyond the moral judgments themselves and instead toward the strength of the justifications underlying those judgments. We need to examine *why* we regard an action as being right or wrong and whether the explanation offered in support of that judgment stands up to scrutiny. Philosophers are especially interested in what *makes* right acts right and wrong acts wrong, often constructing elaborate frameworks to help us determine whether an act is right or wrong.

Two Senses of 'Guilt'

The language of guilt is a staple of our everyday moral discourse. As an effective state, we regularly express its possession by ourselves ('I feel guilty about . . .') and ascribe it to others ('You appear to feel guilty about . . .'). There are also times when we prescribe feelings of guilt by stipulating that a person should feel guilty about something.

But the language of guilt can be deployed without directly referring to our emotions. To say that 'this person is guilty of x' does not necessarily mean that the person does or should feel guilty about x. Rather, we interpret it as a factual statement concerning that person's *moral blameworthiness* for x. It's this meaning of 'guilt', with its focus on moral blameworthiness, that is relevant: we're concerned with the moral propriety of lawyers defending individuals, whom they know are morally blameworthy, for their actions.

There is, however, another sense of the term 'guilt'. As well as being morally blameworthy for an action, I might also be *legally blameworthy* for it. We can say that a person is legally blameworthy for y if the law prohibits individuals from doing y or allowing y to materialize, but that person is nevertheless found by a court of law to have done y or failed to prevent y from arising and that person satisfies the basic criteria for legal responsibility for doing y or allowing y to arise. It is this notion of legal blameworthiness that is captured when a jury returns a verdict of 'guilty' or a defendant pleads guilty to an offense. Consequently, we now have two related, though distinct, senses of 'guilt': moral guilt and legal guilt.

Yet moral guilt does not imply legal guilt, or *vice versa*. I might be morally guilty of insulting somebody, but this does not mean that my actions constitute a criminal offense (or would be deemed so by a jury). Nor does the fact that I have been found guilty in a court of law entail that I am morally guilty. We need only think about laws criminalizing homosexuality to recognize how legal guilt need not entail moral guilt. Given that we can appear to separate legal and moral guilt, there are four scenarios we might visit when looking at the problem of defending the guilty.

We're only concerned here with scenario (i), since the problem of defending the guilty is typically conceived as involving clients whose lawyers believe them to be both legally and morally guilty.

Defending Legally and Morally Guilty Clients

Lalo Salamanca gazes nonchalantly around the courtroom as he waits for his bail hearing to commence. "Who's that?" "That's gotta be his family," replies Saul, "Fred Whalen. The guy who

	Legally Guilty	Not Legally Guilty
Morally Guilty	**(i)** **Legally Guilty +** **Morally Guilty**	**(ii)** **Not Legally Guilty +** **Morally Guilty**
Not Morally Guilty	**(iii)** **Legally Guilty +** **Not Morally Guilty**	**(iv)** **Not Legally Guilty +** **Not Morally Guilty**

died at the TravelWire." Stung by Lalo's failure to recognize the victim's name, Saul briefly turns again in the direction of the sobbing family, prompting him to evaluate the moral status of the defense he's about to provide. The defense in question alleges that an important prosecution witness was tampered with, carrying the implication that Lalo has been wrongly accused of murder due to being deliberately misidentified ("JMM"). As Saul knows that Lalo did in fact murder Fred Whalen, would it be right for Saul to attempt to secure bail for his client?

You may notice that Saul's defense is, in effect, attempting to deliberately mislead—or *lie* to—the court. Cast in these terms, we might instinctively feel that it would be wrong for Saul to attempt to secure bail for Lalo. But what justifications can be offered in support of this position?

One response is that there is something about the act of lying to the court which itself makes Saul's conduct wrongful. According to moral theories of this ilk, we need to look beyond the effects of an action to determine its propriety; some actions are simply prohibited irrespective of whether they produce morally good consequences. An influential contribution to ethics is Immanuel Kant's moral theory.

For Kant, the moral permissibility of an action is determined by its compliance with the moral law (the 'categorical imperative'). The most well-known formulation of the categorical imperative is the Formula of the Universal Law, which states that we should "Act only in accordance with that maxim through which you can at the same time will that it become a universal law." As cryptic as it sounds, Kant's idea is fairly simple. We must first formulate a maxim for our contemplated action. Once we have our maxim, we need to see whether we can will the maxim while also willing it as a universal law of nature. If we can, we are permitted to act according to our maxim; if not, we are under a moral duty not to do so. So how would Kantians approach the issue of a lawyer lying to the court so that their client can avoid criminal sanctions?

A good starting point would be to draw an analogy between lying in court and Kant's discussion of insincere promises. While surveying the different duties which flow from the categorical imperative, Kant considers whether, in order to obtain a loan, a person in financial straits is permitted to promise that they will repay money despite knowing that they will be unable to. His conclusion is that we are under a perfect duty not to make such promises. We must *always* refrain from making lying promises to secure a loan. Kant's reasoning is that if we were to will that making lying promises were a universal law of nature, the very practice of making such promises cannot exist because nobody would believe them. We have a contradiction in conception: I'm conceiving of a world in which I can obtain a loan by making a lying promise but where the practice of making lying promises cannot exist.

Equally, Kantians might consider that the maxim 'If I know that my client is legally and morally guilty, I will lie to the court in order to absolve them of criminal liability' yields a similar result when cast as a law of nature. For if lawyers were to lie to the court to allow their clients to escape justice whenever those clients were guilty, the practice of lying to the court could not exist: the courts would give no weight to counsel's arguments, thereby frustrating the purpose of making deceitful submissions. Kantians would therefore regard our intuitive response to Saul's contemplated defense as well-founded by pointing to the fact that he would be violating his perfect duty not to lie to the court. But is it really convincing to maintain that a lawyer should *never* lie to the court so that their guilty client avoids criminal liability? The absolute nature of this duty seems questionable.

Consider Jemma's case. Jemma is an exceptional doctor who works at Albuquerque Memorial Hospital and specializes in complex, life-saving neurosurgery. She is widely considered to be a pioneer in her field. As the techniques involved in her procedures are cutting-edge, Jemma is the only person in the world capable of performing them. One morning, however, Jemma was caught on CCTV stealing her favorite candy from a local supermarket. After explaining that she will lose her medical license if she is convicted, Jemma asks you to lie to the court by telling the jury that she did not commit the theft and that someone else took the candy. What should you do? On a strict reading of the Kantian position outlined above, the answer seems to be 'nothing': you are prohibited from lying to the court even though Jemma's present and future patients will die without her intervention. This is the case even if, by pure coincidence, you find out that your best friend happens to be one of the patients Jemma is due to operate on. Although Kantians will point out that you are not morally responsible for the tragic consequences of a situation created by Jemma's poor judgment, this does little to allay the feeling that not lying is still somehow *wrong* in this situation.

Looking at Results

In contrast with Kantians, consequentialists judge the morally good or bad character of an action by its results. Consequentialists locate the source of our unease in the fact that we are admitting the consequences of not lying into our evaluation of whether it is the right or wrong thing to do. We're appreciating that the harm caused by our decision to not lie to the court does not outweigh the good resulting from lying, leading us to conclude that we *ought to lie* in Jemma's case. Consequentialism therefore seems like an appealing alternative to Kantianism as it accords with our intuition about what we should do in Jemma's case. But how does consequentialism fare in respect of Saul's dilemma?

For consequentialists of all stripes, the only thing that matters when determining whether an act is right or wrong is consequences. One kind of consequentialism is act consequentialism. The act consequentialist maintains that the right action is the one that produces the most good: if there's a choice between an action that produces 100 units of good and another that yields only 80 units, act-consequentialists believe that we ought to perform the former action. The crucial issue for Saul is whether misleading the court will produce a greater amount of good than any defense which would not mislead the court. And the answer seems straightforward: Saul certainly should not mislead the court because we know from later episodes that Lalo skips bail and intensifies his destructive (and lethal) behavior—something that could have been avoided by not lying.

Yet whilst we have access to information about the actual consequences of Saul's actions, Saul does not. Given that act consequentialism requires us to perform actions which *in fact* produce the most good, how can Saul be sure that he's choosing the right course of action? By requiring lawyers to occasionally lie to the court, moreover, act consequentialism also risks coming into conflict with lawyers' personal values. Being a con-sequentialist saint may demand far more than most lawyers are willing to tolerate.

The conclusions of Kantian ethics and act consequentialism seem to agree on the issue of whether lawyers should lie, with each providing strong justifications against Saul misleading the court in Lalo's bail hearing. The more interesting question is whether lawyers are permitted to provide an honest defense for clients who they know to be legally and morally culpable.

Giving an Honest Defense

In practice, most defendants are likely to accept that their lawyer cannot lie on their behalf. A defendant may therefore instruct her lawyer to still provide a defense (such as the pros-ecution's evidence not being strong enough) without asking the lawyer to suggest that she did not commit the offense. This type of defense recurs throughout *Better Call Saul*, with the two most notable examples being when Jimmy represents the three college students charged with criminal trespass and des-ecrating a corpse ("Uno") and Kim's defense of Jimmy during his ethics hearing ("Chicanery")

We saw that act consequentialists (unlike Kantians) do not place an absolute constraint on lawyers lying to the court when defending guilty clients. Yet the question remains: is it right for lawyers to provide an honest defense for clients they know are morally and legally guilty? For act consequentialists, there appears to be no real difference in the propriety of a lawyer's conduct so long as the net good produced by lying is equivalent to that produced by raising an honest defense. This might strike you as odd—even if a dangerous client would have been convicted irrespective of whether an honest or lying defense is given, surely there is something morally worse about attempt-ing to acquit the client by lying? Some act consequentialists agree with this sentiment and observe that we need to draw a distinction between *actual* and *probable* consequences. Whereas both defenses are of equal standing according to their actual consequences, giving a dishonest defense increases the probability of the defendant being acquitted. Putting forward a dishonest defense is therefore 'more wrong' than offering an honest defense as the probable consequences of the former defense produce less good than the latter.

Rule consequentialism affords a stronger justification for permitting lawyers to honestly defend guilty clients. For rule consequentialists such as Brad Hooker, an act is wrong only if it is prohibited by a rule or set of rules the acceptance of which produces the greatest good. Unlike act consequentialism, rule consequentialism is indirect in its evaluation of our actions: it doesn't look at whether our actions produce the most good, but whether our actions are permitted by rules which produce the most good. This is important because it means that although giving an honest defense may produce less good than other available actions, it's still the right thing to do because it's permitted by rules whose acceptance yields maximal good. So if the general rule 'Lawyers ought to provide an honest defense to all clients' produces the greatest amount of good within society, a lawyer who acquits an unrepentant serial killer by giving an honest defense has still performed the right action. But (along with Michael Huemer) we might question whether this rule really is the one that produces the most good. For it's difficult to see how such a rule would result in more good than one stating that lawyers should only defend their client's interests to the extent that they are consistent with the requirements of justice.

From a Kantian point of view, the interesting thing about providing an honest defense is that it does not seem to be prohibited by a perfect duty. The maxim 'If I know that my client is guilty, I will give an honest defense in order to secure their acquittal' does not create a contradiction in conception when universalized, not least because this is what actually occurs in the real world. Rather, it's more likely that lawyers have an imperfect duty not to try to acquit those known to be guilty. The reason why this duty is imperfect is because the maxim produces a contradiction in my will: since all rational people (myself included) will that substantive justice is realized in all cases, I cannot also will that defense lawyers attempt to cause substantive injustice by using an honest defense to acquit guilty individuals. There is therefore no absolute prohibition against honestly defending guilty clients, but lawyers must *sometimes* refuse to do so by, for example, encouraging a guilty client to accept a plea deal.

Arguably the most intuitive responses to the issues in this area are those theories which focus on the character and motivations of lawyers when making honest or deceitful defenses. Moral theories within this branch of ethics—known as virtue ethics—place a premium on a person's good or virtuous character, with right actions being those which flow from a virtuous disposition. David Hume's sentimentalist virtue ethics is no exception.

In Hume's view, we ought to perform an action if it's the type of action that would be produced by a virtuous motive (a motive approved of by an impartial observer). So should lawyers provide an honest defense for guilty clients?

We might answer 'No' on the basis that defending guilty clients is the type of action driven by bad motives, such as a desire to make money at the expense of justice. But this is too simplistic. The better response takes stock of the fact that we tend to disapprove of individuals, especially lawyers, who are not motivated by the desire to ensure that the legal process treats everyone fairly and justly. On this view, it would be wrong for lawyers not to provide an honest defense for guilty clients since they ought to be motivated by procedural justice, with giving an honest defense being the type of action produced by this motive.

This approach also seems to align with our intuitions in the cases of Saul and Jemma. Saul's decision to lie to the court case is wrong because he ought to have been motivated by procedural justice, yet his true motive was self-interest. The lawyer in Jemma's case, by contrast, would be doing the right thing by lying to the court. She would be acting out of benevolence in order to save the lives of Jemma's patients, and the absence of this motive would, in this particular case, elicit disapproval (even if concern for procedural justice were in its place).

Presenting Mitigation

Now imagine that Lalo was denied bail and put on trial for the murder of Fred Whalen. A couple of days after the jury returned its guilty verdict, Lalo instructs Saul to present mitigation at the sentencing hearing in the hope of avoiding a sentence of life without parole. What should Saul do?

The first thing to note is that would be extremely disadvantageous for Saul to lie about Lalo's legal or moral guilt. Given that the court has already determined that Lalo is guilty of murdering Fred Whalen, denying guilt might be interpreted as a lack of remorse. Nor would fabricating mitigation be helpful: the judge will be skeptical of mitigation that paints a different picture to the one in front of her. If, however, Lalo asks Saul to put his addiction to cocaine and methamphetamine forward as mitigation, is it right for Saul to present it to the judge?

Rule consequentialists would give a qualified 'Yes': Saul can present Lalo's addiction to the judge so as long as acceptance of the rule 'Lawyers ought to provide genuine mitigation for guilty clients' produces the best consequences. Act consequentialists will be less sure of the correct answer. Classical utilitarians such as Jeremy Bentham and John Stuart Mill would ask whether Saul's conduct would yield the greatest amount of net pleasure when compared with that produced by any other action. Let's assume that Saul's plea in mitigation succeeds and that Lalo is granted parole after serving twenty-five years years in prison. After being released, Lalo returns to the drugs trade but does not directly harm anyone ever again due to his age. The question is whether the net pleasure or happiness produced by Lalo having no possibility of release outweighs the pleasure produced by Lalo's release on parole.

We could argue that greater net pleasure follows from keeping Lalo locked up for the rest of his life because he would not be causing harm to people by helping to distribute drugs. But we might also reach the opposite conclusion by questioning whether displeasure inflicted by a spending the rest of one's life in prison outweighs the displeasure felt by those using the drugs he supplies, and whether those drug users would've felt the same degree of displeasure by acquiring the same drugs from another source. And given that Saul has no way of knowing the future consequences of his actions, how can he know whether he is in fact choosing the right course of action? Here, as before, we encounter the difficulties with using act consequentialism as a practical guide for our actions.

Even more problematic for act consequentialism is that it can justify severely unjust punishments. Returning to Jemma's case, suppose Jemma has been found guilty of theft and that her case has caught the attention of an extremist anti-medicine group who will poison New York City's water supply unless she is sentenced to life without parole. When deciding Jemma's sentence, the judge has a choice between giving the sentence of life without parole or imposing a proportionate sentence for theft, resulting in the death of thousands. If our judge is an act consequentialist, Jemma's fate is sealed: she will spend the remainder of her life in prison, this punishment being justified on the ground that it prevents an overwhelming loss of life. But if the judge is indecisive and offers to refrain from imposing the harsher sentence should Jemma's lawyer provide genuine mitigation, the lawyer must condemn Jemma to the harsher sentence through their silence. Imagine paying for that kind of representation!

Kantians are rightly bemused by this outcome and would instead place Jemma's lawyer under an imperfect duty to provide mitigation. Her lawyer's maxim ('If my client is guilty and substantive justice is likely, I will refrain from providing mitigation') clearly entails no contradiction in conception when universalized, but it does produce a contradiction in her will.

No rational person can will her maxim as a universal law and also will that their lawyer would offer mitigation against a harsh sentence were they convicted of stealing candy. In fact, by curbing our ability to pursue our own ends, we would be willing a maxim that would undermine the very thing that Kantians hold dear—our agency.

So, What's the Right Answer?

Surely, you might be asking, there has to an *ultimate* right answer to the questions we've discussed? Perhaps there is, and many philosophers have dedicated their lives to pursuing this elusive, final answer to these important moral questions. But we've been looking at how some ethical theories approach the question of whether lawyers should defend guilty clients, assessing the merits and shortcomings of these different approaches along the way. Each of these moral theories gives us a way of unravelling the knots we encountered, and each provides a blueprint for coherently rearranging the strings so that we can justify or criticize the actions we choose to take.

But if there's one thing we're reminded of when watching *Better Call Saul*, it's that we all have to make peace with the fallibility of ourselves and those around us. It should come as no surprise that our ethical theories, theories by and for imperfect beings, are also imperfect.

4
Better Call the DEA?

Amy E. White

In *Better Call Saul*, the transformation of Jimmy McGill into Saul Goodman, the amoral attorney who defends drug cartel members and, eventually, Walter White in *Breaking Bad*, is brought to life.

This captivating transformation is only possible within the context of the War on Drugs and the current drug policies in the United States. The fictional narrative presented in *Better Call Saul* gives the audience an inside view of the Drug War and clearly illuminates some of the casualties of this campaign. The audience witnesses Jimmy's struggles to tame his conman urges, find love, defend the elderly, and try (albeit in sometimes misguided ways) to do what's right. Even the death of Jimmy's brother doesn't derail his efforts to be a good person. It's only when Jimmy becomes entangled with the trade of illegal drugs and is embraced as a "friend of the cartel," that Jimmy becomes a casualty of the War on Drugs and dissolves fully into Saul Goodman. Unfortunately, once Saul becomes a friend to the cartel, there is no escape. As Nacho Varga ominously informs Jimmy "once you are in, you're in" ("Namaste").

Not only does the audience in *Better Call Saul* see the transformation of Jimmy, but the series also exposes the brutality of drug cartels. Given the lure of such a potentially lucrative endeavor, the audience comes to understand how temptations compel even well-meaning people to do terrible things. Unfortunately, such brutality is not merely fiction. The War on Drugs in the United States plays a crucial function in constructing the environment that many characters in *Better Call Saul* are required to navigate.

History of the War

An important moment in the current War on Drugs in the United States occurred in June 1971 when a proclamation was made by President Richard Nixon that we were at war ("A Brief History of the Drug War"). In his speech, Nixon declared drugs to be our number one public enemy and vowed to enact harsh control methods. This seemingly endless war now involves domestic and foreign efforts to stop the use, distribution, and production of illegal drugs. While the War on Drugs evokes iconic images of former First Lady Nancy Reagan in her red suit urging the population of the United States to "Just say no to drugs," the War has deeply racist roots.

Long before Gustavo Fring opened the first Los Pollos, in the late eighteenth and early nineteenth century, there wasn't a recognized drug problem. Drugs, even heroin and opium, were legal and addiction was seen as a personal problem, not something worthy of government interference. In fact, the Sears Roebuck company offered a syringe and cocaine for sale in the 1890s. Heroin could also be purchased in the catalogue (McKendry, "Sears Once Sold Heroin"). A bit later, certain racial groups, and the drugs associated with those groups, were targets for early restriction. Fears of "drug- crazed, sex-mad" negros committing crimes against white people, especially white women, were played up by the drafters of the Harrison Narcotics Act of 1914. The act was the first substantial attempt by the United States government to restrict drugs. Of course, a racist history may not, in and of itself, be a solid argument to reject the War on Drugs. After all, judging something merely from its origins is clearly fallacious reasoning.

The United States government's next attempt at widespread regulation was the 1919 National Prohibition Act. It's well-known that Prohibition was not successful. Prohibition did not successfully deter most people from drinking. What did happen was that without a legal market, deaths from alcohol poisoning increased, a golden age of crime was ushered in, and NASCAR was founded. In short, the Prohibition Act was a disaster and repelled in 1933. Many authors have argued that the current War on Drugs is also a disaster. In several ways criticisms of the current War on Drugs mimic those given during Prohibition. Nobel Prize laureate Milton Friedman even stated that, "Our experience with the prohibition of drugs is a replay of our experience with the prohibition of alcoholic beverages." Perhaps, like Prohibition, the War on Drugs is a failure and should be halted. It may be that the defense for the War on Drugs is one that even Saul wouldn't be able to convincedly argue.

The Case Against the War

The mission of the War on Drugs is, broadly, to reduce the distribution, use, and production of illegal drugs by making manufacturers, users, and dealers targets for arrest or im- prisonment. In *Better Call Saul,* Hank Schrader is the embodiment of this mission and the DEA. When Hank meets Jimmy and interrogates Krazy-8, his focus is clearly only on arresting anyone involved in the drug trade ("A Guy for This"). This focus becomes an obsessive search for Heisenberg in *Breaking Bad.* Hank seeks to stop the drug trade, often at great personal costs. For Hank the world is clear: drugs, and all aspects of the drugs trade, are bad and must be stopped.

Not unlike arguments that convinced legislators to overturn the prohibition of alcohol, many who oppose our current War on Drugs do so because they claim this mission has failed and will continue to fail. For evidence of the failure, simply ask anyone living in West Virginia, or many other states, about the opioid epidemic surrounding them. Most people in regions where opioid use is most common, can point to the places where addicts gather, and many have family members and friends who have died from overdose. The reality is even worse than the drug use depicted in *Better Call Saul* and *Breaking Bad.*

While anecdotal evidence can be rather weak, the numbers support the personal stories. According to the Centers for Disease Control and Prevention, the number of drug overdose deaths has quadrupled since 1999. Drug offenses also remain the leading cause of arrest in the United States despite decades of pouring money into drug enforcement. Harsh enforcement should, theoretically, make drugs hard to acquire and very expensive. However, drugs are simply everywhere in the United States. Those who wish to use illicit drugs will easily find the means to do so. Not only have the results of current drug control policy been underwhelming at best, but many opponents also argue that this has been a tragic and costly war.

The Drug War is a costly endeavor. Currently prisons in the United States are clogged with drug offenders. Most of these offenders are not like the Salamanca family; they are sitting behind bars for nonviolent drug crimes. This contributes to the United States having the highest incarceration rate in the world. There is also little evidence that those being jailed or imprisoned are dissuaded from further criminal activities or from taking drugs. Within the first two weeks following their release, former prisoners are 129 times more likely than the general public to die of a drug overdose. Given the failure and

the high cost of enforcement of the War and detention of prisoners, proponents of this argument conclude with the claim
that we could better direct funds and should stop this clearly
unwinnable fight. Those who argue for ending the War by legal-
izing drugs, or some drugs, commonly point to the fact that
we could impose a sin tax on the drugs that are legalized.
This revenue, proponents of legalization argue, could be used to
improve education, and enhance rehabilitation options for
addicts.

Another common argument against current drug control
policies in the United States details the unfair enforcement
and unjust sentencing involved in our current War. Even with
smooth talking attorneys like Jimmy, harsh sentencing laws
and mandatory minimums have resulted in offenders serving
long terms for crimes as petty as possession of marijuana.
According to the Drug Policy Alliance, in 2015, 700,000 people
were arrested in the United States for marijuana violations,
ninety percent of the arrests were for mere possession. These
unforgiving sentences, some argue, disproportionately affect
Blacks and Hispanics. This discrepancy is most acute when we
consider the historical differences in sentencing between
cocaine and crack cocaine. Before the Fair Sentencing Act was
passed, it was common for those arrested for crack offenses,
mostly young Black men, to face more severe sentences than
those found with power cocaine. Structural racism helped start
the War and many authors have argued it's what fuels it. Some
commentators on this issue have gone so far as to call the War
on Drugs, a "war on black men" (Block and Obioha). In *The New
Jim Crow*, Michelle Alexander also sees the War on Drugs on
Black men. The War on Drugs is not as transparently discrim-
inatory as Jim Crow; it hides under the banner of the United
States Government's attempt to control drugs; however, the
trauma caused to communities composed mainly of people of
color is undeniable.

There are many similarities between Prohibition and the
current War on Drugs. Under Prohibition, government spending on substance control increased dramatically, risks from
consuming alcohol increased, crime and corruption surrounding alcohol surged, and the consumption rate remained high.
According to Mark Thornton, the prohibition of a legal market
in alcohol elicited a criminal black market and ushered in the
rise of gangsters. Many of the same problems can be seen with
the War on Drugs. Current drug control efforts generate crime,
cause risks to the user, and create corruption. This has caused
some commentators to claim that the War is counterproductive

and that drug control efforts are a major cause of what Americans consider "the drug problem." Milton Friedman argued concerning the War on Drugs, "the very measures you favor are a major source of the evils you deplore." Friedman claimed that the illegality of drugs results in colossal profits that are applied to finance the horrendous techniques favored by drugs lord like Gustavo Fring and the Salamanca family.

The horrendous methods of members of the drug cartels, including ruthless murder, are demonstrated in *Better Call Saul*. Shootouts, not unlike the one portrayed in the episode "Bagman" are, unfortunately, not merely fictional. In the shootout, Jimmy is ambushed in his car by six cartel members while on his way to make a cash drop. Jimmy is traveling with seven million dollars of drug money in the trunk of his car! Thankfully, Mike Ehrmantraut intervenes and kills the cartel members before they can kill Jimmy. Mike is an example of another worry Friedman expressed with the War on Drugs. Friedman argued that illegality creates corruption in law enforcement. The character Mike is a former dirty police officer who accepted bribes and kept quiet about protection agreements. He says:

> You let some things slide, you look the other way. You bust a drug dealer that has more cash than you will ever earn in a lifetime. Some of it doesn't make it into evidence. So what? You took a taste, so did everyone else, that's how you knew you were safe.

Unfortunately, when Mike's son joins the force and is ensnared in the corruption, Mike's tragic path is set ("Five-O").

Between 1925 and 1930, crimes relating to Prohibition increased one thousand percent and homicide rates sored because of the organized crime surrounding the black market. These crimes can mostly be attributed to organized crime groups protecting territories and settling disputes, much like the drug cartels depicted in the show. Lacking legal recourse, disputes are settled with violence. This is driven by potentially astronomical profits. For a visual, just imagine the huge sums of money the Salamancas and Gustavo present to Don Eladio. The potential for such enormous payouts is nearly irresistible.

Competition for territory, deals gone wrong, and a lack of a legal method to seek redress creates a perfect storm of violence. Glimpses of this violence can be seen throughout *Better Call Saul*. Lacking any court of appeal, drug traffickers settle disputes with threats and violence. These disputes often result in innocent bystanders being killed and greatly diminish the quality of many neighborhoods. Drive-by shootings are used to send messages, neighborhood children are recruited to run drugs, addicts flock to abandoned buildings to use, and a living hell is created for residents. As described by Block and Obioha, this cycle of violence disproportionality affects people of color and is caused and perpetuated by the criminalization of drugs.

The cycle is formed quickly and spreads even faster, because habitual users often fund their drug use by recruiting new users. The users recruited can also resort to selling to new users, and the chain goes on and on. From the top cartel leaders, like Eladio Vuente, to the street grunts lining up to buy burner phones from Saul, if a link in the chain is disrupted, another person quicky takes their place and the cycle continues. The black market in drugs is, perhaps, too lucrative to stop. The temptation is enough to make any IT specialist at a pharmaceutical company become a criminal and purchase a yellow flamed Hummer. With the huge profits to be made in illegal drugs, it's not a mystery why this chain is so persistent. If someone like Tuco Salamanca is arrested, there's always a Nacho to take his place.

During Prohibition, the quality of alcohol available on the black market was unregulated. To compensate for increased risk, spirits became more potent and dangerous. This situation is amplified with today's illegal drugs and creates great harms to users. To obtain drugs, a user must engage in criminal activity, and risk extreme dangers, sometimes even death from the drugs they acquire. Users have very little idea what is in the drugs they consume. This is especially dangerous considering the rise of fentanyl and carfentanil in heroin. Overdoses are, unfortunately, common. If there was a legal market, some proponents of ending the War argue, protections could be in place and drugs would likely be less potent and less dangerous. Warning labels and product safety guidelines could result in users who are better informed. Also, licensed sellers would be less likely to sell to children and involve them in the distribution of drugs.

Defenders of decriminalization or legalization of drugs claim that ending the War will not result in a dramatic increase in drug use. We can look at Prohibition for some support for this argument. After abolishing Prohibition, no great evils befell the United States. We did not see a surge of alcohol consumption; we simply saw bootleggers being put out of business and the elimination of most of the costs associated with Prohibition laws. After the repeal of Prohibition, alcohol became safer and organized crime focused efforts elsewhere. The assertion that drug consumption will not increase if we end the War gains empirical support from countries where decriminalized has taken place. Portugal decriminalized possession of small amounts of previously illegal drugs in 2001, and several countries have followed. In general, decriminalization has not resulted in increased use nor social ills. In most cases, decriminalization has been considered very successful and reduced the harms associated with drug use.

Many arguments for ending the Drug War focus on the idea that it does more harm than good. Conversely, another argument centers on a philosophical commitment. In the United States, it's mostly assumed that adult Americans have the right to choose what risks they take, as long as those risks are not likely to involve harm to others. In support of this argument, philosopher John Stuart Mill's famous assertion that the only justification for coercion is to prevent harm can be given (*On Liberty*, Chapter 1). Mill claimed that there should be a principle of liberty employed where citizens are granted a sphere of liberty, protected from intrusion, as long as citizens' actions are not likely to cause harm to others who are not autonomously consenting to the actions. This philosophical commitment was a reason often given for ending Prohibition and is an argument regularly applied to the legalization of many dangerous activities, substances, and items.

If dangerous activities, like mountaineering, skydiving, and smoking tobacco, were prohibited by law, it could rightly be seen as an infringement of liberty. However, the War on Drugs makes the decision to consume drugs, even if harm to others isn't involved, a criminal action. Some authors defending this principle, have noted an inconsistent application in the United States. The United States clearly allows citizens to make some dangerous choices and consume some dangerous substances. For example, alcohol is legal and regulated. However, many authors have argued that alcohol is more dangerous than many drugs that are currently illegal. Thus, to be consistent, and abide by Mill's principle, many argue that the War should end. Of course, it should be clear that, while consuming drugs may fall under the protection of Mill's principle, driving while under the influence of drugs or engaging in dangerous behavior that will likely involve harm to others would remain illegal. This would be consistent with current regulation involving alcohol.

The Case for the War

In response to the accusation that the War on Drugs is a failure, proponents of continuing the fight argue that we haven't lost the War and, especially in some regards, it has been a resounding success. They argue that current drug controls succeed in deterring some potential users from experimenting with drugs, increase the cost of drugs and reduce availability. Some advocates of the War acknowledge that we still have a drug problem but argue that the situation would be much worse if we did not engage in the War.

William Bennett, former Director of the Office of National Drug Control Policy, argued that the war on drugs has prevented an even greater surge of addiction. Bennett argued that wherever drugs have been cheaper and more easily obtained, drug use and addiction have skyrocketed. Because the War keeps prices high and reduces availability, it prevents such a surge from occurring. Drug controls do indeed raise prices and the risks involved in supplying drugs does cause a decrease in their availability. Bennett acknowledged that controls can't keep all drugs from being distributed, produced, and used. However, if the War does keep some drugs from ending up in the hands of users, and if controls keep prices high, the United States is not engaging in a losing battle. If current drug controls can keep a portion of citizens in the United States from becoming addicts, perhaps we are winning the War. If such controls are stopped, the United States might experience a dramatic increase in drug use.

Availability of drugs and sanctions certainly play a role in drug use. Consider the formally popular drug Quaaludes (methaqualone). During the period where Quaaludes were legal and readily available, many Americans used them to sleep, relax and party. Unfortunately, they were also a drug commonly used to assist in sexual assault. (This became common knowledge during the trial of Bill Cosby.) In the early 1980s, the Drug Enforcement Agency and Congress noticed that Quaalude use was problematic. Quaaludes were soon listed as a Schedule 1 drug in the United States. With strict enforcement that cuts the supply and increases the price, we certainly don't see quaaludes being smuggled in the tires of Regalo Heldao trucks or buckets of chicken today.

In support of the link between drug availability and use, defenders of current drug controls often cite a well-known study of service members returning from Vietnam. In the study, Lee Robins documents the effects of widespread availability on drug addiction. While in Vietnam, Robins estimated that around eighty percent of soldiers were offered heroin, and many became frequent users. Use was so prevalent that the United States became concerned that veterans would return and bring their heroin habits back with them. Fortunately, Robins found that while 34 percent of enlisted servicemen in Vietnam tried heroin and 20 percent reported addiction, only five percent of those addicted in Vietnam continued to use heroin in the United States. Reasons given by the servicemen as to why they had stopped included lack of availability and the severe consequences of use in the United States. Defenders of the War point to studies like Robins's to support the claim that strict drug controls do work.

Many advocates of continuing current drug-control efforts argue that, if drugs were readily available, children would also have easier access to them. While age restrictions could be enforced in a legal market, this wouldn't be the case if drug use is only decriminalized. Even if age controls could be enforced, legal substances are simply more available to children. Consider how many children who live in the United Sates have easy access to alcohol or tobacco simply by raiding a parent's pantry. For many children, their first experiences with such substances are due to parental purchases. Furthermore, it could be argued that legalization, or even decriminalization, sends a message that there is societal approval of drug use. This message, especially received by the youth, might be interpreted to mean that drug use isn't seriously problematic. This might also hamper efforts to educate the youth against drug use. Thus, to keep children safe, defenders of the War claim we should continue the fight.

Given the potential for a surge in drug use, defenders of the War argue that legalization or decriminalization would not help the drug problem. They believe that the United States would still face many of the difficulties involved in the drug epidemic, perhaps even on a larger scale. With additional addicts, an increase in available treatment options would be required. However, even if an increase in treatment accessibility were to occur, addicts will often not enter treatment until forced. Because drugs are criminalized, many addicts are currently forced to choose between treatment or jail. If drugs were decriminalized or legalized, they wouldn't be as likely to face such a choice and enter treatment. Thus, defenders of the War claim, if drugs are legalized or decriminalized, the United States would likely have more addicts and lack a necessary tool to make many seek treatment.

In response to the claim that much of the drug problem is caused by the War on Drugs, some defenders of current policy have claimed that it's shortsighted to assume that legalization would cut crime. Drug users would likely still commit crimes to pay for drugs. Even if these drugs were cheaper, many addicts would still be unemployable and turn to crime. If, as some claim, there would be more addicts if the War were ended, it's possible that crime would increase. While crime from the cartel, and friends of the cartel might be lessened, Jimmy would still be busy. Adding to this crime would be users of substances that increase violent behavior, like cocaine, PCP, and methamphetamine. In *Better Call Saul*, the violence created by some drugs is highlighted in the rage and unpredictability that methamphetamine produces in Tuco. If, defenders of the War argue, there were more addicts using drugs that cause violence, violent crime would increase.

In response to the argument that drug use would be safer for the user if we ended the War, defenders of current policy claim this is uncertain. While it's true that legal drugs can be regulated and produced under safety protocols, drugs that are merely decriminalized will still be produced and distributed illegally. The problem of user safety will not improve without enacting other measures by decriminalization alone. Even if drugs were legalized, it could be argued that users might not always be safe. Most legal distribution involves taxes and, this makes drugs still relatively expensive. Unless we distribute drugs for very little, there might still be a black market that would emerge to undercut the regulated one. So the cartel might still continue, along with the violence.

Defenders of current drug policy generally dismiss arguments that claim an inconsistency between alcohol being legal and other drugs remaining illegal. Defenders usually note that comparisons between alcohol and other substances are misleading. While it's true that alcohol can be blamed for quite a bit of violent activity, and many have argued that alcohol use is more likely to result in addiction than other substances, the comparison is flawed. Alcohol might play an outsized role in societal problems because it's legal and easily accessible. As for addition rates, alcohol might appear to be more addictive than other substances because it's easy to keep using. Perhaps, if other drugs were as easily available as alcohol, the comparison would be sound. This flawed comparison is displayed in many studies concerning drug use. For example, a study might conclude that more people who try alcohol become addicted than those who try cocaine. However, this may be because alcohol is legal. Those who tried cocaine, may not have the opportunity to use the drug often. This lack of availability cuts the risk of addiction. If cocaine were legal, addiction rates might be much higher.

While liberty may be important in the United States, many claim that drug use is simply not a victimless crime. Because of this, Mill's principle of liberty should not be appealed to for support in ending the War according to some defenders of current drug policy. Drug use impacts more people than the users. A heartbreaking portrayal of this can be seen in *Breaking Bad*. After Jane Margolis overdoses, her father Donald Margolis spirals out of control ("Phoenix"). This, unfortunately, results in the deaths of many. Families, especially children, of addicts often suffer terribly. Not only can addiction ruin the life of addicts, but they can also take others down with them. Additionally, drug addiction may make addicts less productive employees (if they are employable at all) imposing costs on employers and the economy. Addicts also impose healthcare costs on society generally. In short, this argument in defense of current policy claims that we all pay the costs involved in drug use.

In rebuttal to concerns focusing on liberty, defenders could claim that preventing addiction might increase individual liberty. While an initial decision to ingest a drug may be autonomous and an exercise in individual liberty, some drugs may be so addictive as to make future use less than fully autonomous. Even John Stuart Mill recognized a limit on liberty that might parallel the use of some illicit drugs. Mill claimed that individuals should not be allowed to sell themselves into slavery. His reasoning was that, while a person may freely and voluntarily agree to the sale, their freedom would be fleeting. All future actions of the slave would be controlled by a master. Thus, overall, liberty would be decreased. It is possible that highly addictive drugs mimic the role of such a master, as we see with the demise of Jane in *Breaking Bad*. With the deterrence created by the War on Drugs, we may be saving some people from addiction and preserving their liberty. If enough people were deterred from the use of highly addictive drugs, liberty might be increased overall.

Strategic Withdrawal

The War on Drugs is the battlefield on which many of the characters in *Better Call Saul* are arrayed. Spurred on by the promise of large profits, the cartel draws many friends into its grip. The more the Drug War fails, the more the United States government advocates for it. The reason often given for the failure is that there is a need to increase funding and fight harder! Unfortunately, this logic doesn't account for the possibility that it's the Drug War that is causing much of the drug problem.

Those who want to continue the Drug War claim that decriminalization or legalization would be a very dangerous gamble. However, decriminalization, and even legalization of cannabis, and other drugs, in many states and other countries, has not resulted in a dramatic increase in use. Czechia, the Netherlands, Portugal, and Switzerland are among countries where personal drug use and possession of small amounts of previously illegal drugs is decriminalized. This, in conjunction with a harm reduction program has proven highly effective in reducing crimes, lowering overdose deaths, and even cutting the number of users.

While the United States is different from those countries that have ended their War on Drugs, there seems to be little reason why such strategies would be unworkable. Perhaps this is a case where we better call Saul and leave the DEA out of it.

II

You can be on one side of the law or the other

5

The Sovereign State of Salamanca

WALTER BARTA AND THOMAS PAUL BARNES, ESQ.

Have you ever thought about starting your own country? The Founding Fathers did it, so why can't you?

Ricky Sipes, the would-be client of Saul Goodman, back when Saul was still Jimmy McGill, asks this very question. Ricky gets to thinking he should declare himself king, just like that, so he calls Saul and says he has got a proposition: the lawsuit to end all lawsuits, to secede from the State of New Mexico and create a sovereign territory, the Sovereign Sandia Republic.

Ricky offers Saul a million cash, but when Saul opens up that briefcase and sees Ricky's mugshot on that money, he knows something is sketchy ("Alpine Shepherd Boy"). Of course, this is not *Sandia*, and Ricky is not king; this is still New Mexico, and it is still a democracy—mostly. Saul is one of the best lawyers in Albuquerque and he knows enough about "The Law" to know what Ricky doesn't: you don't get independence by just declaring it; no, you've got to take it

The Court and the Cartel

But what is sovereignty anyway? To answer that we need the theories of Thomas Hobbes, a philosopher in England back in the 1600s, when there were still real kings. Hobbes's writing is about politics: "the causes, generation, and definition of a commonwealth" (*Leviathan*, p. 223). Hobbes asks political questions. How are contracts made? What are the rights and powers of a government? And what preserves and dissolves one? According to Hobbes, a sovereign is a person who uses strength to enforce contracts, defend subjects, and make peace.

In New Mexico they have two big power houses: the Court, of course, but also the Cartel. These institutions overlap in the obvious adversarial sense. The Court upholds the Law and the Cartel undermines the Law. But where does this conflict come from? And why do these institutions have so many similarities? Hobbes would see that both the Court and Cartel have similar structures, founded in the elements of sovereignty. According to Hobbes, war is the natural state of humankind, power organizes from that bloodbath, and state structures emerge from these forces. Hobbes is a realist: to him, if you try and make-do by yourself, life is going be rough—"nasty, brutish and short" (p. 186). He thinks the government is a necessary evil, so big and bad it scares us all straight, like a "Leviathan"—a giant sea monster—which is what he titled his book, *Leviathan*. When a giant monster is breathing down your neck it can be pretty hard to *break bad*.

The Drug War as State of Nature

Hobbes's first big idea is that there is no law in the wilderness. Rather, Hobbes calls it a "State of Nature": a place that contains no justice. This is because it is out of the eye of the sovereign, in nature. And, according to Hobbes, nature is brutal: she does not care whether you live or die.

As Hobbes says, "Where there is no Common Power, there is no Law: where no Law, no Injustice . . . where there is no Common-wealth, there nothing is Unjust" (pp. 188, 202). Justice is nothing but the law of the land as declared by the power presiding over it. We may call it the desert of New Mexico, but names come from men who give them. The desert has no name; it is just a featureless waste. For example, the Kettleman family, after they embezzled all that money from the city, when they felt the heat from the law on their tracks, what did they do? They went camping ("Nacho"). There is nothing like escaping into the wilderness to avoid the law. With a business like the Cartel's, that is what you have to do.

That's why the Cartel always meets there. Whether muling drug money, having a Mexican standoff, hiding bags of embezzled cash, or cooking meth, the wilderness is where the crime can get done, outside of the view of the law. But furthermore, when the state makes something illegal that people still want—the criminalization of certain pharmaceuticals—they create a power vacuum, a wilderness, a State of Nature on their own streets.

Drug-dealers cannot call the cops, even if they are downtown. The streets are a State of Nature when you are wheeling and dealing in the drug-trade. For example, when Nacho Varga, stole from his business partner Pryce, the poor guy calls the Albuquerque PD "not . . . as a criminal" but "as a crime victim," but the cops interrogate Pryce anyway because, what with his secret stashes and pimped out ride, they correctly suspect that he is a drug dealer ("Cobbler"). If the Law wanted to legalize it, they could; but, when it is illegal, they give its control back to nature.

But Hobbes also says there is "general equality" amongst men: we are all equal—but not in the lovey-dovey way—in the I-can-murder-you-and-your-whole-family way. We're all equal in that we're all equally able to kill each other. If they had to, even the weakest person could kill the strongest person, whether it meant by getting allies to gang up him, or by replacing his heart medication, or by head-shotting him from across the desert.

Mike Erhmentraut demonstrates this principle when he gets hired by Pryce for a protection job. Mike is not that small, but the other two guys he is on the job with are big like bouncers. One guy starts talking trash, bragging about his guns, then realizes Mike is not armed—"How do you not pack a gun?"—and gets cocky and challenges Mike. But Mike grabs the gun, chops his throat, and disarms him. After that, the other big guy just runs away. What that shows—besides that Mike's got skills—is that we are all equal, in a sense: a huge guy might seem unbeatable, but a small guy with a quicker hand can take him down ("Pimento"). That is Hobbesian equality for you: equality amongst murderers. Like what they say, the first rule of prison: "pick the biggest guy, punch him as hard as you can . . . assert dominance" ("Sunk Costs"), but just expect them to do the same to you.

So, for Hobbes, because there is no law in the wilderness, and because we are all pretty much equal, it is all versus all. The lack of oversight means that there's no justice, no rights, no decency—just the "Right of Nature": everyone has the right to do what he can for his own good and his own life. Because of this, "every man has a Right to everything" (p. 189) which leads to a "war of every man against every man" (p. 190). Unlike in our typical society where being nice and doing good are virtues; in a war, force and fraud are virtues: shooting people up and ripping people off become great resume filler.

This might seem like injustice, and it is, in a State of government; but, in a State of Nature, it is fair game. As Nacho says, "I like ripping off thieves because they can't go to the cops, they have no recourse" ("Mijo"). In order to get what they want, people seek to use any means necessary, including theft, assault, and murder, and there is nothing there to stop them except the will of someone else. If two men want the same thing, they can become rivals and try to kill each other. There's no court of law to decide that feud, just the gun. As anyone will tell you "Possession's like four tenths of the whatchamacallit . . . [ownership], bro" ("Hero"). Where there is nobody to protect your property rights, what you own is what you can carry away. One time Mike scopes out and sticks up a drug-mule for money. He goes out into the middle of nowhere, fashions a homemade trip wire, pops the mule's tires and cuts them open. Mike gets himself a quarter million cash for the price of a garden hose and some nails. Of course, the mule had hidden a gun under a rock for just such an occasion, but Mike overpowered him ("Nailed"). Later, Hector Salamanca goes out to cap the driver for his mistake. And nobody can say anything; there is no calling 911 in the desert.

Gangs Becoming Government

But according to Hobbes, even though nature does not have laws, from the war of all against all we can deduce some reasonable principles of behavior, or "Laws of Nature": 1. every man ought to seek peace and, when he cannot obtain it, use war; and 2. to protect himself, every man ought to be satisfied with only enough of his rights as he would allow others (p. 190). In other words, hope for peace, but prepare for war; and you do not want to die, so you have got to make some compromises.

Basically, people agree to work together out of fear. This situation of shared trust is what Hobbes calls a "common-wealth" because it's a state of affairs that benefits everybody. Thus, from the desert emerges a State. For example, when Saul Goodman found the Kettlemans in the desert, they had a literal "tug-of-war" over a bag of money, but made a deal in the end: "We're in this together, come what may." Saul points out that the Kettlemans embezzled money and the Miss Kettleman points out that Saul took a bribe. With mutually assured destruction by blackmail, they agree not to turn each other in ("Bingo").

The first time Mike met Gus Fring it went down like that too. Out in the middle of the desert, with mutual fear, they come to an agreement not to draw their weapons. As Gus suggests, "I may assume you're armed. I do not wish to see your gun, and if I don't, you will not see mine" ("Something Beautiful"). This kind of armistice might work, temporarily, if neither party can get the upper hand, or have too much to lose, or have mutual respect, love or interest. Mike is smart enough to know that the best way to keep his head on his shoulders is to satisfy the deal. As he tells it, "If you make a deal with somebody, you keep your word," and he is even willing to quibble over pennies for his principles:

—We're short twenty dollars.

—Agreed amount or no deal.

—Are you really willing to blow up this deal for twenty bucks?

—Are you? ("Pimento")

It's in everybody's best interest that the deal go smoothly, because when bullets start flying you don't know who's going to get hit. Mike is so adamant about this he is even willing to pay back Nacho $25,000 for a deal gone wrong, even though he does not have to ("Off Brand"). He knows trust is worth more than money.

However, Hobbes thinks that honor among thieves is unstable. Both parties are operating out of fear of the other, so the moment they get the chance to stab each other in the back they may take it. For example, Pryce and Nacho did some dealings on the side, but it was always an uneasy arrangement. Pryce even points out how awkwardly these under-the-table deals go down: "How is this supposed to work? Do I hand over the pills first . . . or do I get the money and hand over the pills? I guess it would be fair if we had them over at the same time" ("Pimento"). Pryce's uncertainty is intrinsic to human dealings: you never know if someone is really going to follow through, and the feeling is mutual. Of course, Pryce and Nacho's business only lasts until Nacho gets the chance to screw Pryce over. Even when Nacho says, "I trust you," that may just be the way he knocks you off guard to rob you blind ("Switch").

So, to solve the problem of mistrust, Hobbes thinks we have to have a "Common Power" to "keep [us] all in awe": from the Laws of Nature emerges the need for a powerful party to oversee agreements (p. 185). As Hobbes says, "covenants, without the sword, are . . . of no strength to secure a man at all" (p. 223). In disagreement, both sides must choose a neutral judge to decide, otherwise they could come to blows. This cannot be a disputing party either, because they would be biased. Furthermore, you cannot write laws until you agree on who is writing them.

Rather, the king gets to decide what is good and bad. And, under a king, nobody has to fear promises being broken, because the king will enforce them, so people will tend to keep them. For example, after Nacho steals from Pryce and Pryce calls the cops on Nacho, that does not phase Nacho at all, because they are both criminals, outside of the domain of legal protection; but, when Mike threatens to tell Tuco, Nacho fulfills his end of the bargain because he is scared of Tuco, and drug-dealing is under Tuco's jurisdiction, so to speak. It is easy robbery behind the Cartel's back, but with the Cartel involved there are rules and punishments.

As Mike says, "The stick is Tuco Salamanca" ("Cobbler"). Just as many people obey the law because they're scared of the cops; gangsters keep their word for fear of the Cartel boss. Indeed, implied in the Cartel's structure and function is an acknowledgement of the power of fear as a motivator. When Mike catches some Salamancas in his house, that is exactly what his would-be assassins say: "We were just trying to scare you" ("Bali Ha'i"). They might do worse, but they will not have to, if you obey their rules. That is exactly what happens when Tuco Salamanca kidnaps Jimmy McGill and his skater buddies after they tried to scam Tuco's abuelita.

Out in the desert, might makes right, according to Hobbes, so Saul has nothing but his big mouth to talk Tuco down. Appropriately, when Saul tells Tuco he is an FBI agent running "Operation *King*breaker," Tuco is ecstatic, exclaiming, "that means I'm the king!" and he is not wrong. In that moment Tuco is an acting sovereign, administering his justice, at the point of a gun. Tuco is about to murder those skaters, but instead Saul tries to negotiate: Nacho is concerned about the laws protecting Saul and Saul is scared of Tuco's violent temper. From this they come to an agreement. The conversation goes down something like this:

— You're tough but you're fair. You're all about justice.

— That's what I'm saying: Justice . . . [but] it's not enough.

— Okay, then let's talk proportionality. They're guilty, agreed. Now you have to decide: what's the right sentence?

— Like a judge. ("Mijo")

Tuco administers his own form of "justice" and behaves "like a judge" and jury and executioner.

According to Hobbes, a whole system and structure of rules and affiliations emerges from this mutual fear and common interest. And that is what the Cartel is, a whole hierarchy of positions of authority, made possible and kept together by a common power. Above Tuco are the Drug Lords; Hector Salamanca, Juan Bolsa, and Gus Fring; and above them, the kingpin himself, Don Eladio—as they say, "a lot of eyes on Salamanca" ("Gloves Off"). It is practically a legal system. The number one rule: "You rat, you die." Nacho pulls this line on Mike and Saul, demanding loyalty for protection, showing how important it is to obey the Cartel ("Hero", "Nailed").

When Tuco thinks a drug-dealer is screwing him, he stares them down, gives them his "lie detector", and may even shoot them in the face, if he is feeling like it ("Gloves Off"). That is how the king keeps the serfs in line. After Tuco gets imprisoned for assault though, Nacho moves up to his position, but still has a boss, Hector. When Crazy-8 small-talks to excuse a light payment, Nacho almost lets him off the hook; but when Hector expresses displeasure, Nacho knows he's being too soft, so he beats Crazy-8 to a pulp to teach him the power of the Cartel ("Off Brand"). Even though it is against Nacho's better-nature, he is compelled to employ violence as a member of the power structure.

Later on, after Hector has his stroke, Nacho gets promoted again, to Lalo Salamanca's right-hand man. But Lalo rules him with an even harder fist than Hector. Indeed, through all his loyalties and betrayals, every time one of his bosses gets terminated, Nacho gets a bigger and badder boss to replace him. Then there's Gus Fring. Gus is so tight-laced he might as well be legitimate. He has a bureaucracy like a true businessman. His drug-dealing operation runs as smoothly as the logistics of a corporation, not unlike real corporations made possible by real governments. Indeed, his drug-lord acumen for the Salamancas is directly transferable to his day-job as a fast food manager for the international conglomerate Madrigal Automotive.

But ultimately, all of this structure only stands at all because of the crowned head at the top, the sovereign himself, Don Eladio. Although he mostly just hangs around his pool at his mansion in Mexico, occasionally Eladio does what a king needs to do. Anytime he meets a new recruit, he asks, "You would think to run off with our stuff?" and scares them into obedience, because they know the price of betraying the king. As they say, "You better behave, . . . no second chances" ("Sabrosito").

Hobbes also notes that ancient titles of nobility were assigned by the king to his most loyal soldiers for their service to him during times of war. Similarly, under a Cartel, rewards and titles may be given to those who show loyalty, especially those who risk and sacrifice their lives for the defense of the Cartel. Indeed, many of the gangsters have titles—Drug Lord, Kingpin, or Don—like a Duke or Baron or Earl, and they oversee territory, like feudal lords (pp. 158–59). They even gave a title to Jimmy after he helped out in a jam, dubbing him "friend of the Cartel", a title of honor amongst gangsters ("JMM"). The Cartel, like the Court, in this way makes itself look legit, like the J.D. after Jimmy's name. In that way the Cartel's power structure operates just like a kingdom: a feudal proto-government, just like Hobbes's commonwealth.

But, Hobbes warned that infighting not quelled by the king can weaken and divide the commonwealth, even to the point of civil war. In the same way, the Cartel is held together only very loosely, always feuding with itself. Nacho is constantly plotting to kill his various bosses,—Tuco, Hector, and Lalo—the same guys who vouched for his street cred, but less out of ambition than out of fear of reprisal; just like how, as Hobbes points out, in ancient Rome, for fear of tyranny, Brutus conspired to kill Caesar, the very man who made him senator. But, Nacho's petty schemes are nothing compared to the ongoing feud between Hector and Gus, who hate each other to the core.

These two rival drug lords compete for territory and distribution, always bordering on gang violence. However, they are careful not to break trust, at least publicly. Their conflict is kept in check by the mutual fear of the Common Power of Don Eladio. Don Bolsa is always asking "Did Don Eladio approve this?", and Gus is worried that Hector's rash actions are "endangering the interest of the Cartel" ("Sabrosito"). In the end, the two attempt to settle their dispute because Don Bolsa intervenes on behalf of Eladio ("Lantern"). As between Hector and Gus, a gang can break into rival gangs, just as a kingdom can split during civil war.

The United Cartels of America

The Cartel is nothing compared to the Court when it comes to Common Power. As Jimmy once pointed out to an overly assertive community-service officer, "Out here you might be king douchenozzle, but in court you're little people" ("Fall"). This argument convinces the officer to give him community service hours, out of fear of reprimand. Everybody is king of their own small domain, but in the end everybody has to appeal to the State.

The State is like a Cartel too. The legitimated use of force by police officers is what makes the law function. Whether they are tazing mentally ill shut-ins, roughing up backstreet cell-phone-dealers, or harassing senior citizens, the law is always exerting force. Mike, a former police officer himself, tries to deny this to Saul, saying, "I'm not making you do anything, those are the rules," only to refute himself moments later by forcibly detaining Saul ("Nacho"). The rules only exist through enforcement. Of course, Mike has a history of use and abuse of power. Back in Philadelphia Mike worked for the police department and his whole unit was corrupt. They might as well have been gangsters: looking for a quick buck, killing their partners, covering up crime scenes, stealing stashes from dealers. This was just the way the State worked, just like a gang, as Mike admits:

> You let some things slide. You look the other way. You bust a drug dealer who has more cash than you make in a lifetime. Some of it doesn't make its way back into evidence. So what? You took a taste, so did everyone else. That's how you knew you were safe. It's like killing Caesar; everyone's guilty. Matt wasn't guilty, I was, everyone was. ("Five-O")

No wonder Mike was able to get a job so easily with the Cartel, he had already worked for one: the Philadelphia PD. Protection is protection, whether for suburban housewives or drug-smugglers. Moving from Philadelphia's police officer to Gus's "Safety Officer," Mike's skill set transfers from one sovereign to the other sovereign, from Court to Cartel, no problem. The seamless transition shows how similar the two institutions really are.

The legal procedure is like gang loyalty. The State and police have to execute and kill sometimes to maintain power, and we are told it is justice, but it is also self-preserving, just like a gang maintaining its own power—killing a snitch—using violence to maintain itself. The police and gangs alike get their authority from their ability to protect their members, which lasts as long as they can continue to do so. If captured or conquered, the obligation to the State transfers to the conquering institution. In the case of gangs and police alike, this may simply be whoever seizes the other. For example, if the police cannot adequately defend your neighborhood, you may seek recourse to a gang that can; and if your neighborhood belongs to the territory of a gang, but is seized by force by another gang, your loyalty may flip again, if it provides you protection.

This sinister side of the State infects the courts as well. The corrupt State of legal process maintains power for those in power. What is contract law except the keeping of promises by force, made possible by common fear? Saul's old law firm,

HHM: is it not a Cartel? They use all the tactics of a Cartel, albeit with less blood. For example, they punish Jimmy's girlfriend, Kim Wexler, just because "she should have been looking out for the firm's interests" ("Gloves Off"). Jimmy wants to sue them for that, for putting her in the "cell block" of the documents room, but Kim points out, "if I won, who would hire me?" ("Rebecca").

Kim knows that all law firms work like that, like a Cartel, looking out for number one, preserving their interests. But if you do not buy that, just look at Jimmy McGill himself, the ultimate shyster lawyer. Jimmy plays the game so well he can work with the Court or Cartel. He will tell you, "I'm a lawyer, not a criminal . . . I wasn't trying to rip them off, I just wanted their business," but what's the difference? ("Mijo"). As Saul tells the Kettlemans, under client confidentiality, "I can't take a bribe, but I can take a retainer" ("Hero"). The line rings false because of how identical a bribe and a retainer seem to be in the context. What is the substantive difference? In the one case, you pay Saul and he keeps hush-hush; in the other case, you pay Saul and he keeps client confidentiality. Either way, Jimmy gets paid, whatever the law might say.

Ironically, as Hobbes observes, from all this misfortune and malice comes something beautiful: the common-wealth, a State of Peace, and the good things in life. Gus himself would acknowledge that this is one of the great things about living in a State, protection from violence: "This is America. Here we do not fear. Here those men have no power . . ." ("Sabrosito"). Although the State may assert force, it creates a State of Peace by protecting people from other forces, like gangs: in other words, "the end of Obedience is Protection" (p. 272). By establishing a Common Power, we can create many of the beneficial features of civil society: generosity and good will, accommodation and hospitality, forgiveness and forethought, optimism and civility, distribution and equity, equality under law, due process of law, access to systems of recourse, and even "the golden rule" (pp. 201–217). These are what Hobbes calls his "other Laws of Nature." In Nature, good Samaritans just get shot in the face and left to be found by vultures—or metal detectors ("Coushatta")—but the Common Power protects them and it benefits all of us. We all want life to be fair, even if it is tough.

A State of Fear and Peace

So, when Ricky Sipes says the government is "damned oppressive," he is damned right; he just does not realize that *all* government is oppressive ("Alpine Shepherd Boy"). According to Hobbes, oppression is exactly what makes it a government, an arrangement coerced by the necessity of social contract—"an optional agreement, but not a single one opted out" ("Cobbler").

Most people live in a State of Fear, whether you're afraid of gunshots in the night, or just newspapers falling at your doorstep ("Amarillo"). Just look at Saul Goodman, or should I say Gene Takovic: these days he lives in hiding as a Cinnabon Manager in Omaha. His life is pure fear—whether of customers staring at him, or of opening emergency exits, or of watching cops walk by ("Switch", "Mabel", "Smoke"). Saul is as scared of the Court as he was of the Cartel. We never really get to "be our own boss" because there's always someone above us ("Inflatable"). The Hobbesian State works like that because would-be criminals are wracked by the forethought of judge, jury, and executioner: fear for punishment. We live in a state only made possible by the omnipresent "fear of that Invisible Power" (p. 200).

We may well wonder, as some other philosophers do, whether a society can ever be built contrary to Hobbesian principles on anything besides fear. Hobbes bases his assumptions on a view of human nature: that everyone is selfish. But even if only *some* people were selfish, we would still require some of these state-like structures to protect us. The elimination of self-interest, fear, and oppression is a lovely dream; but, until then, we are all just would-be criminals cowering under the Leviathan .

6

The Morality of Mike's Manifesto

JAKOB R. GIBSON AND TOBIAS T. GIBSON

In the first several scenes of *Better Call Saul* where Mike Ehrmantraut is featured, he's used primarily as a foil to fast-talking attorney Jimmy McGill. Prior to "Five-O," much of Mike's screentime is devoted to thwarting Jimmy's repeated attempts to evade the established rules of the parking area that Mike oversees. Jimmy frequently tries to leave the area without the requisite number of stickers, claiming that Mike is a "troll under a bridge" in "Mijo" or that he will compensate Mike with extra stickers when he returns, before raising the gate himself and driving away in "Nacho." Because of his job as a parking attendant, Mike plays the role of a literal barrier to allowing Jimmy to con his way out of a situation.

More importantly, the early interactions where Mike enforces proper parking validation offer two pieces of insight about his character. First, Mike is a "rules guy." The kind of guy who might say that rules prevent anarchy; or the type of person who has an internal code by which he leads his life. Second, and no less important, he also expects people to live within a certain set of rules. He takes verbal abuse from Jimmy, and eventually responds to a request from Jimmy to let him out despite, yet again, not being properly validated, by saying "I'm not making you do anything. Those are the rules."

Mike's Manifesto

Mike Ehrmantraut is the most interesting of the very flawed characters at the center of *Better Call Saul*. Mike's has a "manifesto," his internalized way of living, his code, and how it is evident in his actions, as organized through his words.

When we get to see Mike away from the parking booth, he's a devoted grandfather who dotes on his granddaughter and helps his daughter-in-law however he can. His demeanor remains unruffled, whether dealing with miscreants like Jimmy McGill, having a gun to his face, or having dinner with his family. Though a man of few words, those words pack a hefty punch. Understanding his thoughts, sense of honor, his manifesto, is critical to understanding the way that Mike walks through Albuquerque.

Mike is in some ways a dichotomy, though not duplicitous. He lives at least two lives: that of the blue-collar parking attendant who attends to his family; and that in the criminal underground, as Gus Fring's *aide de camp* and problem solver to both Gus and Jimmy, in a place where Mike is skilled in the ways of combat and strategy—perhaps more so than any other character in *Better Call Saul*. Yet, in both worlds, he has rules and abides by them. Is Mike's manifesto moral? Or is he a good character with bad character?

"I've known good criminals and bad cops. Bad priests, honorable thieves. You can be on one side of the law or the other. But if you make a deal with somebody, you keep your word."

This may be Mike's most famous line in *Better Call Saul*. It is foundational to his manifesto. In today's society, much of a person's identity and worth is found in the job that one does. The job description of police officer versus that of a prostitute, for example, conjures much about contributions both make to society, but also about their moral worth. But it is important to note that *job* description in not a description of a person's moral worth or identity. There *are* bad cops, who join to a police department and are then enabled to bully the citizens under their care. And there *are* prostitutes who are forced and trapped into the job—who have entered the profession not due to their moral shortcomings, but those of others. In *Better Call Saul* we observe a host of characters in positions requiring moral rectitude who ignore that key tenet and debase their station. The story of *Better Call Saul* is one filled with such characters. The primary focus is the descent of the often flippant Jimmy McGill into the genuinely unethical and sleazy Saul Goodman, and perhaps the parallel descent of his partner Kim Wexler. However, supporting characters such as Mike and his fellow Philadelphia officers are other fine examples of people displaying varying levels of iniquity. Mike himself is a former dirty cop, who takes it upon himself to kill two other dirty cops, Troy Hoffman and Jack Fensky, who set up and murdered his son for refusing to take dirty money.

Thus, it is important to think beyond titles as identity and worth. And, Mike, who simultaneously works as the parking attendant, the fixer for a smarmy attorney and, separately for a violent cartel, wouldn't seem to have much of a moral compass.

Yet Mike's words—and accompanying actions—suggest that he follows a code that the other Albuquerque criminals we are exposed to do not. Mike counsels new and established criminals on conduct—and models behavior in which he doesn't always carry a gun, move to kill a rival at the first offense, or skim money that no knew was in his possession. In other words, unlike many other characters in *Better Call Saul*, he is a logical and rational thinker. Aristotle considered virtue to come with practice and suggested that virtue is not found in excessive emotion, but rather that "virtue finds and chooses the median" (*Nicomachean Ethics*, p. 44). He seemingly would approve of Mike's personality and his counsel toward temperance, but not the presence of his more culpable traits. Mike does not live a good life and based on the limited background we have on him, he never has. He is not someone to emulate, and he is not a hero. But he may retain an element of Aristotelian virtue.

Aristotle writes in Book 1 of *Nicomachean Ethics* that living life with high standards for yourself is virtuous. Thus, to paraphrase Aristotle, "the proper function of a [criminal enforcer in Albuquerque] . . . is the same as the function of a [criminal enforcer in Albuquerque] who has set high standards for himself." Aristotle adds that "pleasure and pain" are the test of virtue. One "who abstains from bodily pleasures . . . is self-controlled. . . . and [one] who endures danger ... is courageous." Based solely on these passages, there is hope for the morality of Mike's manifesto.

"I was hired to do a job. . . . That's as far as it goes."

In what is probably his best trait, Mike is appalled when innocents are attacked. When Mike learns from Nacho that the "good Samaritan" who helped the Salamanca truck driver that Mike hogtied was killed, Mike decides to attack Don Hector, the head of the Salamanca cartel, directly—although he had just told Nacho that he was done with Hector. Mike is thwarted by Gus Fring, who tells Mike "I cannot allow you to kill Hector

Salamanca, but I am not unsympathetic to your sense of justice." Later, after Mike disrupts the Salamancas' drug running, Fring offers compensation, but Mike tells him "What I did, I didn't do for you . . . it's not the kind of thing I want to take money for" and that if Fring wanted his help in the future it'd depend on the work. When Dr. Caldera—the veterinarian who is Mike's conduit into the criminal underworld—offers a loan shark job, Mike declines saying that "I'm not breaking legs."

More substantially, the foundations for Mike's descent into the Albuquerque criminal underworld began in his early years as a Philadelphia police officer, outlined in "Five-O." Mike quickly learned that the way to survive in his precinct was to be a dirty cop and take money or bribes. Unfortunately, the same could not be said for his son, Matty, who joined the same precinct. Though Mike implored Matty to take the money so that his partners, Troy Hoffman and Jack Fensky—and the precinct as a whole—would not be suspicious of Matty's intentions to rat on them, Matty didn't listen and refused to take part in any illicit activities. Hoffman and Fensky killed Matty and covered up his murder as part of a raid on a drug house. A few weeks later, his partners are also found dead next to their patrol car. Both killings were considered to be ambushes, though we know that Mike was behind the deaths of Hoffman and Fensky. He goes to a cop bar where Hoffman and Fensky were and then pretended to be heavily drunk and got them to take him home.

In the bar, and again in the patrol car, Mike tells them that he knows they killed Matty, and that he will make sure that everyone knows the truth about his death. Hoffman and Fensky decide to stage Mike's suicide in an isolated industrial complex. Once they get Mike out of the car, Fensky convinces Hoffman that Mike's death is "for the greater good" in a warped sense. While they have stepped away, Mike takes this opportunity to attack them, though he is shot in the shoulder while doing so.

Some philosophers contend that the morality of an action is entirely dependent on its outcome, while others believe in a strict inviolable code of conduct, regardless of consequence. Immanuel Kant argues that the morality of an action is dependent on the intent behind it, not on the consequences it brings. Despite being responsible for killing Hoffman and Fensky, a normally repugnant act, the fact that Mike was avenging Matty and ridding the streets of murderous police officers—as well as defending himself from possibly being murdered—provide sufficient positive motivation. While killing wantonly would not be something that Kant endorses, the intent that Mike had to set up Hoffman and Fensky arguably has more acceptable underpinnings.

In contrast to Kant, John Stuart Mill believed that the idea of morality is centered around social rules as opposed to self-imposed universal maxims. In Mill's view, an action can be deemed morally wrong if the consensus is that it should be a sanctionable offense, whether those sanctions come in the form of legal or extralegal punishment, public shame, or merely a bad conscience. Many of Mike's actions are clearly illegal, though his reasoning for doing them is generally admirable. As a result, though these actions may be legally punishable, Kant suggests there is room for debate as to whether they are morally reprehensible.

"This Business Requires Restraint"

Given Mike's calm, unruffled demeanor, Stoicism is consistent with his internal code. In modern terms, saying you're a stoic often means that you're devoid of emotion. In contrast, it should be understood that Stoicism is a logical and ethical philosophy, which promotes self-discipline, industriousness, and production. Rather than lacking emotion, Stoics find pleasure in preparation, mindset, and doing a job well. According to Dirk Baltzly, Stoics held "that emotions like fear or envy (or impassioned sexual attachments, or passionate love of anything whatsoever) either were, or arose from, false judgements."

Stoicism is an ancient Greek and Roman philosophy, and there are several famed Stoics, including Seneca and Epictetus. In her survey of historical warrior cultures, Shannon French argues that the Roman virtues were the embodiment of Stoicism. If we "rule over our inner selves," then we "can enjoy those eternal goods which no external force can strip away from you, such as your own good character, honor, and integrity" (p. 68).

The value of Marcus Aurelius's *Meditations* can be seen in the way that Mike lives and works. Aurelius's admonition that "You have power over your mind—not outside events. Realize this, and you will find strength" is readily apparent by the calm demeanor that Mike exudes in exchanges and situations that would lead many or most of us to lose our cool. As Marcus Aurelius further advised, "When another blames you or hates you, or people voice similar criticisms, go to their souls, penetrate inside and see what sort of people they are. You will realize that there is no need to be racked with anxiety that they should hold any particular opinion about you." Whether he is being derided as a "troll under a bridge" by Jimmy for adherence to policy while working as a parking attendant, having guns pulled on him by a "wannabe" bodyguard, or realizing that Werner Zeigler's escape has jeopardized months of work, Mike tries to react to problems calmly. Werner was right to reference the roots of his name, "world plus strength" in German.

In wisdom that resonates to this day, *Meditations* reminds us to "Never let the future disturb you. You will meet it, if you have to, with the same weapons of reason which today arm you against the present." In other words, the time that we spend worrying about what might happen tomorrow, next week, or in a year is wasted. Focusing on issues at hand, now, is the path of the Stoic. Similarly, Mike lives without undue stress worrying about the future. As he tells Jimmy in "Bad Choice Road," "We all make our choices and those choices they put us on a road. And sometimes those choices seem small, but they put you on the road. You think about getting off but eventually, you're back on it." If we make informed, quality choices now, we can improve the path—but being overly concerned about "what ifs" will lead to indecision, and the path may be decided for us.

Beyond his work, Mike exudes a day-to-day Stoic lifestyle. It's common to suggest that a simple, unadorned lifestyle is "Spartan." Perhaps, but it is also Stoic. Aurelius noted that "Very little is needed to make a happy life; it is all within yourself in your way of thinking." His car is a 1988 Chrysler Fifth Avenue, thirteen years old by 2001, when the first season is set. Notably, he has a small home, and there are entire rooms that seem to be empty and unused. He has little furniture and no frivolities around the house.

In a scene so important it is shown twice, at the conclusion of "Marco" and the beginning of "Switch," Jimmy wonders why he didn't just split the embezzled money with Mike. Mike's response is telling: "Me, personally, I was hired to do a job. And I did it. That's as far as it goes."

He also clearly understands that taking up weapons indicates the intent to use those weapons against an enemy or opponent. He goes out of his way not to use force unnecessarily. He doesn't bring a gun when he first meets Nacho. He doesn't kill Tuco when hired to make Tuco "go away"—even when we learn that he has high level sniper skills that are later displayed in "Bagman" when Jimmy is ambushed in the desert while traveling with seven million dollars. He doesn't kill the Salamanca driver, instead leaving the driver hogtied, and unhurt. This leads Nacho to suspect that Mike was the thief, because

"Anyone in the game would've capped him without a second thought," and Nacho starts to wonder "Who's the guy who *won't* pull the trigger?" (emphasis in original line). Mike's willingness to find solutions that don't involve killing is a pattern.

According to Marcus Aurelius, it is wise to "accept the things to which fate binds you and love the people with whom fate brings you together but do so with all your heart." In Mike's case, if there is anything that he truly enjoys beyond the work that he does, it's spending time with and helping his daughter-in-law, Stacey, and granddaughter, Kaylee.

We can see from his interactions with both Stacey and Kaylee that he loves them greatly. He visits with them, picks Kaylee up from school, sits out in front of their house all night to protect them, and helps them find and buy a new house. He attends grief group meetings with Stacey because she asked him to, although it's very clear he doesn't want to be there. His actions speak volumes about how important they are to him, and he clearly loves them with the entirety of his heart. When he tells Stacey that "Anything you need, I'll be there" in "RICO" he means it. Much later, in "Bagman," his love for his family is reaffirmed though they have been less involved in his life. While stranded in the desert together, Jimmy asks why Mike keeps going and doesn't just give up, Mike responds by saying "I have people waiting for me. They don't know what I do, they never will . . . if I live, if I die, it really doesn't make a difference to me, as long as they have what they need. So, when it's my time to go, I will go knowing I did everything I could for them. Now you ask me how I keep going, that's how." His family is the literal reason why he lives.

"I do what I do so they can have a better life."

As Mike ultimately decides that he needs a way to launder his ill-gotten money from the Salamanca cartel truck, he strikes a deal with Gus Fring to become an "employee" at Madrigal Electromotive in "Fall." Fring intends to have him "work" as a logistics consultant for twenty weeks in order to completely launder the money he stole from the Salamancas.

Instead, Mike requests to be listed as a security consultant, and then shows up to work at Madrigal after stealing an access badge from a legitimate employee. Mike then spends the day going around that branch's facilities and assessing problems with its security before presenting his findings to the baffled branch manager who clearly has no idea who Mike is. At one point, Mike goes as far as to order workers to use proper safety equipment, because those are the rules. Lydia, the employee who "hired" Mike, is frustrated by his insistence to do work in return for money that was already his. Lydia concedes eventually, after their meeting in "Breathe," and Mike is brought on as a valuable and increasingly respected member of Fring's staff at Madrigal. That respect seems to be mutual despite Fring's evident willingness to commit acts that are morally reprehensible at best. This may be a result of Fring's moral consistency, relative to the mercurial Jimmy McGill. By Season Five's end, Mike clearly becomes what was known in Japanese samurai culture as a retainer, a warrior bound to his master or leader. Despite his original intentions in the criminal underworld, helping Stacey and Kaylee, he has become entrenched.

His work with and around Gus Fring further illustrates his internal code. When Mike errs regarding Werner, and the construction contractor leaves the secured site to meet his wife at a hotel, thereby compromising the security of the dig when he inadvertently clues Lalo Salamanca in on the job, Mike opts to take care of Werner himself—killing him in the desert—rather than Fring killing him. Mike takes responsibility for his shortcomings. Mike's code is also evident in his views towards Nacho Varga after he learns Fring is using Varga's father as a bargaining chip to keep him in the game—"You have a gun to his father's head, that doesn't sit with me." Fring may not agree with Mike's admonishments, but he always listens to them—and Mike isn't shy about offering them.

We All Make Choices

Aristotle believed that all morally sound and good people must necessarily have no regrets about their actions and must also be content with themselves, whereas "wicked men seek the company of others with whom to spend their days, but they avoid their own company" (p. 254). It's likely that Aristotle would view Mike as a "wicked" person, not because of his actions, but rather because of his obvious inner turmoil. He writes that when wicked men are isolated, they become uneasy by remembering troubling events in their past, and anticipating similar events to come, but that when they are with loved ones they can forget. This seems to be an especially apt description of Mike's life and perspective. As Aristotle says, "bad people are full of regrets," and Mike certainly has plenty of them.

Though Mike adheres to his manifesto, he—like all of us—is imperfect. He spent much of his career with the Philadelphia

Police Department as a dirty cop; his set-up of his son's partner, though eventually an act of both justice and self-defense, is (at best) morally questionable, as is his work in the criminal underground. He works for killers and drug dealers, and though he does try to keep them in check, he never tries to convert them to completely legitimate operations. The one time we see him lose his temper is to Kaylee, his granddaughter, who was asking about her father. As we noted in the outset, Mike Ehrmantraut is both fascinating and flawed.

Which brings us back to *"I've known good criminals and bad cops. Bad priests, honorable thieves. You can be on one side of the law or the other. But if you make a deal with somebody, you keep your word."* This quote is Mike in a nutshell. He aspires and falls short. As Aristotle suggests, he's a bad man filled with regret. But at the end of the day, without fail, his honor is bound in his word.

7

Saul Goodman Stands Before the Law

E.F. HAVEN

JIMMY: Fine you're going to make me walk back and get the stickers? I will walk back and get the stickers!

MIKE: I'm not making you do anything. Those are the rules.

In *Better Call Saul* the Law emerges as a character. The Law is more than just a collection of laws, but something in itself. Lawyers practice *the Law*, not a law. We say the court uses "the full force of *the Law*," not "the full force of laws." From the most upstanding to the sleaziest characters, everyone deals with and is dealt with by the Law. It haunts the actions of the characters like a phantom, always present but never seen. Whether lawyers or criminals, the Law imposes restrictions or distributes justice. It takes a cut as the price of doing business. It discriminates against 1216 Rosella Dr when it should be 1261 Rosella Dr. Jimmy McGill works with it to bring charges against Sandpiper and he works around it when fabricating evidence.

Many people claim to know the Law, yet no one talks to the Law or sees the Law. I want to bring this character out from hiding to ask: how should we understand the Law? And what can Jimmy McGill's journey teach us about the Law? Jimmy McGill transitions to Saul Goodman once he realizes the secret of The Law: The Law is an unfulfillable promise.

To understand the Law, and what this means for Jimmy McGill, we will look at the parable *Before the Law*, by Franz Kafka. Kafka wrote several books which were not published during his lifetime, but after his death, his work became so iconic it even got an adjective in the dictionary—Kafkaesque, which means characteristic or reminiscent of the oppressive or nightmarish qualities of Franz Kafka's fictional world. *Breaking Bad* paid homage to Kafka by naming Season Three, Episode 9, "Kafkaesque." While the translation of the title for our parable is difficult, it is something like "Before the Law." This parable was published separately in his lifetime, but included in his novel *The Trial*.

BEFORE THE LAW stands a doorkeeper. To this doorkeeper there comes a man from the country and prays for admittance to the Law. But the doorkeeper says that he cannot grant admittance at the moment. The man thinks it over and then asks if he will be allowed in later. "It is possible," says the doorkeeper, "but not at the moment." Since the gate stands open, as usual, and the doorkeeper steps to one side, the man stoops to peer through the gateway into the interior. Observing that, the doorkeeper laughs and says: "If you are so drawn to it, just try to go in despite my veto. But take note: I am powerful. And I am only the least of the doorkeepers. From hall to hall there is one doorkeeper after another, each more powerful than the last. The third doorkeeper is already so terrible that even I cannot bear to look at him." These are difficulties the man from the country has not expected; the Law, he thinks, should surely be accessible at all times and to everyone, but as he now takes a closer look at the doorkeeper in his fur coat, with his big sharp nose and long, thin, black Tartar beard, he decides that it is better to wait until he gets permission to enter. The doorkeeper gives him a stool and lets him sit down at one side of the door. There he sits for days and years. He makes many attempts to be admitted, and wearies the doorkeeper by his importunity. The doorkeeper frequently has little interviews with him, asking him questions about his home and many other things, but the questions are put indifferently, as great lords put them, and always finish with the statement that he cannot be let in yet. The man, who has furnished himself with many things for his journey, sacrifices all he has, however valuable, to bribe the doorkeeper. The doorkeeper accepts everything, but always with the remark: "I am only taking it to keep you from thinking you have omitted anything." During these many years the man fixes his attention almost continuously on the doorkeeper. He forgets the other doorkeepers, and this first one seems to him the sole obstacle preventing access to the Law. He curses his bad luck, in his early years boldly and loudly; later, as he grows old, he only grumbles to himself. He becomes childish, and since in his yearlong contemplation of the doorkeeper he has come to know even the fleas in his fur collar, he begs the fleas as well to help him and to change the doorkeeper's mind. At length his eyesight begins to fail, and he does not know whether the world is really darker or whether his eyes are only deceiving him. Yet in his darkness he is now aware of a radiance that streams inextinguishably from the gateway of the Law. Now he has not very long to live. Before he dies, all his experiences in these long years gather themselves in his head to one point, a question he has not yet asked the doorkeeper. He waves him nearer, since he can no longer raise his stiffening body. The doorkeeper has to bend low toward him, for the difference in height between them has altered much to the man's disadvantage. "What do you want to know now?" asks the doorkeeper; "you are insatiable." "Everyone strives to reach the Law." says the man, "so how does it happen that for all these many years no one but myself has ever begged for admittance?" The doorkeeper recognizes that the man has reached his end, and, to let his failing senses catch the words, roars in his ear: "No one else could ever be admitted here, since this gate was made only for you. I am now going to shut it. ("Before the Law")

To understand the parable and the choices Jimmy makes, let us turn to the analysis of Jacques Derrida. Derrida is an Algerian-French Jewish philosopher and the seminal figure of postmodernism. He lived from 1930 to 2004. In the world of philosophy people tend to either love him or hate him, but either way, his influence on philosophy cannot be denied. In his work *Acts of Literature*, Derrida lays out an explanation of this parable. We will see how Saul both parallels and, in the end, diverges from Kafka's "man from country."

Like the man from the country, Jimmy McGill begins standing before the Law. Before in the sense of time, as in *"before* I learned to tie my shoes." He spends years as a conman, bouncing around from con to con, with no direction. Jimmy decides to get his act together. He decides to become a lawyer and enter into the Law. Throughout the show, he is trying to gain access to be taken as a 'real' lawyer.

Jimmy is drawn by the promise of the Law. The Law not only offers him the chance for a new life but it is supposed to be open to everyone. Much like the man from the country, "[there] are difficulties the man from the country has not expected; the Law, he thinks, should surely be accessible at all times and to everyone," Is this not the promise of the Law? All people no matter where they come from should have access to the Law and find justice in the Law.

At the heart of a promise is a deferment. There is something I am promising will come. If I promise that I will pay back the money I owe tomorrow, the promise refers to the paying back of the money. The promise at the moment is deferring the meaning of the promise, to be completed when the promise is completed. In this way, we could take a freeway exit sign as a simple promise. The sign is promising that in one mile there will be an exit. The promise is fulfilled when you get to the exit.

The gatekeepers deny the promise of the Law. Like the man from the country, Jimmy McGill encounters a gatekeeper preventing him from entering the Law. This is captured by Mike working as the gatekeeper at the parking lot. While the courthouse is open, parking fees must be paid. Another gatekeeper is Howard at HMM. Through the first season, Jimmy McGill battles with Howard to get acceptance in the Law and is convinced Howard is the only one stopping him. Much like the man from the country, who "forgets the other doorkeepers, and this first one seems to him the sole obstacle preventing access to the Law. . . . He becomes childish, and in his yearlong contemplation of the doorkeeper he has come to know even the fleas in his fur collar."

Jimmy McGill obsesses about Howard rather than attempting to find entrance into the Law. He goes so far as to get an identical suit and childishly antagonizes him in meetings. As we come to find out, Howard is not keeping him from the Law but is one of his biggest advocates. So, like the gatekeeper in the parable, he is opening the door for him. The real gatekeeper is his brother, Chuck, who goes behind Jimmy's back to have the partners agree not to give Jimmy a job.

The denial of the promise constitutes a secret. Much like a secret society, the Law hides behind the gatekeepers, inaccessible and unknowable. Chuck seeks to keep the secret of the Law a secret, believing that the Law must be protected from people like Jimmy, especially unworthy people who attended the University of American Samoa's correspondence law school. In his work *How to Avoid Speaking: Deniel*, Derrida outlines this kind of secret. Let's say, I know something will happen tomorrow. But having this information is not a secret in itself. There is a lot of information I have that I don't share with others. You don't know what I had for lunch yesterday, but that isn't a secret. It becomes a secret when I actively deny people access to that knowledge. So, for a secret they need to know I am not telling them. I need to announce that I have a secret. It may not be as direct as saying I have a secret. I may simply make a face that suggests I know something. Then when they ask, I say, "Oh, nothing." Thus, the secret occurs when I promise I know something, and then I deny or revoke that promise. Because there is no longer a promise to fulfill, only a reference without anchor remains. I can deny any promise was ever made. If asked, I would say, I didn't say anything.

The Law is not just an unfulfilled promise, but an unfulfillable promise. Unlike secrets that will eventually get revealed, the secret of the Law is for no one to give. The Law can't speak itself. It is inaccessible. At any moment none of those laws are present or enforced. If I sit in silence, I do not hear anything. The Law itself does not enforce anything. I cannot turn over my couch pillows and find the Law hiding in the corner. As Derrida puts it, "The law is silent, and of it nothing is said to us . . . We do not know what it is, who it is, where it is. Is it a thing, a person, a discourse, a voice, a document, or simply a nothing that incessantly defers access to itself, thus forbidding itself in order thereby to become something or someone?" ("Before the Law," p. 208). The Law dictates and defines so much of my life, and yet it is silent. It does not say I should do anything. It isn't saying do this or that. It doesn't even say don't kill someone.

It only speaks through its agents. The court, the officer, the lawyer all speak on behalf of the Law, but none of them are the Law. As the story says, "I am only the least of the doorkeepers. From hall to hall there is one doorkeeper after another, each more powerful than the last. The third doorkeeper is already so terrible that even I cannot bear to look at him." None of the gatekeepers have even seen the Law themselves. Kafka nicely captures this when in *The Trial*, a priest tells this parable to the protagonist. The protagonist after hearing the story protests that the gatekeeper is deceitful. The priest responds by saying some interpret the gatekeeper as the one who is deceived.

> "It is based," answered the priest, "on the doorkeeper's simple-mindedness. The argument is that he does not know the Law from inside, he knows only the way that leads to it, where he patrols up and down. His ideas of the interior are assumed to be childish, and it is supposed that he himself is afraid of the other guardians whom he holds up as bogies before that man. Indeed, he fears them more than he does." (*The Trial*)

The Law presents a unique secret, the unfulfillable promise of the Law. This is a contradiction. What makes the promise a promise is that it can be fulfilled, yet the Law is unfulfillable. This core contradiction in the Law creates many contradictions in our interaction with the Law. For example, the Law appears withdrawn and inaccessible, yet always present, constraining, and affecting us. "It forbids itself and contradicts itself by placing the man into his own contradiction: one cannot reach the law, and in order to have a rapport of respect with it, one must not have a rapport with the law, one must interrupt the relation. One must enter into relation only with the law's representatives, its examples, its guardians" ("Before the Law," pp. 203–04). Another such contradiction, on display throughout *Better Call Saul,* is the noble and yet pedestrian appearance of the Law.

Since the Law is inaccessible, the task of keeping the secret of the Law, is delegated to the gatekeepers. And with it "to this task of keeping, the nobility is delegated." The lawyer acts with the highest of ethical standards, following the letter of the Law. But they also must treat the Law with the highest respect. When yelling at Jimmy, Chuck finally reveals some of his cards saying "The Law is sacred, this isn't a game." The use of the word sacred invokes religious connotations. And why not? For the Law transcends the human experience. Those who practice it are then like priests of a sacred order, a secret society. Derrida writes, "If the nobility is necessary, it is because this essence has no essence, it can neither be nor be there. It is both obscene and unpresentable—and the nobles must be left to take charge of it. One has to be a noble for this. Unless one is God."

On the other side, the Law is also mundane and petty like a gatekeeper. The work of a lawyer consists of paperwork and meaningless hearings. Kim Wexler finds this out all too well. Despite being in the respectable law firm of HHM, she is relegated to document review. The lawyers are petty, fighting over who gets what cases and sending her to a hearing with no chance of winning, just to prove a point.

It's an upstanding, sacred profession, yet it is mundane and petty. This is best seen in a flashback when Jimmy comes over to Chuck's for dinner. Jimmy makes a series of jokes at the expense of lawyers. At the same time, he keeps insisting he knows lawyers are good people. This moment is also revealing because it shows that the gatekeepers of the secret don't necessarily understand it. In response, Chuck becomes upset, showing us that Chuck doesn't understand the secret of the Law, but only sees the nobility in protecting the Law (Season Two, "Rebecca").

Now we can see that the secret of the Law both allows access and closes the door. The lawyer who enters the Law is put in an impossible position. It is impossible for anyone to truly reach the Law and stand in the presence of the Law. As a result, the man from the country and Jimmy are indecisive. They don't make a choice, waiting, often uncertain of themselves. As Derrida describes the man from the country: "Does he decide to renounce entry after appearing determined to enter? Not in the least; he decides to put off deciding, he decides not to decide, he delays and adjourns while he waits."

Jimmy oscillates between choosing the Law and choosing criminality. He's constantly presented with opportunities to enter into the Law, but he can't commit. He takes a job at Davis and Main, only to find himself a round coffee cup in a square cupholder. He stops at the end of Season Two when leaving the courthouse, to ask Mike why he didn't just take the money, wondering why he would even try when he could become a criminal.

However, Jimmy McGill's indecision is different from the man from the country. The man from the country wastes away waiting, forever expecting the promise of the Law to become fulfilled. Jimmy begins to see there will never be room for him in the Law, not without having to sacrifice himself. He can't be the lawyer he wants to be unless he starts his own law firm, where he can call the shots, where he can position himself how he wants in relation to the Law. Jimmy accepts putting himself in the impossible position not on the inside of the Law or outside the Law. As a result, he becomes Saul Goodman. Living outside of the Law. Not as an outlaw. But as one who stands *before* the Law. In this space between the Law and the outlaw (outside the Law), he finds freedom.

> The law is prohibited. But this contradictory self-prohibition allows man the freedom of self-determination, even though this freedom cancels itself through the self-prohibition of entering the law. Before the law, the man is a subject of the law in appearing before it. This is obvious, but since he is before it because he cannot enter it, he is also outside the law (an outlaw). He is neither under the law nor in the law. He is both a subject of the law and an outlaw. (Derrida, "Before the Law," p. 204).

Nothing holds before the Law, but Saul must hold himself. He stands in a contradictory place as neither and both, choosing to embrace the impossible.

It should be noted that only because of this tension can this story exist. If Jimmy simply accepts the nobility of the Law there is no show. And if he doesn't accept, just leaves and goes back to being a conman, there is no show. He does try in the final episode of Season One, finding that he can't return to his old life. Derrida says of the parable, "His resolution of non-resolution brings the story into being and sustains it. Yet permission has never been denied him: it had merely been delayed, adjourned, deferred."

Now that we understand the Law as an unfulfillable promise, that is as a secret, and the inaccessibility of the Law, we have been able to unpack both the parable "Before the Law" and the show *Better Call Saul*. Through this process we can come to see that only by dwelling in this liminal space between the Law and the country, could Jimmy McGill perceive both sides of the promise and the denial of the promise in the Law, letting him in on the secret of the Law. Only in this space could Saul Goodman appear as the best and worst lawyer. Unlike the man from the country, he needed to understand the secret of the Law and rather than seek access to the Law accept its inaccessibility.

In this way, the show *Better Call Saul* embodies the truth of the Law. Saul Goodman is exceptional at his job, not because he follows the Law as it is presented but because he knows the dirty secret of what the Law is: the undesirable, unexplainable secret that the Law is a phantom; it doesn't exist.

III

Put on your big boy pants and face reality

8
Self-Hatred as Identity

CONALL CASH

When Walter White 'broke bad', he expressed the frustration and resentment of a hard-working, middle-class husband and father who could no longer tolerate the indignity of his predicament or the disrespect he experienced in daily life.

Breaking Bad was a show about an ambitious and proud man who felt that the world had done him wrong, whose terminal cancer diagnosis propelled him to finally break with 'normal' society and reassert his ambition and self-importance in the criminal world. However much he changes over the show's five seasons, Walt never loses the sense that *other people*—from his colleagues at Gray Matter to Hank Schrader to Gus Fring—are at fault, preventing him from having the good life and the recognition he deserves.

The central characters of the prequel, *Better Call Saul*, are more ambiguous. The transformations of Jimmy McGill and Mike Ehrmantraut into the criminal figures they will eventually become do not take place primarily through a sense of resentment towards *others*, as does Walt's. Instead, their loathing and anger is above all directed at *themselves*. The originality and dramatic force of *Better Call Saul* stems above all from the fact that its central narrative arc—the transition of Jimmy and Mike into the characters they will be on *Breaking Bad*—takes place through their gradual acceptance of a negative image of themselves, or what the contemporary philosopher Martin Hägglund calls a "negative self-relation" (*This Life*, p. 185).

In asking themselves the question, 'How does a person *become* Saul Goodman the sleazy lawyer, or Mike Ehrmantraut the druglord's henchman?', Vince Gilligan, Peter Gould, and the other writers on *Better Call Saul* open up some profound and difficult philosophical questions about identity and person-hood: How does a person develop a self-image, or sense of self? Is it possible to live and sustain a life on the basis of a negative self-relation, a negative conception of yourself? Is it truly pos-sible to hate yourself? How do you live with becoming what you know to be the worst version of yourself?

To see how *Better Call Saul* helps us think about these questions, we need to go further into its world, and examine how the negative self-relations of both Jimmy and Mike pro-vide compelling responses to the narrative problem of back-story or pre-history faced by the show's creators. In a sense, both *Breaking Bad* and *Better Call Saul* are works of pre-history, and mark themselves as such from their beginnings. Both draw much of their dramatic power from their reversal of the TV convention of an *open* and *optimistic* future: from the first episode of each series, we know where it's going to end, and that the ending will not be a happy one. Walt is given that terminal diagnosis in *Breaking Bad*'s "Pilot," and this fate hangs over the subsequent sixty-one episodes of the series, with every new assertion of Walt's lust for power occurring against the backdrop of our (and his) knowledge that it will soon come crashing down. The entire series, we can say, is the pre-history of Walt's death, as he builds himself up into a leg-end (as the great Heisenberg) whose immortal glory he thinks will survive his mortal end.

This sense of pre-history—the sense that what we're watching is the build-up to an impending and unavoidable crash—weighs all the more on the viewer of *Better Call Saul*. From before the show begins, we know what awaits both Jimmy and Mike: namely, that they will become the char- acters we meet in Season Two of *Breaking Bad*, their involvement with Gus Fring and Walter White ultimately leading Mike to his death and Jimmy/Saul into hiding, where he will find himself "managing a Cinnabon in Omaha"—a job we find him performing in a flash-forward in the opening scene of *Better Call Saul*'s first episode, "Uno."

With this set-up, we know from the beginning that the drama of the series will be driven not so much by 'what hap-pens' as by the question of how these two characters 'become who they are' (to borrow a phrase from Friedrich Nietzsche). Liberated to a significant extent from the more superficial pleasures of wondering *what* will happen, the viewer can focus their attention on the *how* and the *why*. The wealth of context and prior investment in these characters that is available to us as viewers of *Better Call Saul* allows us to build an increasingly complex picture of their motivations, in terms of their respective conceptions of themselves as people.

This can be observed, for one thing, in how we let ourselves be mesmerised by sometimes absurdly intricate narrative detail, like Jimmy's switching of the address on some documents from "1621" to "1612"—our immersion in these details speaks to our interest in seeing how the narrative world whose outcomes we know in advance will fit together in a more complex and determinate form throughout this pre-history, and what nuances of character will be filled out in the process of enlarging this world.

I Broke My Boy

How, then, do Jimmy and Mike each come to take on the negative self-relations I evoked above; and why does this provide the key to bringing the fictional world of the series to a dramatically compelling whole? We can start with Mike, whose story is the simpler of the two, and acts as a minor variation on the major theme that is Jimmy's transformation.

Mike moves to Albuquerque, New Mexico from Philadelphia to be close to his daughter-in-law and granddaughter, his only living family following the death of his son, Matty, who was a rookie in the same Philadelphia police precinct Mike had worked on for decades. As we learn in the Season One episode, "Five-O," Mike is saddled with guilt, not simply for failing to prevent Matty's murder by two dirty cops, but for having made his son "debase" himself by advising him to accept their dirty money for his own safety. When Matty is offered stolen money from a drug bust by a colleague, he hesitates and goes to his father, asking him what he should do.

Mike tells him to take the money so as not to put himself in danger, and when Matty resists, Mike reveals to his son that he himself has been "going along," taking part in police corruption so as not to get into any trouble from his colleagues, for years. At the close of "Five-O," Mike tells all of this to Stacey, Matty's widow, in an astounding speech that gains its dramatic power from how far removed its emotional rawness is from the dour, taciturn manner Mike maintains on all other occasions. Crucially, this scene reveals how deeply Mike's self-conception has turned towards self-hatred, and how fundamental this will be to his character going forward in the series:

> He put me up on a pedestal. And I had to show him that I was down in the gutter with the rest of 'em. I broke my boy. . . . He was the

strongest person that I ever knew. He'd 've never done it, not even to save himself. I was the only one. I was the only one that could get him to debase himself like that. And it was for nothin'. I made him lesser. I made him like me. And the bastards killed him anyway.

For as long as his son looked up to him as a great man, Mike could at least half-believe it himself, finding strength and a reason to live by looking to the future that his son would be a part of, this son who would be better and stronger than Mike knows himself to be. In "breaking" his son, Mike breaks his conception of himself as a decent man, and breaks every last possibility of a future in which he might be absolved from guilt, in which he might be able to live in some form of self-acceptance. From now on, his life is over. All that he lives for now is to make money for his granddaughter, knowing that nothing he does will allow him to forgive himself. Having "broken" the one person who could make him think well of himself, there is now nothing stopping him from "debasing" himself ever further, falling deeper into the criminal world. Whereas the tragic irony of Walter White's accumulation of money was that he could never have enough to satisfy his pride, Mike's tragedy is a more self-conscious one: he is under no illusions that life in the underworld will make him "feel alive," as it does Walt. Instead, he will gradually let himself be led into working for Gus Fring, putting away drug money for his granddaughter's inheritance as the only positive legacy he can leave to the world, precisely because he knows that nothing will make him feel alive ever again.

A Chimp with a Machine Gun

Jimmy, like Mike, has defined his sense of self through his relationship to a blood relative: in his case it is his older brother, Chuck. As with Mike, it will be the recognition that he can never be good in the eyes of this beloved family member that will lead Jimmy further into ethically and legally "flexible" territory. Jimmy moves to Albuquerque from his home town of Cicero, Illinois, after Chuck—a prominent lawyer in Albuquerque—saves him from a prison sentence for a prank gone awry. Moving to New Mexico and vowing to play it straight upon his release, Jimmy goes to work in the mailroom at Chuck's firm, Hamlin, Hamlin, and McGill (HHM), and gradually works at getting a law degree by correspondence from the University of American Samoa.

HHM declines to invite Jimmy to work for them after he passes the bar, and so he struggles to make it in private practice, resenting HHM's figurehead, Howard Hamlin, for denying him the opportunity to work alongside his brother. In Season One's "Pimento," Chuck convinces Jimmy to bring his first big case to HHM, assuring him that a case of its size is too great for Jimmy to handle alone. Assuming that by bringing HHM the case they will finally invite him to join the firm and continue working on it with them, Jimmy is distraught and enraged when Howard turns him down once again, telling him that the firm don't want him, and offering him only a fee for referring them the case.

But in the final minutes of the episode, Jimmy is faced with the truth: it was his brother Chuck all along who worked behind the scenes to prevent him from getting a job at the firm. Jimmy confronts Chuck, demanding to know why his brother was working to undermine him all this time, and the contempt underlying all of Chuck's love and affection for Jimmy is brought to the surface:

> You're not a real lawyer. University of American Samoa, for Christ's sake? An online course? What a joke. I worked my ass off to get where I am, and you take these shortcuts and you think suddenly you're my peer? You do what I do because you're funny and you can make people laugh? I committed my life to this. You don't slide into it like a cheap pair of slippers and then reap all the rewards.

When Jimmy, close to breaking down, replies, "I thought you were proud of me," Chuck insists, "I was! When you straightened out and got a job in the mailroom, I was very proud." Proud, in other words, of his brother occupying a respectable position, as long as it is well below his own. Chuck, after a lifetime of disappointment in his brother, is certain that his low opinion of Jimmy is deserved, and that Jimmy himself will be better off if he accepts it and stops trying to be something more than he really is: "I know you. I know what you were, what you are—people don't change. You're Slippin' Jimmy. And Slippin' Jimmy I can handle just fine, but Slippin' Jimmy with a law degree is like a chimp with a machine gun. The law is sacred! . . . On some level, you know I'm right."

Jimmy, the ne'er-do-well younger brother, longs for Chuck's recognition of him as a good person, a good brother, and a good lawyer. But to Chuck, anything Jimmy does to try and prove himself will only be another scheme, a ploy to manipulate his way into favor. Growing up with a kind but weak father who ran a neighborhood store, the two brothers define themselves through their different responses to this upbringing. Chuck, the older brother, takes upon himself a sense of responsibility and ambition, committed to becoming a cultured and respectable man who will care and provide for his parents as they grow old, becoming the strong presence that was lacking in his own childhood.

A Sheep in Wolf's Clothing

As Chuck goes off to university, his younger brother Jimmy is left at home to help out at the store, witnessing his father's failures and humiliations as he lets people rip him off and allows the business to fall slowly into ruin. In Season Two's "Rebecca," Chuck reveals his knowledge that Jimmy had been stealing money out of the register at their father's store for years. Chuck remains incensed by the fact that he could never get his parents to see the truth about their younger son: "Dad wouldn't hear it. Not his Jimmy," Chuck recounts. Their father died not long after his business went under; "at the funeral," Chuck wryly reports, "no one cried louder than Jimmy." For Chuck, Jimmy will always be this selfish and irresponsible child, not even conscious of the consequences of his own actions, while the sober, responsible, all-seeing Chuck is left to "pick up the pieces" left in Jimmy's wake.

Yet as we learn in a flashback scene in "Inflatable," two episodes later, Jimmy's behavior at their father's store cannot so clearly be put down to selfishness and irresponsibility. After pleading in vain with his father not to hand over money to a scammer, young Jimmy is forced to face the fact that his father will never stand up for himself, will never have the savvy to look out for his own and his family's interests. Seeing the conflict between father and son, the scammer decides to give Jimmy a life lesson, while the father is out of earshot: "There are wolves and sheep in this world, kid. Figure out which one you're gonna be." When the man leaves and young Jimmy pockets some cash out of the register—for the first time, it seems—he does so with a look of dejection and anger on his face.

What Chuck fails to appreciate in his judgment of his kid brother is that Jimmy's turn to the scamming and trickery of "Slippin' Jimmy" is an act of disappointment and contempt towards his father for his failure to notice him: Jimmy steals because he knows he will get away with it, and he hates his dad for letting him do so. In stealing, he confirms his disappointment in his father for neglecting to hold him to a standard, for neglecting to care enough to notice his youngest son falling through the cracks. And, we may assume, his stealing also expresses some anger at his older brother for going away and leaving him to live with this neglectful, absent-minded father, putting him in a situation where the only way he can seek attention is as a jokester and a scam artist.

To Chuck's mind, Jimmy is a wolf in sheep's clothing, full of laughs and smiles as he scams the gullible. But what we learn is that he is really something like the opposite: a vulnerable sheep who dons the costume of a wolf because it is the only way he feels he can be noticed. With every success he has scamming or stealing, he only reconfirms his low opinion of himself, as someone who can get away with murder because no one cares enough to pay attention to what's really going on with him.

In the present timeline of the opening seasons of the show, Jimmy sees the possibility of gaining some sense of recognition and self-respect by being a good brother to Chuck, and by making Chuck proud of him through his achievements as a lawyer. But this is something he will never succeed in, and in our advance knowledge of the person he will become as Saul Goodman, we spend the series filling in the detail of how Jimmy will be led to abandon his hopes of proving himself as a respectable lawyer and man, to Chuck and to himself. The power and tragedy of their relationship stems from the fact that for each of them, having a positive self-conception requires demanding something of the other that they are unwilling to give. Chuck needs to "keep Jimmy down" (both physically down in the mailroom, and symbolically down in the world of the weak and insignificant) in order to confirm his sense of himself as the responsible, decent one, the one who has carried the family name (as he reveals in "Rebecca," he is even named after his father) and made it shine in respectable society. Jimmy, meanwhile, needs his brother to see the good and the talent in him, needs to be treated by him as a peer, and this recognition is the thing Chuck is most incapable of giving.

As the series develops and Jimmy finds himself 'slipping' into his old ways, making what Mike calls "flexible" use of his new legal wiles (Chuck's nightmare of "a chimp with a machine gun"), he has the pleasure of finding out that he is good at something that can bring him wealth and a kind of recognition. But this pleasure is tainted by the knowledge that with every such success he is only confirming Chuck's negative image of him, that he is becoming that monstrosity, "Slippin' Jimmy with a law degree," and letting Chuck be right about him once again. The more he's forced to see that nothing will ever be enough to gain Chuck's recognition and respect, the more he accepts the image of himself he has received from Chuck, seeing himself as a crook and a scammer who will never be any good. His every revenge in outsmarting Chuck—a cycle that reaches its greatest heights in the trial sequence in Season Three's "Chicanery"—only makes him accept all the more the worst image of himself, as the one who can succeed by trickery because he will never truly be accepted as legitimate and respectable, least of all by himself.

Jimmy's transformation into Saul is a result of his gradual acceptance of this image of himself as "not a real lawyer," as the showman and the joker who bends the rules to get ahead, rather than putting in the decent hard work of a real, upstanding servant of the law. At first he is immersed in a struggle with Chuck and with himself, and is tormented with worry and guilt at his own worst actions in the conflict with his brother. But eventually, as the possibility of things ever being any different diminishes, his conscious bitterness and sadness fade away, to the point where he effectively becomes the mask he wears, and Jimmy gives way entirely to Saul. The key turning point is Chuck's death by fire at his home, which occurs in the Season Three finale "Lantern," and which Jimmy discovers in Season Four's opener, "Smoke." Racked with despair and worry about what led to his brother's death, Jimmy makes it through the funeral in a daze. Then, Howard Hamlin comes to him to express his own remorse for forcing Chuck's resignation, worried that he may have driven his former partner to suicide. Jimmy, while realising in this moment that he himself has played a role in Chuck's final unraveling, seizes upon Howard's sense of responsibility as an opportunity to free himself from despair and guilt: "Well, Howard," he responds, "I guess that's your cross to bear." Upon speaking these words, Jimmy stands up, walks across his apartment, and resumes his everyday activities with a smile.

In letting Howard take on the remorse that he himself has been feeling, Jimmy appears to 'let go' of his own negative feelings, his negative self-relation. But it has not gone anywhere; at best, we can say that it has become unconscious. In 'forgetting' his bad feelings, Jimmy embraces the persona of a happy miscreant, unconcerned by the laws he may be breaking or the ethics he may be betraying. In doing so, he accepts Chuck's vision of him, Chuck's assertion that he will never be a respectable peer or upstanding citizen. He accepts the version of himself that Chuck urges him to give in to during their final conversation, in "Lantern": "You have regrets? I'm telling you, don't bother! What's the point? You're just gonna keep hurting people. If you're not going to change your behavior—and you won't—why not just skip the whole exercise?"

The slow build of the show's five seasons so far takes us to the point where Jimmy McGill has begun to morph into the caricature of the person that is Saul Goodman, with Jimmy's conscious negative self-relation replaced by Saul's happy-go-lucky superficiality and hedonism. The latter, we now understand, is the mask with which he protects himself from conscious recognition that he is becoming the person Chuck told him he would—"Slippin' Jimmy with a law degree," "a chimp with a machine gun"—while we, the viewers, are the only ones to appreciate the tragedy that he need not have become this person if Chuck hadn't *needed* him to, for the sake of preserving his own sense of superiority and virtue. The mask of Saul eventually becomes Jimmy's true face, a face plastered around Albuquerque, captioned by the cheesiest of slogans: "Better Call Saul."

Being and Nothingness at a Cinnabon in Omaha

Both Mike and Jimmy define themselves through a negative self-relation, through an essentially self-loathing conception of themselves. In different ways, this self-loathing is what leads them to become the people they are by the time we meet them in *Breaking Bad.*

For Mike, it takes the form of an acceptance of the irreversibility of his guilt for "breaking" his son, such that, knowing that he will never be a good person in his own eyes, he can compromise himself further, devoting what is left of his own life to stashing away drug money for his granddaughter, looking towards a future world whose goodness and decency will be assured only by his own absence from it.

For Jimmy, becoming Saul Goodman is the answer to the problem of knowing that he will never gain the recognition from his brother that could allow him to feel himself to be a good person. His self-hatred becomes unconscious, but with every success he enjoys as Saul, he reconfirms to himself that he is nothing other than the lying, cheating, conniving trickster his brother told him he would always be.

The stories of Mike and Jimmy offer a compelling exploration of the phenomenon of negative self-relation. Philosophically speaking, this is not an easy question to think through, and rich character studies like those provided by *Better Call Saul* can illuminate it through their efforts to answer concrete narrative questions, like the question of how Mike and Jimmy become the Mike and Saul we know from *Breaking Bad*. The question of negative self-relation is philosophically challenging because it confronts us with the problem of how someone can simultaneously be the *subject* and the *object* of a negative judgment.

As Jean-Paul Sartre argues in *Being and Nothingness*, when we speak negatively of ourselves—such as when we say the words, "I am evil"—we are treating ourselves as objects, creating a separation between the consciousness that speaks and the one whom consciousness is speaking about, even if both are located in the same physical body. Sartre argues that "I am not and cannot be evil for myself," that no one can truly regard themselves as evil (p. 365). Sartre's point is that if I declare myself to be evil, I am no longer referring to myself as I experience myself, but to a foreign object. To truly *be* evil for myself (to *treat* myself as evil), I would have to willingly act as the evil person I take myself to be. But if I willingly do something, I am doing it because I affirm it, because I take it to be *good*. Thus the attitude of self-hatred has something contradictory about it. The judgement that I am evil is always the judgement of *an other*, and when I bring this judgement upon myself, I do so by seeing myself as an other, through the eyes of other people.

In a sense, this is exactly what Mike and Jimmy both do. Mike takes on a negative image of himself by internalising his son's disappointment in him, a disappointment that is redoubled by his failure to save his son's life; while Jimmy takes on Chuck's image of him, letting himself become the low-life Chuck needed him to be. They each sustain the identity of someone who has decided he will never be any good, and through this they reach deeper into worlds and behaviors they themselves—at least initially—see as immoral. But what *Better Call Saul* shows is a far more dynamic and layered process than the one Sartre describes. Sartre's refusal of the concept of the unconscious, expressed at an earlier point in *Being and Nothingness*, may point to the limitations of his analysis of the phenomenon of self-hatred (pp. 92–95).

Jimmy cannot function by *consciously* hating himself, since, as Sartre shows, when we hate ourselves in an explicit and conscious way, we judge ourselves from the outside, and affirm as good some other way of living from the one we've been practicing. If Jimmy hated himself in this manner, he would be hating a person he doesn't want to be, and would not be able to continue living in this unjustifiable way. Once Jimmy becomes Saul, he is clearly no longer judging himself explicitly like this. But this is because his self-hatred has become unconscious: he can avoid being weighed down by it in daily life only by taking on the worst image of himself, and forgetting the part of himself that ever thought he could be any different. It may in fact be Sartre's final, unfinished work, *The Idiot of the Family*, which offers more insight into the character of Jimmy McGill. This book, concerned with the childhood and youth of the novelist Gustave Flaubert, is a study of the difficulties experienced by a younger brother born and raised in the shadow of a beloved eldest son, who finds the world a strange and lonely place, and becomes a kind of inventor and trickster in an effort to make the world notice him.

Going into *Better Call Saul*'s final season, however, one big question remains about how much Saul really has 'forgotten'. The name of this question is: Kim Wexler. Kim's fate, still unknown, holds the missing piece in the puzzle of how Jimmy becomes Saul, and what remains of Jimmy McGill in the hollowed-out Cinnabon manager going by the name of Gene Takavic.

Does Kim have to die for Jimmy to complete his conversion into the sleazy, contented trickster, Saul Goodman, with no one left alive who has ever believed in him? Or does his conversion hide a secret, with Kim's protection playing a role all along in Jimmy's embrace of the mask of Saul? Whatever the answer, for it to work, it will have to contribute to the picture that has so far been developed of Jimmy's negative self-relation. *Better Call Saul*'s achievement stems not so much from its answers to the question of *what happened* to these two men to make them into the people they eventually become, but rather from what it shows us about *how* they each take on a negative self-relation, as the only avenue left to them to go on living.[1]

---

[1] The ideas presented in this chapter draw on extensive conversations about *Better Call Saul* I've had with Jonathan Davenport. All errors remain my own.

9

The Prequel versus Free Will

Landon Frim

> If I had to do it all over again, I would maybe do some things differently. I just thought you should know that.
>
> —Jimmy McGill

What can a fictional TV show tell us about free will? Can it demonstrate this chapter's bold claim that free will is a nonsensical concept? Perhaps that's asking too much.

But while works of fiction can't *demonstrate* a philosophical point, they may *illustrate* one. Here, the hit series *Better Call Saul* is uniquely qualified for the task. And that's because it's a prequel. A prequel is, by its very nature, an earlier story that explains a later one—in this case, the events of Vince Gilligan's *Breaking Bad* universe. A prequel illustrates the point that, however surprising or dramatic a situation may be, there's always some causal explanation behind it. As such, prequels embody that logical doctrine known as the "principle of sufficient reason." Broadly stated: *For every event there is some cause.*

It doesn't matter if "the event" in question is a drug war, a plane crash, or that you ordered tequila instead of a Moscow Mule at lunch; there has to be some causal story about why that event (and not any other) came to pass. Otherwise, we lapse into an unscientific, unintelligible world where some things happen for literally no reason at all. So, we might ask, how does a frustrated schoolteacher come to operate a crystal meth empire? Why did he partner with a "criminal" lawyer named Saul Goodman? And how did Goodman position himself as a flashy consultant-to-criminals in the first place?

The benefit of the principle of sufficient reason is that there are always answers to these questions; it's just a matter of tracing the story—the intricate pattern of causes and effects—back ever further. There's always a story behind the story, a prequel to the prequel to the prequel, *ad infinitum*. In Mike Ehrmantraut's words, "We all make our choices. And those choices . . . they put us on a road. Sometimes those choices seem small, but they put you on the road" ("Bad Choice Road"). The principle of sufficient reason agrees, but adds that there are reasons why you made those choices in the first place. There's no beginning or end to this road; It's infinitely long, and we're always, already on it.

The *Better Call Saul* universe tells us that, as with any deal, there's a price that must be paid. The cost of buying into the principle of sufficient reason is the shocking realization that things could not have been otherwise. We may protest all we like, and with Saul Goodman (then called Jimmy McGill), insist that, "If I had to do it all over again, I would maybe do some things differently." ("Lantern") But in a universe governed by the principle of sufficient reason, what philosophers call a "deterministic" universe, that is mere fantasy. There are no do-overs and no "could-have-beens," but equally, there is no room for regret. What did happen had to happen.

In the face of such a reality, most people recoil in horror. Their condemnation of the deterministic universe typically boils down to three basic complaints: 1. it makes the world boring, 2. it casts life as amoral, and 3. it degrades human beings as mindless. Determinism, so it is argued, transforms us all into thoughtless, irresponsible puppets, passively jostled here or there by strings that stretch back millennia. But these complaints miss the mark, and in fact, are nothing more than myths. A closer look at *Better Call Saul*—as a prequel—can help us to demolish these myths. The deterministic universe, one free of "free will," can be a fascinating, morally significant place where people's decisions and life projects really matter.

But First . . . Heisenberg!

You can hardly mention the debate between determinism and free will without someone piping up three seconds later with the epiphany, *"But quantum mechanics says . . ."* And it doesn't matter if the interloper is a theoretical physicist, or a self-help guru, or if they even bother to finish their sentence. Everybody knows that quantum mechanics disproves, once and for all, a deterministic universe of cause-and-effect. Randomness is at the very foundation of things. Therefore, they surmise, free will must be real.

Within quantum mechanics, "Heisenberg's uncertainty principle" expresses the idea that there are fundamental limits to how much we can know about the world. That's why Walter White takes on the persona "Heisenberg" in the *Breaking Bad* series. He's transformed from a browbeaten teacher who always follows the rules, to a dangerous, *unpredictable* meth kingpin.

The problem with simply invoking "quantum mechanics" is that it confuses a mathematical model with reality itself. The model suggests that the qualities of particles (their position and momentum) can only be known "stochastically," or in other words, as a matter of probability. Therefore, there's no such thing as certainty when it comes to the fundamental building blocks of the universe.

But does this mean that the world, *itself*, is uncertain or indeterminate? Are there no "hard facts" with definite causes, but only spontaneous, indeterminate happenings (at least at the level of individual particles)? Many physicists think so, while others disagree. Serious scientists have developed nearly a dozen, mutually-conflicting interpretations of quantum mechanics with differing stances on the "determinism" question. An example of a deterministic interpretation of quantum mechanics, currently held by some physicists and philosophers, is the so-called "pilot-wave theory" which was first proposed by Louis de Broglie and later developed by David Bohm. (See Wayne Myrvold, "Philosophical Issues in Quantum Theory.") Which of these theories makes the most sense is a topic which far exceeds our discussion here. What is clear, however, is that simply uttering the phrase "quantum mechanics"—as though it were some kind of magical spell—is insufficient to settle any philosophical debates in a serious way.

But let's get to the point: Does quantum indeterminacy (supposing it's real) prove the existence of free will? Heisenberg himself (the uncertainty principle's namesake, and not the fictional drug lord) thought that it did. The contemporary physicist, Michio Kaku, takes a similar line, proclaiming that, "No one can determine your future events given your past history. There is always the wildcard" ("Why Physics Ends the Free Will Debate").

Yet here, again, we see a basic confusion. That's because randomness ("the wildcard") in no way equals "free will." Free will is the idea that we supposedly make rational, deliberate decisions without being caused to do so. Mere randomness or spontaneity simply doesn't get you there. An uncaused spasm or convulsion is not the stuff of meaningful choice. Thus, even if quantum indeterminacy were true, and even if it applied to people just as well as particles, this picture does nothing for the cause of free will. Indeterminism suggests the presence, not of "free choice," but rather of a mindless, erratic flux.

So much for Heisenberg. With mere "uncertainty" set aside, we can move on to the three most popular myths levied against the deterministic universe.

Myth 1: Determinism is Boring

What makes for a good story? According to some partisans of free will, it's the unpredictability of unforced choices and the idea that the future is radically "open." Anything could happen. By contrast, a world governed by mechanical cause-and-effect is a terribly dull place. If everything is explicable in light of what came before it, then there can be no real novelty or drama. The adventurous life of the protagonist is replaced by the dull, monotonous grind of the cosmic machine. In that case, even the most valiant hero or dastardly villain is but a cog within this clockwork universe. This, at least, is the common claim.

Now, obviously, it's sloppy reasoning to say that the universe must be a certain way because that would make things more interesting for us humans. So what if a universe full of free will is more intriguing than a "dull" determinism? A universe populated by technicolor jackalopes might also be more exciting, but that's no reason to believe in them. Oddly, such wishful thinking is not limited to the daydreams of "lay people," but can be found within the works of some of the most esteemed philosophical minds.

The philosopher William James defended free will, at least partly, because it provides more "subjective satisfaction" than does determinism. After all, he says, "What interest, zest, or excitement can there be in achieving the right way, unless we are enabled to feel that the wrong way is also possible?" ("The Dilemma of Determinism"). Similarly, the French theorist Bruno Latour complained that determinism went against the "narrativity" that made worldly events meaningful for us humans (*Facing Gaia*, p. 72).

But even if wishful thinking is a poor way to do philosophy, there's a more basic problem with the claim, "Determinism is boring." Simply put, it's just not true. Determinism—the intelligible connections between events—is the *only* thing that makes for a compelling narrative. To make this perfectly clear, consider the following two stories:

Story One

Walter White, a high school chemistry teacher, becomes an unlikely producer and distributor of crystal meth in the Albuquerque, New Mexico area. Why? Because White was diagnosed with terminal lung cancer and is anxious to provide for his family after his demise. In danger of being exposed by the DEA, White hires a local lawyer, "Saul Goodman" as his advisor and consigliere. Why choose Goodman? White finds Goodman because he actively markets himself to Albuquerque's criminal class. He dresses in ostentatious, flashy clothing, and even changed his name from Jimmy McGill to Saul Goodman (a play on the phrase "S'all Good Man") to match this new persona. Why did he do that? Goodman (aka., McGill) developed this unsavory client base when he sold untraceable burner phones in a seedy restaurant parking lot. Why did McGill sell burner phones? Because his law license was suspended. And why did this happen? Because he was caught breaking into his brother's house to falsify some legal documents. Why? Because his brother, Chuck (also a lawyer), stole a client away from Jimmy's then girlfriend, Kim Wexler. Besides, Jimmy and Chuck had a longstanding rivalry owing to their diametrically opposed personalities. Chuck is the consummate rule-follower, if rather pretentious. Jimmy is a longtime cynic when it comes to the law. And why did they develop such different personalities? Well, there are reasons. These reasons stretch back to their childhood in Cicero, Illinois, but at this point you should just watch the series!

Story Two

Walter White, a high school chemistry teacher, decides to produce and distribute crystal meth. He does so of his own free will. Period. No streaming subscription necessary.

Which story is more intriguing? There's really no contest. It's precisely the circumstances, personalities, and agendas *behind* a character's choices that make for a meaningful storyline. The ubiquitous "because . . ." (the explanatory *cause*) is the very essence of telling a tale. These causes may be external to a character's mind, like a cancer diagnosis, a DEA investigation, or a suspended law license. Or, they may be internal features of a character's psyche, such as romantic love, fraternal jealousy, fear, ambition, or greed.

Either way, the thing that explains a character's decisions is exactly what makes those choices at all meaningful, and thus, potentially exciting. And, of course, even our inner states (emotions, intentions, and desires), don't come about spontaneously. We are bold or meek, principled or cynical, passionate or unfeeling *for some reason.*

To be fair, the proponents of free will never claim that our decisions are *totally* independent of causes and influences. Not believing in pure randomness, they soberly agree that both "nature" and "nurture" matter when it comes to how we behave and the choices we make. Their reasonable-sounding claim is only that there is some small element of freedom, some wiggle room, when it comes to our actions. And *this,* they claim, is where all the drama in life is to be found—within that small, unaccountable domain of unforced decision.

But then, the advocates of free will are faced with a stark dilemma: Within that small space supposedly left for free choice, do we choose *for some reason* or not? If we do choose for some reason, then their arguments truly amount to nothing; the "wiggle room" disappears entirely and they reveal themselves, in the end, to have been good determinists all along. Yet if they answer the other way—if, within our range of possibilities, we choose for literally no reason at all—then this lands us back in the meaningless (and thus boring) world of indeterminacy. Heisenberg comes knocking again, as it were. Our vaunted "free will" is nothing more than a random spasm (albeit one occurring within some limited framework).

Either response to this dilemma critically undermines the free will position. What remains clear is that the drama in real life, as in fiction, is to be found in its intricate patterns and connections, not in their (total or partial) absence.

Myth 2: Determinism is Amoral

Perhaps the deterministic world can be exciting, but is it moral? Can one be ethical in a universe that lacks free will? Tellingly, *Better Call Saul* follows the exploits of a criminal defense attorney. The whole series is an extended meditation on guilt and the question, "How did it come to this?"

When it comes to the law, "mitigating circumstances" are those factors that lessen the seriousness or culpability of a criminal act. The thinking goes that we deserve less blame if we committed a crime while suffering from an emotional breakdown, a cognitive disability, or some other burden on our judgment. Crimes done in the "heat of passion" or by persons suffering "diminished capacity" may be treated with more leniency as opposed to, say, a premeditated murder done "in cold blood" by a fully competent adult.

But all this raises the question: What counts as a "fully responsible" criminal act? A skillful lawyer might explain away even the most depraved misdeeds if they can point to sufficiently mitigating circumstances. That's what McGill attempts in the episode "Uno" when defending three young men who broke into a funeral home. His closing argument stretches the notion of mitigating circumstances to the max:

> Think back. Your brain—It's just not all there yet. If we were all held responsible for what we did when we were nineteen . . . Let me tell you. The juices are flowing. The red corpuscles are corpuscling, the grass is green, and it's soft, and summer's gonna last forever. . . . But if you're being honest, I mean, well, really honest, you'll recall that you also had an underdeveloped nineteen-year-old brain. Me, personally . . . If I were held accountable for some of the stupid decisions I made when I was nineteen . . . Oh, boy, wow. ("Uno")

It turns out that the three defendants didn't just break into a funeral home, but also removed a head from one of the corpses before having sex with it. Needless to say, this wasn't a simple case of criminal trespass. Jimmy's closing argument fails, and the three young men are sent to prison. He can't get the jury to believe that "underdeveloped nineteen-year-old brains" and "corpuscling corpuscles" excuse sexually violating a corpse.

Fair enough. But the question remains: Is *anybody* truly responsible for their misdeeds, however disgusting or violent? If everything happens for some reason, and if those reasons— those causes and effects—stretch back from before you were born, then does the category of "guilt" even make sense? Maybe the deterministic universe is amoral after all?

On the other hand, perhaps what we really need to do is to rethink our definition of morality. The conventional view of ethics is that people are good or bad because they choose to be. That's supposedly why premeditated murderers *deserve* to go to jail, to say nothing of corpse desecrators. "Just deserts" and "free will" appear to be inextricably linked; you can't have the one without the other.

But then, why not discard both concepts together? We don't need either of them to do ethics. A murder is devastating because it ends a life, causes pain and suffering in the victim, and extended emotional trauma for their loved ones. Stipulating that the murder was intentional, *but also* that these intentions were totally spontaneous, only confuses matters. Murder is bad because its effects are bad. That's enough to pass moral judgment.

We can naturalize our ethics to include words like "suffering," "joy," and "wellbeing," but leave out concepts like "sin," "blame," and "guilt." The former list are merely subjective states that can be experienced by living, breathing human beings. They are desirable or undesirable according to our ordinary human natures. The latter list is made up of confused pseudo-concepts. Words like "blame" and "guilt" spring from an essentially supernatural idea of evil. One imagines a mysterious, dark desire to do wrong—just because.

Yet the problem with the notion of willful "evil" is that the more premeditated a misdeed is, the clearer it becomes that it was done *for reasons*. That's what "premeditated" means after all. It's a crime done, not just out of momentary passion, but from some planned, deliberate intention. The question then becomes, were our so-called "reasons" reasonable, or were they confused?

In Season One of *Better Call Saul*, we meet perhaps the two most comically self-deluded criminals in the entire series. Craig and Betsy Kettleman embezzle $1.6 million dollars from Bernalillo County where Craig was treasurer. This is clearly a premeditated white-collar crime, and not some spontaneous act of passion. It required planning, and math, and subterfuge. But in the episode "Hero," when Jimmy suggests they give the money back, their rationale for the crime lurches wildly from "it wasn't illegal" to "it was illegal, but fair."

> BETSY KETTLEMAN: We are not giving this back. We are not guilty. This money belongs to us. We are—well, I mean, Craig earned it.
>
> CRAIG KETTLEMAN: I worked very hard. You know, weekends, holidays.
>
> BETSY KETTLEMAN: All unpaid, always. And really, just because you're salaried, doesn't mean you don't deserve overtime. I think that's only fair.
>
> CRAIG KETTLEMAN: I mean, really, that's what this is about, right?
>
> BETSY KETTLEMAN: Fairness, right. . . .
>
> CRAIG KETTLEMAN: I mean, not just what's legal. If you want to talk about legal . . . slavery, that used to be legal. Human slavery. So . . . ("Hero")

Do Craig and Betsy believe their own defense? Who knows? Maybe they realize, deep down, that stealing the money was wrong, but that this knowledge was overwhelmed by the irresistible impulse to get rich. Or perhaps they're truly as deluded as they seem, and they actually believe that embezzling

$1.6 million is a fair remedy for not being paid overtime. Either way, what we have here is a disorder of proper reasoning. The fact that the crime took a long time to commit, and was planned in advance, in no way changes the fact that it was born of some mixture of delusion, ignorance, or impulsivity.

Any criminal deed, supposing it's truly wrong, will be the same. In the words of Socrates, "No one goes willingly toward the bad" (Plato, *Protagoras*, 358d). If a person clearly understands that doing X is wrong, then they will not do it. That's counterintuitive because we can imagine all sorts of people (including ourselves) doing selfish, violent things because it makes us feel good, even though we know it to be wrong. But what's really occurring here is a kind of self-delusion or a breakdown in reason. In the split-second where we steal, lie, or harm another, we convince ourselves that it *is*, in fact, the right thing to do. We tell ourselves all sorts of self-exculpatory tales, such as "they had it coming," or that "everyone bends the rules sometimes," or simply that "it's time I got mine." But no one truly thinks they are doing an unjustifiably bad thing at the very moment of action. (That's indeed why the action can occur in the first place!)

A crime of passion is one where our thinking is distorted or overwhelmed all at once. A premeditated crime is one where our reasoning breaks down over a longer stretch of time. But how this question of timing makes certain crimes more "willful" than others is terribly unclear. Disordered thinking is disordered thinking, no matter how subtle or gradual our confusion. And no one *chooses*, out of the blue, to think poorly. At any rate, we don't need to pretend that harmful acts are done voluntarily to call them harmful. The effects speak for themselves.

Myth 3: Determinism is Mindless

If ethics is ultimately about the *effects* of our behavior, then doesn't this discount things like intentions, motivations, and inner beliefs altogether? Determinism assigns a causal explanation for even the most heinous criminal trespasses, but in so doing, it seems to set up a universe which is essentially "mindless." Our inner states don't matter because they, like everything else, are merely the result of previous circumstances.

However, this too is a myth. The deterministic universe is one which fully recognizes the existence of minds, along with all the things that minds do: weighing alternatives, anticipating consequences, and judging results. What's more, just as we can judge some actions as better than others, so too can we perceive that some minds function better than others. That's a controversial-sounding claim, but one well-illustrated within the _Better Call Saul_ series.

Nacho Varga and Tuco Salamanca both worked for the Juárez Cartel, and at one time, Tuco was Nacho's immediate boss. But the similarities really end there. The personalities of the two are drawn in high relief so as to accentuate their starkly opposite natures. Nacho is calm and collected, even in the face of extreme violence. Tuco, by contrast, is a bundle of impulses, emotions, and paranoia. His mood swerves erratically from maniacal laughter to unfettered rage. Tuco's long-standing drug habit (at first "biker crank" and then crystal meth) doesn't help matters ("Gloves Off").

And because of this, he's easily manipulated. In "Mijo," Jimmy convinces Tuco not to kill his two associates by appealing to Tuco's outsized sense of pride. "Now you have to decide, what's the right sentence? Like a judge." Being compared to a judge? That's exactly the thing to kick Tuco's egomania into overdrive, and it works.

A mind can be judged functionally—according to whether it follows its own, logical rules (Nacho), or if it's constantly compelled from the outside (Tuco). In the latter case, it's immaterial whether the mind is overcome by a chemical substance, delusions of grandeur, or simple ignorance. In each instance, something gets in the way of its own, logical deliberation.

Still, if proper reasoning is something objective (logic is logic after all), then it seems to deprive the mind of genuinely free choice. Either we clearly perceive what's rational, and act accordingly, or we're overwhelmed by other stimuli (drugs, paranoia, flattery), and our thinking breaks down. We _necessarily_ choose what's right, or we are _caused_ to choose what's wrong.

But this doesn't mean that the mind is a non-entity. By way of analogy, a machine may not freely design itself nor does it choose how well it operates; it nonetheless exists, and one can judge how efficiently it functions all the same. So too are minds more or less active or passive, autonomous or enslaved by external passions. They exist, even if they don't spontaneously _choose_ to exist.

Besides, "knowing what is right" (especially in the moral sense), often presents itself to the mind as an unwelcome, but nonetheless irresistible fact. In "Lantern," Jimmy has a sudden realization: He can help his elderly client, Mrs. Landry, but only if he thoroughly discredits himself in front of the whole retirement community. Sitting with his girlfriend, Kim Wexler, this realization hits Jimmy like a ton of bricks.

JIMMY: No. Oh, shit.

KIM: What? What is it?

JIMMY: [*Chuckles*] Mrs. Landry.

KIM: You figured it out.

JIMMY: Yeah. But I really, really don't wanna do it.

Jimmy *says* he doesn't want to do it. Who wants to purposefully invite the hatred of a crowd of adorable seniors? But really, it's no choice at all. Jimmy sees all too clearly that it's within his power to help Mrs. Landry, and what's more, it's the right thing to do. He is moved by the sheer force of his own good reasons. We might say that Jimmy is "powerless" to resist this force, but that's not quite right either. For "reason" is that very quality by which we judge the power (the functionality) of a mind. He *has* to help Ms. Landry, but this necessity springs from his own thinking, and not from some outside manipulation.

Acting Lessons

Within the deterministic universe, there may be no "free choices," but there are such things as power, morality, and reason. These qualities are enough to make for a dramatic story and a meaningful existence. That every life (fictional or real) can be explained by some prequel takes nothing at all away from it.

Whatever circumstances got us to this point, we're here now, in the middle of things; we are actors in this story, and not mere observers of it. And actors act, for they cannot do otherwise. Criminal or pillar of society; showman or recluse—these are all ways of acting and shaping our future. The life-decisions we make aren't free, but regardless, they are genuine decisions with real effects. And since we do possess a mind, then we will necessarily seek out what we believe is best, and act on it, to the best of our abilities. In this, we have no choice.

10
Slippin' Identity

KRISTINA ŠEKRST

> I know you! I know what you are. People don't change. You're Slippin'
> Jimmy.
>
> —CHARLES LINDBERGH MCGILL, JR. to James McGill, "Pimento"

Instead of saying "You're a liar. A conman. A dishonest man.
A cheater," it was enough for Chuck just to state that he was
"Slippin' Jimmy." All of the character traits that make Slippin'
Jimmy a Slippin' Jimmy are already present in the name.

"Saul Goodman" seems to refer to a different person than
"James McGill." The former is a quick-witted and somewhat
sleazy lawyer, while James McGill is an underdog living in the
shadow of his more successful brother and colleagues. Gene
Takavic is a quiet and emotionally broken shopping-mall manager, while Viktor Saint Claire is a fictitious wealthy man drinking
expensive tequilas and thinking about becoming even richer.

They all seem like different characters even though they
are all, in fact, the same human being. However, they seem like
different people since not only the alias changes, but the main
character traits as well.

What's It Like to Be Jimmy?

In countries that allow such a practice, it's not unusual for
patients with dementia to request euthanasia. One peculiar
case involved a seventy-four-year-old woman signing a
written declaration stating she wanted to be euthanized at
the moment her demented state took over her life. However,
when the time came, she started fighting for her life. It was
as if a different person had signed the former consent and the
new person was incapable of reaffirming it.

So, what does being the person that one is amount to? The problem of personal identity tries to answer questions such as: *Who is Jimmy? What are the things that make Jimmy the person he is? What is it to be a person? What does it take for a person to exist from one point to another?* If Jimmy is just his body, then the introductory case might seem simple: we're dealing with the same person. Saul Goodman is the same person as James McGill, Slippin' Jimmy, Viktor Saint Claire and Gene Takavic. And even Bob Odenkirk!

Yet this somehow doesn't feel right. A more intuitive notion is that personal identity has more to do with someone's mind as opposed to their body. The idea here is that personal identity requires some kind of *psychological continuity.* Psychological continuity refers to a kind of autobiographical memory. Jimmy remembers himself being himself yesterday or even years and decades ago, having the same beliefs, views, desires, intuitions, and personality traits. If Jimmy would equate his identity with his consciousness only, it would seem as if he was losing his identity every time he went to sleep. But what does not change? Jimmy's inner mental world in general. It's an intuitive position in which your thoughts, desires, fears and character are what makes a person exactly that person. Jimmy can lose his hair or change his appearance, we would still feel as nothing has changed about who Jimmy really is.

Seems good, everything we need is just some old-fashioned psychological continuity! However, if we take a closer look at psychological continuity, a number of examples come to mind that raise the question of the type and amount of psychological continuity needed to ground personal identity. We have mentioned that all of us lose consciousness for at least a couple of hours per day. We just don't consider sleeping to be a kind of a break in our psychological continuity ("I need at least eight hours of psychological discontinuity" doesn't seem to be a valid excuse to be late for work, but I encourage the reader to try his luck.). We might argue that a longer or different type of break in psychological continuity is needed to lose personal identity. However, if Jimmy slips into a coma that might take weeks, months, or even years, is he really that different when he wakes up?

Is Hector Salamanca still Hector Salamanca after waking up from a coma? I wouldn't dare to ask him that. If we were to wake up from a coma, most of us would probably claim we were still the same person. Intuitively, unconscious moments somehow don't seem to count, but again they do if they're a different type of (un)consciousness, such as in the case of

Alzheimer's disease, dementia, or various psychological ill-nesses. However, we don't have to think about rare events such as comas or diseases, all of us have lost the memories and beliefs we had in the first couple of years of our lives, and yet continued to consider those kids as us. So, it doesn't seem that psychological continuity is what grounds personal identity, or at least the sole thing responsible for it.

Physical Self

If Jimmy's psychological continuity is not enough to ground his identity, maybe there's something worth checking out regarding his physical continuity. Such a stance is often called the *brute-physical view*. Similar to psychological continuity, we can talk about *bodily continuity:* a way to state that there is a threshold limiting how much of our body stays the same so that we're still considered the same person. It seems easy to attack such a position, even a graduate of the University of American Samoa could do it. No one would deny a person their identity if the human being in question is missing some organs or limbs. Again, there might be a threshold (in the words of Monty Python, "it's just a flesh wound!"), similar to psychological continuity.

However, even though the technology is currently not as developed, we might propose a thought experiment involving a brain transplant. If Jimmy's brain was transplanted into another body, most of us would intuitively feel that the old body didn't matter anymore. There might be another issue at stake as well that might turn the tables. Suppose Jimmy had cancer spreading through his brain, which could be resolved by replacing it with a donated one. If such a procedure were possible, it might provide him with new memories and traits. If that happened, our intuition would again feel as if some point of identity has been broken. On the other hand, if Jimmy's mental states, desires, beliefs, and personality did somehow stay the same, this would feel as if Jimmy had gotten a lung transplant: he would still feel like Jimmy, the same way Walter White would still feel like Walter White after a lung trans-plant. So, it appears that Jimmy's mind does seem to matter a great deal in regard to his identity after all.

Once Upon a Time

Perhaps the notion of personal identity then consists of a combination of both psychological and bodily continuity, and both sides of the coin might influence the other. Consider the case of Phineas Gage, an American railroad foreman who survived an accident in which an iron rod was driven through his head, which destroyed his left frontal lobe. After long and exhaustive treatment, he was left blind in his left eye and retained some facial weakness, but no obvious neurological deficits. Had the story ended here, it would have been another example of a medical triumph. However, it seems that the injury had significant consequences on both his behavior and personality. His friends were stating that he was "no longer Gage." Compare this to the episode "Blood Money" of *Breaking Bad* when Hank tells Walter White: "I don't know who you are. I don't even know who I'm talking to," being shocked to discover that fundamental character traits he thought Walter possessed are now different. One might even argue that Walter's tumor was changing his behavior.

One way of trying to tackle the question of personal identity is to abandon the mind-body problems altogether. Maybe some portions of our minds are important, maybe some aspect of our bodily continuity weighs in as well. *Narrativism* is the view that states that we persist from one moment to another as the same person—having the same personal identity—because we're able to tell the same story about our- selves. Jimmy doesn't have to be Homer and write an epic about his life, but he would have a general idea of what sort of a human being he is in some fundamental sense. He would tell the same story about his half-an-hour-ago self as he would now. But he probably wouldn't do it for his fetal phase, early childhood, or maybe even himself from years or months ago.

Imagine Jimmy on a first date with Kim. She would ask him to tell her about herself. You have some, coherent or not, idea about who you are, what your beliefs, desires, attitudes, or traits are. That's the narrativist account. Sometimes it's not accurate, but even a lie might be a part of who Jimmy really is and how other people see him if he presents himself like that.

One intuitive motivation for narrativism is the fact that sometimes other people help us identify some parts of our lives. People are going to tell you how you acted when you were a kid, even if you don't remember it now. So, it's not only Jimmy who's telling his life story, it might also be others. But he's still the guy who's telling what to accept and what not. Somebody might tell you you did some nasty stuff while drunk, and you might deny such a narrative because that *just isn't you.*

That said, consider the seventy-four-year-old dementia patient mentioned previously. She wouldn't tell the same story as her former self had. And the whole *Better Call Saul* series, along with *Breaking Bad* as well, is illustrating how a person's identity changes with different circumstances. Walter White from the beginning of *Breaking Bad* doesn't seem to us like the same person as Heisenberg from the final episode, and we're bound to see Jimmy McGill become Saul Goodman and slip into a new personal identity. But there are other character developments we might see as identity changes from different perspectives. Charles McGill, suffering from an apparent psychological disorder, is not fully considered the same person he was by his former peers, even though he is treated the same by his brother Jimmy.

Slippin' Jimmy

Let's presume the nature of personal identity has something to do with the story a person tells about himself. The story Jimmy is telling is actually *constituting his identity*—it's who he really is. This doesn't mean he can start telling everybody that he's the world's best lawyer, it will probably only constitute his identity as a liar. Even though he doesn't feel like the same person he was when he was two years old, he will still tell his life story including those years. It might seem wrong to include something he doesn't remember as a part of his identity. Narratives, of course, don't arise out of thin air, and he's not the only participant in the story, even though he's at its center. Parental reminiscence and other people's stories still constitute a big portion of a person's identity. Remember the time you were hearing about all the things you did when you were really drunk? You still may have done some embarrassing things, and not remembering them doesn't excuse you from the possible repercussions on your identity. I know, philosophy is dangerous.

However, this isn't the only story that should be considered. Chuck's mistake lies in the fact that he thinks that only one story forms the complete Jimmy McGill's identity: that of Slippin' Jimmy. In his past, Jimmy did stage slip and fall accidents to make quick cash. But in "Slip," Jimmy is claiming that Slippin' Jimmy is "back in Cicero, dead and buried." In "Wiedersehen," there's a heartbreaking scene between Jimmy and Kim: "You look at me and you see Slippin' Jimmy", says disheartened Jimmy, once more rejecting his former identity. A past Jimmy is being *Jimmy* if he has narratives supporting such a connection. He's the narrator and the protagonist, and he's the one to decide what he takes to be his own life. That way, Jimmy can consider Slippin' Jimmy to be a past part of him, but not feel it's constituting his identity right now.

In the narrative process, one might be self-delusional or say one thing and do another. For example, Jimmy might claim he never lies. We know that this is not the case. Jimmy also might try the fake it till you make it tactic. He might start telling people he's not afraid of anything, even though he is. It would still be a part of his narrative and a part of his personality. But can we require accuracy? We aren't perfect computers remembering every little thing in detail, nor do we constantly act according to some predefined principles. Jimmy's narrative might even describe events that never happened: sometimes, a hidden trauma or a story one made up can be a huge part of one's identity. Okay, then Jimmy might still claim he was Shakespeare, right? He could also state that he was an honorable man, and such a description would constitute his story. But the others are here to believe it or not.

It seems that pure narrativism wouldn't work without adding a certain kind of a reality constraint: Jimmy's life story doesn't have to be entirely true or perfect, but his memories need to be *grounded in reality*, at least in principle. Jimmy may give up on certain aspects of himself or try to act like a different person. If we didn't allow that, then turning a new leaf would be impossible. Or even realizing one liked tomatoes or cigarettes after all. Producing a narrative is understood *dispositionally*: Jimmy doesn't need to recite thousands of pages of his life story (even though we all, unfortunately, know a person who does that), but in certain circumstances, he might. He doesn't need to tell everything about James McGill, the lawyer, but he might if asked.

Saul Goodman

In *Breaking Bad*, we were only seeing the Saul side of James McGill. In such circumstances, that really was his identity. It was a story we as the audience learned to believe, but now we have different narratives to choose from. James McGill has presented his alter ego Saul Goodman to the world as "the last line of defense for the little guy," "a righter of wrongs," a "friend to the friendless." Since he's the protagonist of the story, such a description seems ultimately identity-constituting. But is James McGill really Saul Goodman, just by sharing the same physical body and psychological continuity? We have seen various objections to arguments considering psychological or physical continuity. Or is it like the case of a person believing he was Shakespeare? If narrativism is such a necessary prerequisite of our identity, then any continuity break would end our existence. Imagine that, no need for suicide, Jimmy just needs to stop telling his story and bang, he's done. Do remember that one's constituting narrative is only a *disposition*: he doesn't need to actually recite it, but he has to have the ability to do so in some way.

However, this again raises the problems of psychological continuity as a marker for identity. If someone's suffering from dementia, his life story is now different, or maybe even completely lost. Some people have argued that Chuck McGill is suffering from early-onset dementia. From a narrativist standpoint, the former Chuck McGill is gone, because it seems that he no longer possesses the disposition to tell the *real* story of Chuck McGill he once was. If mental trauma isn't widespread, Chuck might have "good days" in which he remembers it, but if not, then the breaking of the narrative really constitutes a new life story, a new person, and a new identity to converse with. In real life, old habits may always creep back. Chuck can give up on some narratives, but then they might come back. But he will always have *a* narrative to tell, there's no way to escape it. Chuck might end up as a different person, willingly or not.

Narrativists often emphasize that our narratives are prone to revision. Our memory isn't perfect, our life choices change. In "Quite a Ride," Jimmy proclaims: "I'm gonna be a damn good lawyer. And people are gonna know about it." And we really, really want to believe that. However, we have mentioned that often Jimmy's autobiographical point of view isn't enough. First, it has to be somewhat grounded in reality. Second, Jimmy might not have been aware of some important or less important moments in his life. None of us was aware of the most important moment of our life—our birth. However, if the society is influencing Jimmy's narrative, can we safely state that James McGill *is* Slippin' Jimmy, and that would constitute his identity? Now we go back to the criterion of being grounded in reality. This is where we as the audience need to decide whether James McGill acting like the best lawyer ever is grounded in reality or is Slippin' Jimmy often taking over? We might even say that Chuck's identity is also at stake because of his seemingly psychological fear of electricity.

Gene Takavic

In flash-forward sequences at the beginning of each season, James McGill, now under yet another alias Gene Takavic, works behind the counter in a store called Cinnabon. Winding down after work, we see Gene watching an old VHS tape of Saul Goodman's TV commercials from his former life. Gene begins to cry. James McGill was disowning his Slippin' Jimmy identity, but it seems that he was really trying, and maybe even—to his standards—succeeding, to be the best lawyer ever. In "Switch", he carves the initials SG into a wall. It seems that James McGill is genuinely identifying with his Saul Goodman persona.

Consider again the question of *persistence*. Does Saul Goodman *exist* anymore? Jimmy, wanted by the police, apparently can't narrate his Saul Goodman story anymore. Other people can, but the autobiographical part is missing, even though it's dying to come out. Perhaps we could survive without narrative continuity, maybe it's possible that Saul Goodman is still "alive." It seems wrong to think that one moment, narrative continuity matters, and suddenly it doesn't. Therefore, we need to weaken our claim: it might not be *necessary* for us to persist from one point to another, but it might be *sufficient*. It's not enough for Jimmy to just kick the ball while playing soccer to score a goal, but it's a necessary step, he can't use a cannon, according to the rules of the game. But for it to be sufficient (enough), it needs to pass over the goal line and include the necessary conditions.

Jimmy doesn't need to remember his early childhood to consider it a part of his identity, and he did survive without narrative continuity, the same way Saul Goodman doesn't need narrative continuity to make a comeback as Jimmy's (perhaps *true*) identity. But if Jimmy compares himself from a current standpoint to himself at some point in the past, he might establish a new narrative continuity, the same way Gene can recall his former Saul Goodman self by remembering the person he once was and reidentifying as such. Of course, this doesn't tell us when exactly an identity was created. This seems like an easy way out, Jimmy can just establish a narrative continuity whenever he wants to. How convenient!

There isn't an easy way out or a right way to answer the persistence question, and it seems that the most satisfying answer lies in the combination of all the mentioned criteria. But the notion of persistence isn't the only relevant question in this argument. The *characterization question* asks what makes us the people we are, what are our beliefs, desires, wishes, preferences, and similar mental states. Narratives are presented as an adequate answer. Even if we might not be sure when Jimmy persists from one point in time to another, we can argue that Jimmy's narrative is pinpointing at least the *necessary* conditions of what it is like to be Jimmy.

If Jimmy's having an identity crisis, then he's not sure of the very fundamentals of his identity and whether they're necessary, sufficient, or neither. However, it seems intuitive that other people can't tell him what his *fundamental* character traits are since their narrative isn't as important as his regarding *his* life story. His is necessary, theirs *might* be sufficient. And being Slippin' Jimmy or Saul Goodman presupposes different necessary characteristic properties. Chuck or Kim can accuse Jimmy of being Slippin' Jimmy, but if he identifies his most fundamental character traits to be those of Saul Goodman, nobody can take that away from him, maybe not even himself.

James McGill

So, who is James McGill? A little bit of everything, and it depends on the point of time we're observing. He really was Slippin' Jimmy and Saul Goodman at different points in his life. He's superficially Gene Takavic, but this doesn't bear any identity-altering changes except for the silly mustache.

Narrativism explains how different identities can be distinguished even if we're seemingly dealing with the same body (and therefore presupposing the same mind). The only thing that matters is that Jimmy is able to tell a new story about who he really is. Starting a new chapter is taken literally, as a way of reaffirming or abandoning your former identity. Sometimes other people contribute to his story, and sometimes not. Sometimes it's not easy to tell when or where an identity shift took place. But James McGill can transform into Saul Goodman or back into Slippin' Jimmy, not in a weird werewolf way, but as a change of heart and mind great enough for himself and other people to consider him a different person. When such a shift happens, the person formerly known as James is now telling a new story about who he really is. And we're here to listen. In the words of a wise scholar, Lalo Salamanca, "Tell me again. I just want to hear the story."

11

The Self-Deception Road

DARCI DOLL

A commonly accepted truism in philosophy is that it is good to have true beliefs, bad to have false beliefs. Even outside of philosophy, this principle seems to hold. We praise those who correctly identify what's true and incorporate that into their beliefs; we criticize those who believe things that are false.

Yet we can't ignore the fact that it's easier said than done to have only true beliefs. Some truths are beyond simple consideration and require advanced thought or study. In addition to this, there are many people who wish to deceive us. Whether it be a slick-talking scam artist or a blustering, seemingly authoritative attorney, there are those who would benefit from us having false beliefs and at least some of these people actively attempt to make this so. In these cases, the source of the false belief is interpersonal deception.

Interpersonal deception is fairly easy to define. Interpersonal deception occurs when someone intentionally imparts false information to someone with the intent to deceive. This form of deception need not require that the deceiver knows the actual truth. Rather, all that is required is that the person is knowingly convincing someone else to believe a false belief. In this sense, we can come up with examples of interpersonal deception easily.

When Jimmy and Kim scam people in hotel bars, they're engaging in deception to get free tequila (though arguably it's more for the thrill than the actual tequila). While the motivation to deceive others and the philosophical analysis of what it means to be deceived is interesting, there is a more perplexing philosophical problem regarding deception: self-deception. Self-deception is when we deceive *ourselves*.

From looking at interpersonal deception, we might conclude that *self*-deception also involves being aware of the deceit.
How can we knowingly deceive ourselves? In practice, however,
the deceived individual does not believe they are being
deceived. Rather, they believe the deception wholeheartedly.
Most people are aware that they may have false beliefs, but typically speaking will modify those beliefs when provided with
evidence of the falsity.

Self-deception, then, involves an inability to rationally recognize that certain beliefs are false. Herein is the contradiction. An individual can convince themselves to believe
something false, yet fail to be able to recognize that the belief
is false. The individual *doing* the deceiving is likely to be
unaware that they're being deceived. This is unique to other
types of deception where a person knowingly deceives another
with intent to deceive. The lack of demonstrable intent to
deceive is often missing in cases of self-deception. There are
many examples of self-deception in *Better Call Saul*. Many of
the primary characters operate under false beliefs and even
maintain those beliefs when challenged. We see self-deception
in Jimmy's evolution into becoming Saul Goodman; Kim's self-
deception that makes her relationship with Jimmy possible;
Chuck's self-deception about his health. These examples, plus
the many more not listed, illustrate the question: how do we
manage to deceive ourselves?

It is possible that a person has a false belief because of lack
of evidence. In this case, we hardly would consider this to be
a form a self-deception. Self-deception appears to be more
nuanced and doesn't apply every time there is a false belief.
Rather, there seems to be a requirement that there is something beyond insufficient evidence that is obstructing the
belief. Gregg Ten Elshof notes that self-deception can occur
when "we manage our own beliefs without an eye on main
progress toward the truth. It is most likely to occur when we
have strong emotional attachments to belief on some topic.
When we have no attachments, the general desire to believe
what's true is likely to guide our inquiry" (*I Told Me So*, p. 27).

With self-deception we seem to have made a bargain with
ourselves. We consciously (or subconsciously) agree to remain
ignorant. In fact, there is a phenomenon where exposure to evidence contradicting a belief not only fails to change the belief but
may actually cause the belief to become stronger (psychologists
call this the backfire effect). Additionally, we can know about the
possibility of self-deception (and the backfire effect) and still be
unable to recognize our own self-deception. This complicates

the problem: how are we supposed to recognize self-deception when our beliefs seem true?

One way that a person can be both the deceived and the deceiver is through what Ten Elshof calls "attention management." Deception can occur when you focus your attention only on the things that you care about, or want to believe. By being selective with your attention, you can filter through things that you don't want to believe. In doing this, you are exercising control over what you believe and selecting which sources of evidence are viewed as being reliable or necessary. Attention management can result in selecting information that favors, or confirms, our beliefs. This selective attention can also focus on information that goes against our beliefs with the intent to discredit those beliefs (such as in the backfire effect above).

A second method of self-deception is procrastination. In this case, the person puts off confronting the belief until it becomes a non-issue. By putting off examining the belief, you can diminish the need to be held accountable by the belief. I can be sincerely moved by humanitarian aid and can vow to do more to help my fellow humans. But for some reason, I can't (or won't) act now and by putting off the good acts until later, I can diminish the urgency of the belief. I may feel guilt in not acting, but I deceive myself into believing that it's okay because I'll do it *later*. By putting off holding myself accountable for my beliefs, I can deceive myself into believing that I *will* eventually hold myself accountable. Even the strongest moral beliefs may diminish or disappear if pro- longed long enough. In some ways attention management can work with procrastination. In choosing to prolong addressing our belief/ holding ourselves accountable we can also select what we're paying attention to as a means of distraction.

A third form of self-deception is what Ten Elshof calls perspective shifting. In perspective shifting, the person adjusts what they are paying attention to or how they choose to perceive something. When we adjust our perspective, we often focus on the perspective that we find most desirable. One way to adjust perspective is by looking at a situation through the eyes of others. Perhaps I don't give much humanitarian aid and I feel guilty. However, my friends may think of me as being generous and charitable because of the ways I've helped them. In shifting my perspective from the general humanitarian aid to the local aid appreciated by my friends, I can see myself as charitable and avoid being confronted with the truth.

One of the more common forms of self-deception is rationalization. Rationalization happens when we try to justify prob-

lematic beliefs. These reasons are given in a way that creates
room for justifying the belief or behavior. Kim may rationalize
accepting Jimmy's behavior because she thinks that overall
he's a good person who means well. She gives reasons to ignore
the red flags Jimmy raises and as a result feels justified in
maintaining a relationship with him.

These four means of self-deception are present throughout
Better Call Saul. The prominent characters all struggle with
self-deception and move through these four forms.

Chuck versus Electricity

One of the more intriguing, and possibly most obvious, examples of self-deception is Chuck's illness: electromagnetic hypersensitivity. We are first introduced to Chuck's sensitivity to
electricity in "Uno." We see, without a complete explanation,
the desperate lengths that Chuck and Jimmy go to, to accommodate Chuck's illness: grounding before entering the building, removing everything with batteries, removing all
electricity from the residence. Even with these extreme means,
Chuck is still sensitive to the electricity outside of the house
(and as a result is housebound) and relies entirely on Jimmy to
have some semblance of a functioning life.

When Chuck's disease is first introduced, its severity and
rarity are clear. Additional details, like treatment and progno-
sis, are initially omitted. We soon get the official diagnosis in
"Alpine Shepherd Boy" when Chuck is admitted into the hospital. In this episode, it is shown that his illness results in both
physical and psychological damage. When the electricity in his
hospital room is diminished, Chuck is revived and is able to
explain that while Jimmy has oversimplified his condition, it's
not a totally inaccurate representation of his illness. He has
developed a sensitivity to electricity that, in this case, can
essentially render him catatonic. It's also accompanied by
excruciating physical pain. Jimmy's protectiveness of Chuck
coupled with Chuck's calm, rational demeanor as he describes
his condition, makes Chuck's condition appear plausible and
deeply concerning.

In response to the Doctor's doubts Chuck claims, "Anyone
who's spent more than a few minutes with me knows this isn't
some sort of delusion." After the doctor tricks Chuck by turning on the electric bed without result she argues that he needs
psychological help. Jimmy concedes that he won't say that
Chuck's condition is one hundred percent real, but Chuck is
smarter than the both of them. The implication here being that

someone as intelligent as Chuck wouldn't succumb to a baseless delusion; there must be something legitimate going on that is causing Chuck's pain and suffering.

Jimmy's insistence that there must be a legitimate physical medical cause to Chuck's condition despite the evidence to the contrary is a sign of the effectiveness of Chuck's self-deception. Chuck has convinced himself that his condition is a physical medical condition caused by a sensitivity to electricity. Unlike the forms of self-deception that are discussed above, Chuck's illness has an underlying psychological cause. His condition is very real; however, he is deceived about it being a physical illness when it's actually psychological.

In "Uno" Chuck believes that he will beat the condition and will return to Hamlin, Hamlin, and McGill (HHM). Howard Hamlin, appears to go along with this, but it's uncertain whether he believes the full extent of Chuck's condition. It's likely that Howard realizes this is psychological and is trying to assist Chuck to the best of his ability. To whatever extent people believe in Chuck's condition, essentially everyone in his life works with him in some way to accommodate his illness. In this case, Chuck may be engaged in both attention management and perception shifting. Chuck is reinforcing his self-deception about his illness with the confirmation of the people around him who agree (whether sincerely or not) with his condition. This shared perception allows Chuck to confirm his belief that he has a debilitating physical medical condition. Additionally, Chuck is able to focus his attention on activities and decisions that confirm his belief in the physical nature of his condition.

While it's apparent that Chuck is believing something that is false, one may question whether this counts as self-deception. Chuck, after all, appears to have a debilitating chronic psychological condition. Consideration of this condition, and minimizing its damage should be the priority. As we see in the series, Chuck is eventually able to (at least temporarily) manage his condition. With a carefully regimented routine under the guidance of a medical professional, Chuck is able to regain some semblance of normalcy. When Jimmy visits Chuck in "Lantern," Chuck has restored electricity to his home. They exchange tense words and Jimmy's hopes for reconciliation are dashed when Chuck said Jimmy never really mattered to him.

Despite the progress, Chuck backslides and becomes obsessed with the idea that electricity is still getting into his home. Tragically, in what Howard later says was not an accident, Chuck dies when one of the gas lanterns ignites a pile of papers. The original cause of his psychological disorder remains unknown and his relapse after his brief recovery was unanticipated by those who loved him and marked a tragic and dark end to Chuck McGill. Despite the underlying psychological cause, Chuck still engaged in self-deception. By ignoring the evidence that his condition was psychological, perspective switching and attention management he reinforced a deceptive belief. By accommodating Chuck's needs due to his condition his self-deception about the *cause* and *nature* of his disorder, helped or hurt remain intact. The true extent of the levels of deception taken to accommodate his condition will likely never be appreciated.

Chuck versus Jimmy

Chuck's perception of his condition was likely a psychological coping mechanism and in some ways differs from traditional self-deception. In Chuck's case, he is accommodating a dangerous psychological condition and had found a coping mechanism. It's unclear whether he would have been in a better state if he had been forced to address his condition, for example in the medically suggested thirty-day psychological examinations.

As a character, Chuck's mind, intelligence, and integrity rendered him an apparent hero of the series. Those who knew him looked up to him, Jimmy sought to live up to his image and his expectations. Someone as rational as Chuck, even with a dangerous psychological condition, seems an unlikely candidate for self-deception. After all, it seems that a shrewd rational mind like Chuck's would rationally examine his beliefs and be less prone to self-deception. However, his self-deception of Jimmy is one that prevented him from seeing Jimmy's full potential. Deceiving himself about Jimmy's true nature may have been a contributing cause for Jimmy's return to his "Slippin' Jimmy" ways.

Chuck sees Jimmy as a scamming con artist. Others, however, see the potential for good in Jimmy. Howard calls Jimmy "Charlie Hustle" because of the way he hustled his way through life. In Howard's meaning, he's not using hustle as a pejorative term referring to ripping people off or scamming them. Rather, it's a compliment to Jimmy's determination and willingness to work hard to achieve his goals. Jimmy is a hard worker at HHM. He secretly works to go to law school and pass the bar exam. He fights to prove himself worthy of being accepted as a lawyer at HHM. When the latter fails, Jimmy claws his way through life working as a public defender, eventually expanding into a successful foray into elder care.

What Howard sees in Jimmy is the opposite of what Chuck sees in him. Unlike Howard, Chuck can only see Jimmy's bad traits. He has directed his attention toward the "Slippin' Jimmy" character traits and refuses to pay attention to the "good" character traits that Howard and others see.

For Chuck, Jimmy will always be the criminally inclined "Slippin' Jimmy" from their childhood. He has a clear understanding of where Jimmy belongs and, despite Jimmy's best attempts to prove otherwise, it's not within the noble profession of a (successful) law career. In "Uno," Chuck tells Jimmy to take pride in the value of being a public defender. He tells Jimmy that it's a noble profession and not about the money. Jimmy protests that the money is important and Chuck appears to encourage him to take pride in his work and to see the value in it. However, as the series develops, we see the ways in which Chuck limits Jimmy based on his assumption that Jimmy is destined for nothing but failure. Because of this, Chuck takes steps to limit Jimmy's legal career and experience as he doesn't see him as a "real" lawyer and wants Jimmy separated from "real" law. In this same episode, Chuck encourages Jimmy to strike out on his own and change his last name per Howard's request, and not ride on someone else's (Chuck's and HHM's) coattails.

This is another instance where we believe Chuck is being supportive, but it is more likely that Chuck does not like being associated with Jimmy, especially within the legal sphere. In this case, Chuck is rationalizing his interference with Jimmy's career. For Chuck, he may be harming Jimmy's career, but he's helping more people by keeping Jimmy out of "legitimate" law. Through this rationalization, Chuck is able to confirm his deceptive belief that Jimmy is *only* bad and that he can't be a "legitimate" lawyer. In "Pimento," Chuck said he was proud of Jimmy when he was in the mailroom but, "I know what you were, what you are. You're Slippin' Jimmy. And Slippin' Jimmy I can handle just fine. But Slippin' Jimmy with a law degree is like a chimp with a machine gun." Despite Jimmy's best efforts and accomplishments, Chuck refuses to allow himself to see Jimmy as anything but a con man. He is so invested in Slippin' Jimmy being all his brother is, Chuck goes so far as to sabotage Jimmy's chances of success. While it cannot be denied that Jimmy has a proclivity for questionable activity, we can only wonder what would have happened if Chuck hadn't sabotaged him along the way.

Chuck rationalizes it through the conclusion that he's protecting people from Slippin' Jimmy; however, by failing to let

Jimmy be better Chuck's condemned him to be Slippin' Jimmy. Once he realizes that Chuck has no faith in him, Jimmy loses the faith in himself and becomes convinced that he can't be more than Slippin' Jimmy and that his legitimate law career is out of his league. When Jimmy still tries to help Chuck in "Klick" by confessing that he altered the Mesa Verde documents, Chuck finally had the ammunition to remove Jimmy from the noble profession of the law.

Jimmy versus Slippin' Jimmy

James M. McGill, Esq. has lofty goals. He wants to be a successful lawyer and wants his efforts to be worth something. His ability to relate to people, to get people to open up and trust him (the very traits that helped him con people on the streets of Chicago) helps him establish a steady client base. Jimmy continues to improve himself until he realizes Chuck's sabotage and gives up his legal career and goes back to scamming people.

Up until this point, Jimmy's bending of the rules had significantly diminished since he was first hired in the HHM mailroom. He had a colorful interpretation of the rules of law, but he still tried to keep things legitimate. He uses little scams and grifts, he's got a talent for it after all, but overall he is striving for legitimacy. In "Mijo" Jimmy plans to scam the Kettlemans to get them as clients but doesn't go through with it. Later, he takes a retainer from the money the Kettlemans stole and says "Upon this rock, I will build my church." He sees this as seed money for his firm and a foray into a more successful legal career. He's determined to become a better person and gets the Kettlemans to take a deal and returns the retainer because "it's the right thing." In these early episodes, we see a Jimmy who is still determined to become a person distinct from Slippin' Jimmy. Yet, after losing Chuck's support, Jimmy loses his faith in himself and stops seeing the law as a legitimate business. Jimmy returns to ripping people off and scamming, and even gets Kim to join in on the grifts, telling her that the job at Davis and Main (DM) would be wrong for him and would be a waste of his time.

From Chuck's perspective, Jimmy is deceiving himself that he can become a legitimate lawyer. At this point in Jimmy's life, it seems that he has come to accept that he was deceiving himself about being a legitimate lawyer. For years he had suppressed Slippin' Jimmy and had fought to make a legitimate career as a lawyer. With Chuck's insistence that he'll always be Slippin' Jimmy, Jimmy seems to have decided to stop deceiving himself about his true nature. Using perspective shifting, Jimmy begins to see himself through Chuck's eyes and concludes that he can only be Slippin' Jimmy. Despite Kim's insistance that he's a good lawyer and should take the job at DM, Jimmy seems to have started to accepted his fate—he's no more than Slippin' Jimmy. Due to Chuck's persception of Jimmy, Jimmy deceives himself into believing that he can *only* be Slippin' Jimmy.

By the end of "Switch," Jimmy resists his fate and accepts the position at DM. At DM, Jimmy has all of the signs of legal success. A nice office, a car, salary, and the opportunity to keep working with his Sandpaper clients. Jimmy finds, soon, that he still wants to do things his way, not the proper way. Despite finally having a "legitimate" legal career Jimmy isn't satisfied with doing things the right way. He engages in scams, acts without permission at the detriment of his standing at DM. Jimmy uses rationalization to justify this. He may not have asked for permission to air a commercial, but he got so many calls and new clients that the end justified the means. He may have broken rules about solicitation by targeting seniors in Texas, but he got more clients for the class action suit. While others will point out that he's behaving wrongly, Jimmy is okay with it because he's deceiving himself with rationalization. For him, his behaviors may not be orthodox, but they're effective and that makes them okay.

Jimmy's unorthodox methods lead Chuck to confirm that he's no more than Slippin' Jimmy, and have caused Jimmy's legitimacy to be called into question. When trying to help Kim get reinstated to her position, she dares him to go one day without breaking the rules of the New Mexico Bar Association. She's challenging him to do it the right way, not the Jimmy way. Realizing he can't do things the right way, Jimmy finds a creative way to be released from his position at DM and encourages Kim to leave HHM and become partners with him. Kim asks if they're partners, what type of partner he'd be. At first he says he'd play it straight and then corrects himself; he can't do it unless he does it his way. "I have to go into it as me. So. Yeah. Colorful, I guess" ("Inflatable"). Jimmy is fighting the conflicting senses of self and trying to establish a path that suits him accurately. In this progression we see Jimmy's conflict with self-deception. Through perspective shifting he believed he could only be Slippin' Jimmy. Through rationalization and attention management, he's now able to think about himself as something somewhere between James M. McGill and Slippin' Jimmy.

By "Lantern," Jimmy is trying to continue to rebuild his life by apologizing to Chuck and trying to make amends. Despite his best intentions, the reconciliation is unsuccessful. In response to his apology to Chuck, Chuck asks why he bothers have regrets at all.

—What's the point?

—What do you mean?

—Well look at you. You're in so much pain. Why are you putting yourself through all this [*Jimmy tries to interject*] I'm telling you, don't bother. What's the point? You're just gonna keep hurting people.

—That's not true.

—Jimmy, this is what you do. You hurt people, over and over and over. And then there's this show of remorse.

—It's not a show.

—I know you don't think it's a show. I don't doubt your emotions are real. . . . If you're not going to change your behavior, and you won't, why not skip the whole exercise? . . . in the end you're going to hurt everyone around you. You can't help it. So stop apologizing and accept it. Embrace it. Frankly, I'd have more respect for you if you did.

In this exchange, Chuck once again reveals his opinion of Jimmy. Jimmy, to Chuck, is someone who can't help but hurt people and should accept that about himself instead of going through the charade of remorse. We can imagine the amount of pain Jimmy experiences as a result of this conversation. This pain is likely made worse by the fact that Chuck will die shortly after and any attempt at resolution, no matter how slim the chances, is eliminated. For most of the next season, Jimmy struggles with understanding which version of his self is the real one. While not practicing law, he tries to play it straight selling cellphones. Quickly he turns it into a more lucrative, and less legal, operation.

This side job leads to his associate, Huell, getting in trouble with the law. With Kim's initiative, they're able to pull off a scam that gets Huell released. Feeling again conflicted about reverting to his Slippin' Jimmy ways, Jimmy tells Kim he's sorry for the danger he's brought her way and that he'll never do it again. In response, Kim passionately kisses him and says "Let's do it again." Jimmy is again trying to move away from his morally questionable ways, but Kim reels him back in. With her support of conning people, Jimmy is able to further rationalize his behaviors.

With encouragement and support from Kim, Jimmy finds justification for his behavior and finds himself resorting to his scamming ways. By now, the self-deception seems to have evolved to the point that Jimmy believes he can be a good person *and* engage in his scams. He's rationalizing his behavior by changing what he perceives to be a good person. With Kim's blessing, Jimmy can see himself as a colorful, but good, character and not Slippin' Jimmy.

In "Winner," Jimmy finally seems to resolve the conflict. In an attempt to improve his image and demonstrate remorse for altering documents and framing Chuck, Jimmy engages in a campaign that makes him look more charitable. In doing this he agrees to be on a scholarship board for a scholarship granted in Chuck's memory. Jimmy identifies with a candi- date, a young girl caught shoplifting. He fights on her behalf, arguing for her chance at redempton and the positive influ- ence her experiences may have; however, the board disagrees.

Jimmy confronts the young woman, Kristy, and tells her that he fought for her, but she was never going to get the scholarship. The whole process is a lie that is stacked against her. But so what? If they won't give it to her, she should take it from them. Cut corners, rise higher, and the more they hate her, the more she should make them suffer. "Remember, the winner takes all." Jimmy is being more honest with himself about the system and his role in it. Thanks to Kim's support of his behavior he is able to rationalize his way of doing things and can procrastinate becoming better.

He identifies with Kristy and the way that she worked hard to redeem herself, but redemption wasn't ever actually on the table. He realizes that his previous plans of playing a fairly straight and legal way to success was always rigged against him and he needs to stick to his strengths. The full weight of his decision is made clear when he is up for his appeal for reinstatement. He makes an emotional appeal about how low he was going to stoop by using the letter he received from Chuck upon the reading of his will. He makes an impassioned plea, sharing his remorse and frustration with his past actions. His efforts are fruitful and he is reinstated.

When Kim congratulates him, she quickly learns that it was all a ploy. He had realized his original plan wouldn't work, so he played to his strengths and deceived the board. Kim's celebratory look of pride diminishes as she realizes he had duped her and the board. Jimmy had decided that life as Jimmy or James M. McGill was not to be. Just as with Kristy, he realized that the system was flawed and convinces himself that *he* isn't the problem, the *system* is. So he decides to lean into it. He rationalizes his decision by telling himself that the system is corrupt and he can do more good by becoming Saul Goodman.

Saul versus Jimmy

As Jimmy is taken through the process of reinstatement, he announces that he will need to change his name to Saul Goodman. In "Magic Man," when asked about his name change, he says that he can't be Jimmy anymore. Jimmy will always be Chuck McGill's loser little brother. In embracing Saul, he has settled the debate between whether he was James, Jimmy, or Slippin' Jimmy. He has stopped deceiving himself about who he is and who he wants to be and how he wants to accomplish it. He has decided to embrace his strengths to finally achieve his success.

Throughout the remainder of Season Five, Kim alternates between protesting the Saul persona and working with him on scams. She lets him help her scam one of her public defense clients into taking a deal he didn't want. She enlists Saul's help with a tenant, Mr. Acker, Mesa Verde wants to evict to the detriment of her client, Mesa Verde. Saul tells Kim this is her play and he'll follow her lead. However, ultimately, he bypasses Kim and does what's best for himself and Mr. Acker. No longer deceiving himself about the person he is and the person he wants to be, Saul is coming into his own and, in his own way, is flourishing. That is, until he gets further involved with the problems of the cartel and jeopardizes his own life and Kim's.

From what we remember from *Breaking Bad*, Saul Goodman will continue to be a "criminal" lawyer, and a successful one at that. He gets deeper into the game and gets stronger ties to those involved in the cartel's business. Aside from the black and white flash-forwards that we see in *Better Call Saul*, the life and career of Saul Goodman is a good one. He's finally embraced himself and has stopped deceiving himself about what type of man he is. With the self-acceptance comes a reduction of self-deception. Does this mean the problem of self-deception has been resolved for Saul?

Jimmy is a complicated case of self-deception. He's in denial that he can be anything except Slippin' Jimmy. He then is in denial that he's a good person. His self-deception directs him into these personas but each lacks true authenticity. We may never fully understand who Jimmy is; moreover, he may not either.

Saul versus Morality

Thus far we've discussed the ways in which Chuck and Jimmy have deceived themselves by engaging in all-too-familiar deceptive practices. The question that likely still remains is: So what? What's the harm if a person believes something that happens to be false? If they're not intentionally lying to themselves about something, is there actually a problem?

Self-deception, ususlly called Self-deceit, was a major concern of English and Scottish writers of the eighteenth century. It's worth mentioning two of these, Joseph Butler and Adam Smith.

For Joseph Butler, self-deception is a threat to morality. In being deceived about your self, you can damage your conscience and be unable to properly guide moral action. A person who is incorrect about themselves may also be incorrect about their moral character, which, for Butler and many others, is a significant moral problem.

We can see evidence of this in Jimmy's evolution of identities. As Jimmy, he engaged in some minor morally questionable behavior but aimed to live a good life and experienced remorse. As Slippin' Jimmy, his moral boundaries were less strong and he engaged in more immoral behavior with little (if any) sign of guilt or remorse. As Saul, it seems he finally embraced Chuck's advice not to go through the exercise of pretending to have remorse. He owns that he is a person of questionable moral character and uses that as an asset. Butler sees this acceptance of immorality as tied to a cycle of self-deception. Saul keeps telling himself it's okay to behave the way he is, that he has it under control, and that reinforces his immoral behavior. Moreover, by maintaining some type of ignorance about the type of person he is, Saul is setting himself up to be in a position that he would act in ways that he wouldn't if he were being honest and fully informed about his character.

Similarly, Adam Smith held that self-deception can have a blinding effect and interferes with moral judgment. In refusing to fully consider your own character, including any faults, you're put in a position where you think that you are of a better moral character than you are. Saul, for example, in accepting his "true" self blinds himself to the fact that he is an immoral person. Further, he may not think that it's *bad* to be immoral. The self-deception may go beyond being in denial about what his character is to being in denial that having bad character is itself a bad thing.

If Butler and Smith are right, our main character's (be he Jimmy, James, Slippin' Jimmy, or Saul) self-deception weakens his moral character and can interfere with his success in life. The crimes that are committed start off small, but evolved into even bigger and more harmful crimes. We see this with the evolution into Saul. Saul Goodman seems to be a success. He has the money and the fame. But as we see in the flash-forward, he's left living in hiding with minimal benefits. By all appearances he is alone. In the long term, self-deception is his undoing.

IV

Confidence is good—facts on your side, better

12
A Cave of His Own Making

TIMOTHY J. GOLDEN

> My brother is not a bad person. He has a good heart. It's just—he
> can't help himself. And everyone's left picking up the pieces.
>
> —CHARLES "CHUCK" McGILL

What I find so interesting about *Better Call Saul* are the relationships in Jimmy McGill's background. As the story unfolds in each episode, it's easy to see that the "Saul Goodman" whom we have all come to know and love—or hate—from *Breaking Bad* has many complex relationships that help to make him the compelling character that he is.

Of course, Bob Odenkirk's excellent acting has a lot to do with Jimmy's charisma and charm, but it is how these attributes of Jimmy present themselves in his relationships that make Jimmy so compelling. For example, Jimmy's relationship with Kim Wexler seems to move between a complete disgust that Kim directs at Jimmy for his irresponsibility and manipulation on one hand and a Bonnie and Clyde–styled couple committed to con artistry on the other hand. What a rollercoaster of a relationship!

And then there's Jimmy's relationship with his big brother, Charles "Chuck" McGill. Despite Jimmy's charm and his charismatic ability to manipulate, it is in this relationship that Chuck seems to be in total control, even in his own death. Chuck is unable to overcome his hypochondria and yet is perfectly capable of being rational enough to discern Jimmy's role in the Mesa Verde numerical transposition scandal. But why?

Chuck's Life in a Cave

One way to answer our question about Chuck's ability to point out Jimmy's involvement in the Mesa Verde scandal while

being unable to overcome his hypochondria is to interpret
Chuck with Plato's famous "Allegory of the Cave," which is
found in Book VII of Plato's dialogue, *Republic*. Plato, speaking
through Socrates, tells the story of people who are chained to
their seats in a cave so that they can only see what is in front
of them. Behind these people are another group of people who
are carrying various objects in front of a fire. The light
from the fire casts shadows of the objects onto the cave wall in
front of the prisoners, who, looking at the shadows, wrongly
assume that the shadows of the objects are the actual objects
themselves. One day, a prisoner escapes the cave and sees what
is actually happening. This same prisoner goes outside of the
cave and beholds a world that is very different from the one
inside the cave; a world that the rest of the prisoners do not
even know exists. When this prisoner returns to the cave and
tries to liberate the other prisoners, they reject what he has to
say and even want to kill him. The point of the Allegory of the
Cave is straightforward: the world that we see inside the cave
is not the true reality. All we see in this world are shadows that
we believe are real, but actually are not. Beyond this world of
the cave (the world in which we live) there is a true reality that
none of us will ever see, except those who are enlightened
enough to make it out of the cave through the use of philosophy
(our reasoning) that will help us distinguish between the false
reality that we see and the true reality that our reason can
know.

So, we often associate Plato's Allegory of the Cave with
intellectual freedom from the bondage of our social and cultural beliefs—the chains that bind us and force us to look forward inside of the cave. But here I want to think of the Allegory
of the Cave differently. Instead of the cave being a place where
we're imprisoned against our will, Chuck enslaves himself
through the use of his imagination in a way that thrusts responsibility onto Jimmy to care for him as punishment for his
past wrongs, all while helping him to avoid responsibility for a
healthy relationship with Jimmy.

We can see the reasons why Chuck wants to get back at
Jimmy in the episode titled "Rebecca." In "Rebecca," Chuck
explains the family background to Kim, detailing how his and
Jimmy's father was good-natured to a fault. According to
Chuck, their father was unable to recognize wrongdoing at all,
often allowing customers to take store merchandise without
paying for it. In fact, his father indulged Jimmy so much that
although Jimmy stole money from the register for years, he
was never held accountable for any of his thefts because their

father refused to believe that Jimmy would steal from him. Not long after Chuck discovered the thefts, their father died and, according to Chuck, no one cried harder at the funeral than Jimmy.

Chuck sees in Jimmy's unpunished thefts a fundamental failure to hold Jimmy accountable for his actions that has resulted in Jimmy living a life of deceit and manipulation, abiding by a corrupt code of ethics based on an "end justifies the means" sort of analysis. As Chuck points out to Kim in "Rebecca," Jimmy "is not a bad person. He has a good heart. It's just—he can't help himself. And everyone's left picking up the pieces." It is important to point out that Chuck is having this conversation with Kim after Jimmy blunders a job opportunity with a prestigious law firm on the strength of Kim's recom- mendation. Forced into a situation that made both her and her law firm look bad before the legal community, Kim is being punished by doing the dreaded task of "doc review"—the grunt work of litigation—as opposed to being a front-line member of the law firm who directly handles legal matters for clients. Chuck, then, having seen the damage that Jimmy has done to Kim, is trying to provide Kim with some background so that she can better understand why Jimmy cannot be trusted.

Since Jimmy has never been held accountable, then, what better way for Chuck to teach Jimmy a lesson than to put him in a situation that will require him to think of others before himself? Enter Chuck's hypochondria, which will enable him to retreat into a fictitious world of denial—a cave of his own making—in an attempt to keep Jimmy accountable directly to him. This retreat into a cave of his own making accomplishes two things for Chuck: first, it keeps Jimmy close to Chuck, so Chuck can hold Jimmy accountable for caring for him, and second, it enables Chuck to pursue vengeance against Jimmy for all of the harm that Jimmy did to their father and their family; again, harm for which Jimmy has not been held accountable.

Plato's motivation in the cave allegory is to support his theories of reality and knowledge; he wants to show that we must move from the darkness of the cave to the enlightenment of truth. In contrast, Chuck must build and remain in a cave in order to bring Jimmy "to the light" of his wrongdoing. And it is Chuck's imagination-driven vengeance toward Jimmy to punish him for past wrongs that, rather than lead Chuck out of the cave, drives him deeper into it. Although Chuck's imagination helps him construct a cave to imprison Jimmy, Chuck also imprisons himself using his imagination—what Aristotle called *phantasia*—in ways that cause him to be a good lawyer with high levels of rational discernment, but a bad brother with low levels of love and respect for Jimmy.

Good Lawyer, Bad Brother

Aristotle wrote extensively about the nature of the human soul and about what makes us virtuous. Philosophers call the former "psychology" and the latter "ethics." The root word for psychology is the Greek word *psuche*, which means "soul." The sort of psychology that interested Aristotle is unlike what we know psychology to be today, which is a rigorous, scientific discipline concerned with the study of human behavior.

For Aristotle, psychology was that subfield in philosophy committed to presenting a rational account of the human soul, which explained its composition and its relationship to the physical body as well as its relationship to the rest of the natural world. When I reference "Aristotle's psychology," then, I am referring to Aristotle's attempt to present a rational account of the human soul in relation to the body and the rest of nature (plants and animals). Aristotle's psychology is connected to his ethics, which, again, is about the sorts of things that one must do to be virtuous; that is, to be considered "courageous," "kind," and the like.

Aristotle explains his psychology in his work titled *De Anima*. There, he points out that the human soul has three faculties: nutrition, perception, and reason. This three-fold division of the soul is also compared with other parts of nature such as plants, which Aristotle argues only have the faculty of nutrition. That is, vegetation is able to assimilate nutrients into its biological structures to grow and develop according to its various kinds. Perception is not present in vegetation. Animals, however, have both nutrition and perception. Animals not only eat, but, in the case of predatory animal species, they use sensory organs such as the eyes and the olfactory system to capture their prey.

Lastly, humans, Aristotle argues, have both perception (our five senses) and nutrition (humans need food), but they also have reason, a faculty that enables an intelligence which Aristotle believes is not present in any other living thing in nature. Reason is what Aristotle refers to as *idios*—the Greek term for "peculiar"—to human beings. And it is this insight about peculiarity that connects Aristotle's psychology to his ethics, because Aristotle points out, in his famous "function argument" that we evaluate the quality of a thing by how well that thing performs its essential function. The essential function of a thing is that which is peculiar or *idios* that thing. For example, we call a knife or other cutting instrument a "good" knife or cutting instrument if it cuts crisply and sharply, because cutting is peculiar to cutting instruments, and we call a clock a "good" clock if it keeps the correct time, because keeping the correct time is peculiar to instruments that are designed to measure time.

Applying this same reasoning to human beings, Aristotle, arguing from his psychology in *De Anima*, concludes in his ethics that since reason is unique to human beings, we measure the quality of a human being by how well that human being performs the essential function of reasoning. And we perform the essential function of reasoning in our moral life by choosing a virtuous course of conduct that lies at a mid-point between two extremes, which are vices. So, the virtue of courage, for example, is found at a mid-point between the deficiency of cowardice and the excess of foolhardiness, and the virtue of kindness is found at a mid-point between the extreme vices of meanness and self-sacrifice. Philosophers often refer to this as Aristotle's "Golden Mean."

Understanding Chuck's relationship with Jimmy in these Aristotelian terms is insightful. First, consider the relationship between Aristotle's psychology and his ethics, and then apply that to how Chuck treats Jimmy. Consider that in Aristotle's psychology, there is an intermediate place between perception and reason that Aristotle calls *phantasia*, or imagination. Although it too is peculiar to human beings, imagination falls below reason, making one who is overly imaginative irrational, sort of like Don Quixote, who believes that windmills are enemies and charges at them as though he is in battle, or sort of like Chuck, whose hypochondria—a form of imagination or *phantasia*—has him convinced that he has "electromagnetic hypersensitivity."

On the one hand, then, Chuck is functioning at a subrational level because of his imagination, but on the other hand, Chuck is able to function at a rational level to serve his clients as a lawyer, exhibiting ethical conduct toward his clients like Mesa Verde. Chuck's imagination thus has him behaving irrationally toward Jimmy because he wants vengeance on Jimmy for his past wrongs by making him completely responsible to "care" for him because of his "illness," but Chuck does not allow his imagination to compromise the rationality that he needs to fulfill his lawyerly obligations to his clients.

We can argue that imagination—that mid-point between-perception and reason in Chuck's soul—is well below the ratio-nal mid-point necessary for Chuck to be a virtuous brother toward Jimmy. In other words, Aristotle's psychological, imagi-native mid-point that Chuck embraces to exact vengeance on Jimmy, morally speaking, represents the deficient vice of meanness toward Jimmy that is well below the virtue of kind-ness that Chuck needs to be a good brother. Here, Chuck's hypochondriacal irrationality of perception results in a moral irrationality—a vice-driven disposition of meanness—toward Jimmy. But not only does Chuck's psychologically deficient use of imagination manifest itself as the moral vice of meanness that falls below the moral virtue of kindness, it also manifests itself as the moral vice of cowardice that falls below the moral virtue of courage, for if Chuck was committed to moving for-ward in right relationship with Jimmy, he would have the courage to do so without resorting to a cave of his own making because of his preoccupation with Jimmy's prior wrongdoings.

So, although Chuck's hypochondria is on display for all to see, he can attain the rationality that he needs to be a good lawyer, while being woefully deficient of the morality that it takes for him to be a good brother. Chuck is thus an ethical and functional lawyer committed to reason but an unethical and dysfunctional brother unable to commit to Jimmy.

In this way Chuck's rationality is at once keen enough to discern his brother's involvement in the Mesa Verde numeri-cal transposition scandal—this is the meanness toward Jimmy disguised as an attempt to hold Jimmy "accountable" for his past wrongs—but dull enough to maintain his hypochondria, keeping Chuck in a cave of his own making that shows his cow-ardice toward a future in right relationship with his brother. If Chuck were able to relinquish his preoccupation with Jimmy's past, then he would have the kindness and the courage to move forward into a future with a functional relationship toward his brother. As we will see in the next section, the past demands very little of us besides recollection. But the future demands much more from us in what the philosopher Søren Kierkegaard called a "repetition."

From Past to Future

Chuck's behavior toward Jimmy is oriented toward the past; he wants Jimmy to be held accountable for his past wrongdo-ings. So, Chuck creates a Platonic cave of his own making that imprisons himself and Jimmy, all while severely compromising his humanity because of an insidious use of his imagination that results in an attitude of meanness toward Jimmy and a sense of cowardice to be in a right relationship with him.

There is thus, on the one hand, Chuck's bizarre commitment to his hypochondria, which is thoroughly irrational, and, on the other hand, Chuck's commitment to rationality as a practicing lawyer that enables him both to be faithful to his clients and to accurately theorize, investigate, and accuse Jimmy in the Mesa Verde numerical transposition scandal. For Chuck, then, Jimmy's past—and his own—are the impetus for the dysfunctional relationship between Chuck and Jimmy that shows itself on the screen.

What would it take for Chuck to see Jimmy differently? How could Chuck's relationship with Jimmy be improved? We know that an overwhelming sense of past-oriented vengeance directs Chuck in his relationship with Jimmy. But what if Chuck's orientation toward Jimmy was future-oriented instead of past-oriented? What if Chuck could step away from Jimmy's past wrongs and his sense of vengeance long enough to accept Jimmy on his own terms rather than attempt to make Jimmy into who Chuck thinks Jimmy should be through his own sense of justice, imprisoning himself and Jimmy in a cave of his own making?

In his novella, *Repetition*, Kierkegaard, writing through a pseudonym named "Constantin Constantius," tells the story of a young man in love who reaches out to Constantin for help because he is having difficulty in his relationship with a woman. The young man is in love—he is engaged to be married, but wants to break the engagement and does not know how to do it. Through a series of letters, the young man explains his predicament and would like some advice from Constantin on what to do. But Constantin, because he is an intellectual observer, cannot give any advice to the young man.

Constantin's character represents a sort of stale intellectual figure who is so busy thinking about abstract concepts that he is unable to live in the concrete reality of the here and now. He's too much of a thinker and not much of a doer and thus cannot move forward himself, let alone advise the young man on how to move forward in his relationship with his fiancée. Constantin can only look backward; that is, he is preoccupied with his past, trying to recapture moments that he has enjoyed, such as his trip to Berlin.

No matter how hard Constantin tries to duplicate the experience from his trip to Berlin, he remains unsatisfied. Nothing is ever quite the same or as enjoyable as it was during his previous trip to Berlin. The young man's request for help, then, is like asking the blind to lead the blind: the young man does not know what to do to move forward and neither does Constantin. Constantin can only look backward in search of reproducing feelings of comfort and happiness, and the young man is paralyzed by a crisis of indecision.

Kierkegaard has names for both the condition of the young man and for Constantin. Neither Constantin nor the young man are capable of making the movement that Constantin calls "repetition." A repetition is a forward, future-oriented movement that can perhaps best be explained with reference to marriage, which is the young man's dilemma. When someone marries, they make a commitment to their spouse that contemplates a life-long, love relationship in which a promise is made to love the spouse repeatedly and perpetually. Each day in the marriage ought to be lived with a sense of passion toward the spouse to love them more each day than the day before.

This does not mean passion in an idealistic, naive, romantic sense, but rather in the sense of a sobering, life-long, and exclusive moral commitment that extends into the future. It is simply unrealistic to think that each day of the marriage will be filled with romantic passion. But it does mean that each day of the marriage will result in a deeper sense of commitment than the day before. It will not always feel good and it will not always make the spouses "happy." It will, however, fortify the spousal bond the more the commitment is lived each day into the future. The repetition is found not only in the commitment itself but also in the object of that commitment: the same person must be loved with the same passionate commitment each day in perpetuity.

In contrast to the ethical, forward-moving concept of repetition is the aesthetic, backward-moving concept of "recollection." By "aesthetic," Kierkegaard means that when we make the backward gaze of recollection, we do so based on feeling and sensibility. The ethical move of repetition is not based on feeling; it is based on a passionate commitment, as in the marriage example above. Constantin cannot help the young man in love because he is recollecting his past, attempting to recreate the experiences from his trip to Berlin. He is so overwhelmed by chasing the feeling of the experiences that he had in Berlin that he cannot bring himself to move forward.

And this is the problem with Chuck: he is unable to move forward in a functional, mature, ethically-committed relationship with his brother (a repetition) because he wants to hold him accountable for his past so he can feel his vengeance and experience the satisfactory feeling of being vindicated (a recollection). So, Chuck is committed to a static ideal of aesthetic pleasure in which Jimmy is punished for his wrongs and Chuck feels vindicated, but Chuck cannot make the movement of ethical repetition to move forward in relationship with Jimmy. So it is that Chuck can discern Jimmy's involvement in the Mesa Verde numerical transposition scandal, but Chuck cannot move forward and simply be Jimmy's brother.

Truth in Fiction

Philosophy is concerned with truth. Philosophers want to explain the world in ways that provide a sense of rational satisfaction. We recognize this sort of truth in Aristotle. Aristotle does what a good philosopher should: he provides a rational account of the soul (psychology) and its connection to moral virtue (ethics). But philosophical truth—rational explanation—is not the only kind of truth that exists. In fact, there are other sorts of truths that we find when we encounter fiction.

Plato uses a fictitious story about a cave in order to make his points about reality and knowledge. And Kierkegaard uses a fictitious story about Constantin Constantius, a man who cannot move forward because he keeps looking backward. Although they present us with different accounts of truth— Plato and Kierkegaard present us with a literary form of truth and Aristotle with a more traditional philosophical form of truth—all three of these philosophers not only help us to shed light on the relationship between Chuck and Jimmy but also, through reflection on that fictional relationship, may help us better understand some of our own relationships in real life. Philosophy and *Better Call Saul* are dialogue partners that help us better understand the world—and each other—through both traditional philosophical argument (Aristotle) and fiction (Plato and Kierkegaard).

Even as we learn these philosophical lessons from Plato's and Kierkegaard's uses of fiction, we can also learn from the fictions presented in *Better Call Saul* as it relates to Chuck and Jimmy. From Plato's use of fiction, we learn about the fiction within fiction that comes to us from Chuck, a fictional character who puts himself in a cave of his own making. And from Kierkegaard's use of fiction, we learn about Chuck's inability to accept Jimmy as he is and move forward as his brother because he would rather move backward and feel vindicated.

The more traditional philosophical sense of truth is also helpful to us, as Aristotle's psychology and his ethics both bring Chuck's moral shortcomings into sharper focus because of a destructive use of his imagination: the imagined and irrational "electromagnetic sensitivity" prevents Chuck from attaining the moral virtues of kindness and courage, and instead leaves Chuck with the vices of meanness and cowardice directed at Jimmy.

So, there's truth in philosophy. And there's truth in fiction, too. Just ask Chuck and Jimmy.

13

Chuckrates v. The Saulphists

Walter Barta and
Thomas Paul Barnes, Esq.

**Court's Record: Rehearing of James McGill before
the Disciplinary Board of the Supreme Court of
New Mexico**

Opening Statement for the Prosecution:
Charles McGill Esq.

Should we tell the truth and lose? Or tell a lie and win? Of
course, it would be best to tell the truth *and* win, but sometimes the world is not so easy. Just look at my brother, Jimmy.
Just a few months ago he was working as a public defender,
representing three teenaged boys. After rehearsing long and
hard at the bathroom urinal, Jimmy emerges into the courtroom with a grandiloquent display of impassioned speech. He
uses every trick in the book: compliments the jury, speaks like
an old friend, appeals to their sympathy, ingratiates himself,
flatters their decency, cites their personal experiences, and
plucks at every other string in their hearts. Jimmy has done
his job defending his clients, there's just one problem: the
truth. Without saying a single word, the prosecutor wheels out
a television and plays a videotape showing the incontrovertible
fact: the boys had indeed committed the crime ("Uno").

This is the classic conflict of dialectic versus rhetoric, a
dichotomy as old as human thought, arising again even now, in
this very trial. I, Charles McGill versus my brother, James
McGill. Philosophy on one side and sophistry on the other. Logos
versus pathos. Facts versus feelings. We have a tense relationship because we embody two divergent versions of lawyerly conduct. But don't be fooled: my brother Jimmy practices
speechcraft. In the words of the ancient Athenian philosopher

Socrates, he is "a rhetorician rather than a reasoner" (Plato, *Gorgias*, 471).

To give historical context, in ancient Athens philosophy was born. Socrates, the father of philosophy, lived in pursuit of truth. However, quite tragically, Socrates was tried and put to death by the Athenian courts. His alleged crimes were advanced by intellectual rivals of Socrates, the Sophists, who had a different worldview, a different disposition towards truth, and a different agenda for the role of speech in human affairs. Socrates, the philosophical method, the pursuit of truth on the one side; Sophists, the rhetorical method, the pursuit of ends via words on the other: this ideological dichotomy maps onto us.

In Plato's dialogues, the philosopher is defined as someone who practices dialectic: is doubtful, loves knowledge, studies humanity, devours books, and "rejoices at beholding reality", and . . . "gazing upon the truth" (*Sophist*, 253; *Phaedrus*, 229). The philosopher's dialectic, otherwise known as the Socratic method, is a practice of error-identification and correction; earnest dialogue; cross-examination—with the aim of finding out who is truly wise—deep reflection; reasoned inquiry; and consideration of different positions—wherever the argument leads (*Theaetetus*, 168–69; *Apology*, 41b; *Crito*, 46b–d, 48c). Metaphorically, the philosopher leads us out of ignorance, as if out of a dark cave (*Republic* VII, 514a–520a).

In contrast to the philosopher, the sophist is a different breed of intellectual. Plato characterizes sophists as those who use pseudo-education to convince men to pay them to sound intelligent, who perform the "juggling of words" for private gain, who imitate knowledge, who are not interested in the truth, and may be hostile to it (*Sophist*, 223, 268). They are fake philosophers. Rhetoric is the tool of the sophist, for which reason he is also dubbed a rhetorician. Rhetoric, sometimes known as sophistry, is a practice of creating a "feast of discourse," disregarding truth and honesty in favor of "pleasure and grace," spending time composing, focusing on style over substance, deceiving in hopes of fame, using opinion and persuasion, to "steal away the hearts of his hearers"; in other words, "flattery" (*Phaedrus* , 227–28, 234, 240, 257, 260–61; *Gorgias* , 449, 453, 463). Unlike the philosopher, the sophist attempts to push listeners back into the dark cave of images and idiocy.

As I hope to show you during this trial, my brother Jimmy is guilty of sophistry in the first degree. In every way, Jimmy typifies many of the negative attributes of the sophist. Sophists like Jimmy think they know things, when they really just know how to talk about things; they can flip-flop fluidly on any issue; they have "no need of truth" and only care about winning; they create false belief; and take the job from a more qualified candidate (*Apology*, 22c; *Phaedrus*, 261, 272, 277; *Gorgias*, 455–56, 459, 464–65). Worst of all, the sophist "makes the weaker argument defeat the stronger" (*Apology*, 19b). He could convince you of anything, without scruple, if it served his case, and you'd believe him. Jimmy is a sophist, and because of this he is "not a real lawyer," as I will prove ("Pimento").

Opening Statement for the Defense: James McGill Esq.

Well, give it up to my brother, Chuck!—say what you want, the man can write a speech. And thanks for the history lesson by the way, and the dictionary entries, very educational, hope everybody's still awake—haha! Though I'm glad Chuck brings up Socrates, because that guy was a total hack. He bullied his way about Athens, making fun of people, being a know-it-all, claiming he was the "wisest man in Athens," trying to discredit law-abiding public servants, such as yourselves.

You know, Aristophanes, another Greek guy, wrote this play *The Clouds* just to satirize Socrates's kooky ideas. See, to Aristophanes, Socrates simply was a sophist: Socrates's pretenses to truth are just another rhetorical device, indecipherable from the very claims other sophists would make.

Another philosopher, Isocrates, different guy, similar name, identified himself as a sophist and didn't think it was incompatible with philosophy. Meaning: sophists are not as bad and philosophers are not as good as Chuck thinks.

Furthermore, in Plato's *Republic*, Socrates says that the poets should be banished from the state (*Republic* III, 401; *Republic* X, 595). He thought that artists were all liars, corrupting the perfect ideas of the ideal government. But who would want truth at the expense of beauty?

See, even though I'm on trial here, Chuck is too—hear me out. His claims of my alleged dishonesty depend on his own claims to intellectual integrity; his slander of my character presumes the excellence of his own. Mister golden boy over here thinks he's smarter than all of us, and he'll tell you too. He is going to claim he's a good man, in pursuit of justice and truth, a regular philosopher "pure and true", but that's just as much a spun yarn as anything I will spin you (*Sophist*, 253). If you believe that, let me tell you another: he hates me, and he may not say it, but he will express it in his tone. Sure, Chuck thinks he's the "real lawyer," but we're all Sophists here. He's just as susceptible to rhetoric as the best of us. Chuck is no more a true philosopher than I am Kevin Costner; he's a *faux*-losopher, which means I'm just as much a lawyer as he is—as I hope to persuade you, thank you . . .

Prosecutor's Witness Examination

CHARLES: Jimmy, would you call yourself a sophist?

JAMES: Well, I sometimes sleep on the sofa in my office.

CHARLES: Always the joker . . . Do you consider yourself a talker? Do you have the gift of the gab?

JAMES: Well, you cornered me there, Chuck. If I say "Yes" then I've said something and confessed; if I say "No" I've said something and contradicted myself. Help me out here, should I plead the fifth?

CHARLES: Your honor, he's avoiding the question . . . But anyways, Jimmy, do you rehearse these oral performances of yours? Like an actor? Like an *orator*? You have accents and voices and such, correct?

JAMES: Of course, who doesn't? Even *Saturday Night Live* rehearses.

CHARLES: And Jimmy, you don't have a secretary, do you? So, is that *you* impersonating one on the phone?

JAMES: I do dabble in some *poetic* license. It gives the clients confidence.

CHARLES: So, impressions, images, "imitations thrice removed from the truth," nothing real about them? (*Republic X*, 599). And you're great at quoting popular movies, right?

JAMES: "It's show time!" "Here's Johnny!" "You will atone!"

CHARLES: And the wordplay, you're so good at it. Give us some?

JAMES: "Need a will? Call McGill!" "Gimme Jimmy!" "S'all Good, man"!

CHARLES: . . . as if a legal hearing were a *poetry* reading. Tell me, what did you buy after your first big paycheck?

JAMES: The good things in life: a suit, a tie, a haircut, and a billboard.

CHARLES: So, "appearances only and not realities": you like to dress well, don't you? (*Republic X*, 599). And didn't you use those purchases to impersonate my firm's logo and stage a man falling off the billboard just to look like a hero? ("Hero")

JAMES: Firstly, McGill is my name, what am I supposed to do, use a *fake one*? Secondly, I saved the man's life, thanks.

CHARLES: That wasn't your only publicity stunt, was it? Didn't you get fired running an unauthorized commercial for Davis and Main hurting "their image, their reputation"? ("Gloves Off")

JAMES: Sure, I might've gone behind the boss's back, but I attracted two hundred plus clients when it aired. I quit because of . . . personality differences: I played bagpipes, hated wasting water flushing, and wore colorful shirts—we're lawyers, not undertakers, right? But let me tell you, if you break your arm and stay home binge-watching *To Kill a Mockingbird*, you better hope for my commercial on the breaks. Everybody loves my commercials! ("Lantern")

CHARLES: Rationalization . . . You just never "stop selling" do you? It's just solicitation after solicitation and then selling us that it wasn't?

JAMES: If by solicitation you mean client outreach! I give the people what they want. If someone wants to brag, I let him brag; cry, I let him cry; sell, I let him think I'm buying.

CHARLES: Equivocation . . . So, you'd engage in logical fallacies for a case?

JAMES: Fallacy, shmallacy! What's it matter if I win?

CHARLES: So, ends justify the means? Is it true that you even charmed a drug-lord?

JAMES: Tuco? I talked him "down from the death sentence to six months probation . . ."—I told him what he wanted to hear, appealed to his sense of justice—not the letter of the law, but the spirit—, tickled his soft side—his love for his abuelita—, and I saved two lives—" . . . I'm the best lawyer ever" ("Mijo").

CHARLES: Exaggeration . . . And do you think you're so relatable to criminals because of your dirty past?

JAMES: Dirty? Sure, I will get my hands dirty. I'll dig around trashcans for you. I will write your cease-and-desist on toilet paper if I have to. I will sweet talk, dirty talk, whatever you need, baby! I will talk loudly if you're deaf; dress like a cowboy, if you're into that; and give you the Cajun preacher when you need savin'. Or I'll shut up, if you want: that's not lying, that's just confidentiality.

CHARLES: Evasion . . . I'll rephrase: why was your old nickname "Slippin' Jimmy"? Haven't I bailed you out of jail? ("Nacho").

JAMES: I've made some "slip ups," sure, haven't we all?

CHARLES: Hasty generalization . . . But, ergo, you admit to being a showman and a conman?

JAMES: Well, all I am hearing you saying is that "I'm extremely lovable" ("Expenses"). Is that a crime? In my book, that's a public service. What you call rhetoric, I call "razzmatazz," "gravitas," "production value," "moxie," not to mention zealous advocacy! Sure, I want to evoke sympathy, produce passions, stir virtues in my audience. Why? Because I care about people. That's the difference between me and you. I cried hardest at Dad's funeral, when you hardly cried at all. I have been babysitting you for years, but you won't even hire me. And I lied to you to make you feel better in this trial too, because I care.

CHARLES: So, you admit to sophistry?

JAMES: Well, isn't that a "fine thing": gratifying others? (*Gorgias*, 462)

CHARLES: The prosecutor rests.

Defendant's Witness Examination

JAMES: So, Chuck, you're very philosophical, right? Not sophistic at all?

CHARLES: Well, my primary consideration is the avoidance of logical fallacies, because I uphold the truth in all situations. I believe I have a noble purpose, to serve the city and its interests, even in the face of opposition, even when the city itself objects. Like Socrates, I care whether I am "acting justly or unjustly, like a good man or a bad one" (*Apology*, 28b).

JAMES: Yah, you're so Socratic, down to the quoting Latin and Greek? Even when the cops come knocking at your door, you're the guy standing there arguing about probable cause and case law. And you have the best memory: you can quote obscure cases, exact addresses, statutes, dates? You even use deductive logic in casual conversations. And, you pride yourself on professionalism and job performance. Just the other night, when I hauled in a bag of shredded documents from Sandpiper, you're the one who put those puzzle pieces back together. That's how much you care about truth, justice, and righteousness: a regular philosopher, like Socrates?

CHARLES: Well, thank you for the "*flattery,*" Jimmy . . . (*Gorgias*, 465). Guilty as charged.

JAMES: And, as you know, Socrates was a dead-beat dad, right? (Plato, *Apology* 31b) He spent so much time philosophizing he neglected his wife and kids? And you're divorced, right Chuck? Was your marriage also Socratic?

CHARLES: False equivalency. My wife and I grew apart, due to my work, perhaps.

JAMES: Do you remember that dinner we had, the three of us, all awkward silences? But I started telling lawyer jokes and your wife was eating them up. Could you tell a joke to save your marriage? To win this case? I'll concede right now, if you can make one joke! ("Rebecca")

CHARLES: I will not make a laughingstock of the Law.

JAMES: Tough crowd . . . Well, let me tell you one. Do you remember when Howard Hamlin poached my clients? He said, "You can get so caught up in the idea of winning, you forget to listen to your heart" ("Uno"). Just like Socrates said to Crito, that goodness is more important than your life; but a tad self-serving, from the winner to the loser, don't you think?

CHARLES: You think I'm a hypocrite, but my firm earns all our clients. We reject referral fees, abhor solicitations, and make no illegal deals. If it were my say, I would overturn *State Bar v. Arizona* and prohibit law firms from advertisement entirely.

JAMES: Well, on that subject, you know that Socrates was so annoying that his nickname was the "gadfly" of Athens, because he was like "some stinging fly" on a lazy horse (*Apology*, 30e). Likewise, didn't you annoy Howard so much that he offered to buy you out of the firm? ("Lantern")

CHARLES: I never compromise truth and justice, even for niceties and pleasantries.

JAMES: Some would call that hard truth; others might call it just rude. Is that what you did on our Mom's deathbed? You never even told me Mom's last words—what were they, Chuck? ("Klick")

CHARLES: . . . "Jimmy," these questions are offensive . . .

JAMES: Well, as Socrates says, "Please do not be offended if I tell you the truth" (*Apology*, 31d–e). Or would you like me to be more . . . rhetorical?

CHARLES: Truth is one thing; slander is another.

JAMES: Well, speaking of illnesses, you're aware Socrates heard voices, right? He called them his daemon or "prophetic voice" and took their advice? (*Apology*, 31b–c, 40a) Do you have any similar psychiatric conditions?

CHARLES: If caring about the truth is a psychiatric condition.

JAMES: So, what you're saying is you're the "wisest man" in Albuquerque? (*Apology*, 22b)

CHARLES: Jimmy, that's a non-sequitur, it does not follow. But, yes, I was named as such in the latest printing of the *Albuquerque Oracle*. I work hard, cut no corners, dot my i's and cross my t's. If there's a crack in the defense, I'll find it. I did graduate from Georgetown. So, perhaps I am the wisest.

JAMES: So, by inference, you're smarter than me?

CHARLES: Well you're not a *real lawyer*.

JAMES: Real lawyer? Don't I have a JD? Didn't I pass the Bar Exam?

CHARLES: No *real lawyer* would do what you've done!

JAMES: You say you hate fallacies, but isn't that the No-True-Scotsman fallacy? We'll call it, the "No-Real-Lawyer" fallacy?

CHARLES: I . . . Well . . . Um . . . The verdict will decide that. The members of the board are wise: I am sure they will reach the right decision.

JAMES: But, if they ruled against you, with me, it would not be wise? Would they not be *real lawyers*?

CHARLES: I . . . Well . . . Um . . .

JAMES: Do you not believe in "democracy"? (*Crito*, 48a)

CHARLES: I . . . Um . . . Well . . . Um . . . Of course I believe in . . . I'm not on trial here! You think you're so funny! But you're the joke! Don't listen to this nonsense! You have to listen to me! What I am saying is *true*! And I don't care what the judges decide! I am smarter than all of you! I am the wisest man in Albuquerque!

JAMES: The defense rests.

Closing Statement for the Prosecution: Charles McGill Esq.

Well, members of the board, I apologize for my . . . language. I will conclude with a story reminding the board of what the Law really is. According to Plato's dialogues, on the night of his execution, Socrates was visited by his close friend, Crito, who offered to break the philosopher out of prison, but Socrates stayed in Athens even though he knew it meant certain death. Why? Because justice is more important than any one individual. The Law is the greatest achievement of mankind and the realization of all our greatest values. You see, the legal system itself might be characterized in a sense as a Socratic Method. Legal procedures include many Socratic tools, everything that the first philosophers stood for: the cross-examination of witnesses, questions and answers, the law as a logical procedure, expertise above popular opinion, evidentiary substance and standard, contracts and agreements, discipline, and rational abeyance (*Crito*, 51c–53b).

Socrates believed in truth, justice, and rightness. He came to these beliefs through reasoning, even engaging in hypothetical debate with "The Laws" as he imagined them. The Laws used logic and reason to defend their authority, asking Socrates: can you deny that by running away from your execution you would destroy yourself, the laws and the whole state— "Do you imagine that a city can continue to exist . . . if the legal judgements . . . in it have no force . . . ?" (*Crito*, 50a–b). The Laws trap Socrates in a logical double bind. They suggest that it would be illogical and hypocritical for Socrates to disobey them, after a lifetime of serving them and being served by them. This is what Law—and lawyering—is about. Socrates abandoned sophistry for the sake of philosophy, even though it cost him his own life.

And that's how we see it at my law firm. For example, you may be familiar with the embezzlement case we handled recently. The Kettlemans came to HHM because, as they said, "We heard you win cases." But we believe in the law over and above winning cases. We advised them to return stolen money, make "the county whole again," and plea out, because it was the law, it was justice, it was right, and, they fired us ("Bingo"). Justice is the cost of business.

This conflict of dialectic and rhetoric is the true stake of this trial, just as it was in ancient Athens in the trial of Socrates. In these trials, Socrates and I attempt to use reason, while Jimmy and the sophists attempt to use persuasion. In his own trial, Socrates refused to use rhetoric, focusing on the soundness of arguments; reviling and refuting the rhetoric of his accusers. This is what is important to the Law, not sophistry; and this is why the Athenians made a mistake in condemning him, a mistake that you should not make in this trial: whether rhetoric or dialectic wins is up to you.

But let me remind you of the facts of this case. Jimmy cares so little about the truth that he is willing to switch around addresses in briefings for his own gain. Similarly, he switches around words to enchant you, but don't be deceived. That is all it is, switching of words: transpositional errors. He has used trickeries of language to make his case, and now he wants to sway you with pity, but you heard his tape-recorded confession. Tape recorders don't lie. Jimmy said so himself, "you got every detail exactly right" ("Klick"). In the spirit of English Common Law and its Socratic foundations; Jimmy is a sophist!

Closing Statement for the Defense:
James McGill Esp.

Bottom line: Chuck wants you to believe that the law is just logic . . . But the law is also a persuasive process—see, I'm persuading you right now! This was true in ancient Athens, and it's true today in Albuquerque. Justice is the will of the jury; and people are fickle. Although the legal system may be Socratic in practice, it also includes many Sophistic methods: the use of juries, thereby the appeal to opinions; opening and closing speeches; laws legislated, created, and destroyed by oration; judges elected and appointed; and the priority of conviction over truth.

Rhetoricians like Gorgias pride themselves on the power of their art over the legal system (*Gorgias*, 452). Socrates himself said, "In courts of law, men literally care nothing about truth, but only about conviction . . ." (*Phaedrus*, 272). Socrates complained that rhetoric had so influenced the Athenian courts that his own trial was a result of it; furthermore, that his "plain-speaking" was a liability in court, not a boon; and, that being honorable in public life would lead to one's demise. As Socrates's friend Crito said, "All the same, one might object, 'the people have the power to put us to death'," (*Crito*, 44d). Indeed, Socrates lost the trial and was put to death. In fact, he might have gotten a slap on the wrist, if he had not insulted the jurymen so thoroughly—when they asked him what would be a fitting fine, he asked them for a salary! Socrates knowingly sabotaged his own trial. Socrates called himself the wisest, while calling others mere pretenders, calling the speeches "flowery . . . artificial language," "student exercise," "effrontery and impudence," and refusing to "weep and wail" for the sympathy of the jury (*Apology*, 17b–c, 38d). By rejecting rhetoric, Socrates dug his own grave, because the truth was not enough to save him. In the words of Socrates's follower Phaedrus, "mere knowledge of the truth will not give you the art of persuasion" (*Phaedrus*, 272).

That's just how the Law works. For example, in the Sandpiper lawsuit, everyone was on board with Miss Landry waiting for a higher settlement. But somebody got around to spreading rumors about her, and then everyone hated her and wanted to settle right away. One yoga-class later and they changed their minds back ("Fall"). So, I grease the wheels of justice—give a beanie baby to a clerk, give the prosecutor a sandwich, trap 'em in an elevator—it's the only way to get stuff done around here!

And, let's be honest, don't philosophers use rhetoric too? Socrates seemed to believe that he didn't use rhetoric at all, even going so far as to say he had "not the slightest skill as a speaker—unless . . . they mean one who speaks the truth" (*Apology*, 17a–b). But please, humble-brag much: isn't that statement itself rhetorical? Socrates, of course, changes peoples' minds merely by asking questions. In a sense, dialectic, as an art of speaking, must overlap and integrate with rhetoric, a co-extensive art of speaking. And fun fact: although Socrates wanted to criminalize poems; on his deathbed, he started writing them (*Phaedo*, 60d–e). And Plato, Socrates's most famous follower, wrote—wait for it—dialogues! Rhetorical liberties much?

So as for this trial, like the Athenian trial: sure, I told Chuck all that stuff on the tape, but think about what he did to get that tape. He played a "sob story con job on me" to provoke my alleged confession. He lied to me and recorded me without permission. Then he let my friend Ernesto hear the tape, knowing Ernesto would tell Kim, and that Kim would tell me, which he knew would get me angry enough to bust into his house.

He planned the whole con, which I would have seen through, if I hadn't loved my brother. It worked on me better than any legal argument, precisely because he used my techniques ("Witness"). And I'm the sophist here? He said it himself, "play-acting . . . theater," from his own confession. Chuck may not be a formal hypocrite, but he seems willfully blind to the self-serving nature of his self-righteousness. That's just what a sophist would do: use rhetoric when it served and reject it when it didn't. In as many words, this case all boils down to rhetoric versus rhetoric: "Your word against mine" ("Klick").

Opinion of the New Mexico Disciplinary Board

There are two men whose characters are on trial here today and two questions to answer.

Firstly, is Chuck Socratic? Well, he would like to think so, and has said as much in arguments that prove and exemplify the Socratic ideal. But Chuck, like Socrates before him, seems unable to know when debate should end, and seems oblivious to his own use of rhetoric and his own biases, even in the midst of a mental breakdown. In as much, Chuck's appeal to justice and truth is compelling, but sometimes feels insensitive, self-righteous, or even malicious. Sure, "Let justice be done, though the heavens fall!" but this seems to forget the purpose of law: the good of the people ("Chicanery"). Sorry Chuck, we predict your malpractice insurance premiums will go up after this, you may be bought out from your own firm, we just hope you don't do anything too rash . . .

Secondly, is Jimmy a Sophist? In many ways, he is the quintessential sophist. He scams, persuades, and connives his way through the legal process—even in this very hearing. But Jimmy has heart: he seems to be in touch with something beyond the law, something at the root of the law: empathy. His appeal to feeling may not be logically valid, but it at least acknowledges that the good feeling of people is the common goal that lawyers share. But, we should be warned that *we*, as *the audience*, are seduced by Jimmy, his role as a television personality. The Jimmy on television acts rhetorically towards us, making us sympathize with the "pitiful hero," forgiving his unscrupulous ways. We have fun watching because we are in on the con but lulled into forgetting that we are being conned ourselves. Because Jimmy is so likeable and persuasive, we sympathize with him, even when we may know that Chuck is right. As Plato would say, "poets and story-tellers are guilty . . . when they tell us . . . that injustice is profitable when undetected" (*Republic* III, 392). But, Jimmy may get his comeuppance in the end, just as Chuck predicts, if he continues down his road of sophistry: "the truth will come out" ("Alpine Shepherd Boy"). Maybe in a few years he'll find himself on the wrong side of the law—who knows. In this way, as a work of tragedy, Jimmy's story may stop short of valorizing his crimes.

Perhaps Chuck and Jimmy were at their best when working together, using each other's strengths, synergizing dialectic, and rhetoric. Unfortunately though, the truth is a muddled and messy mixture of words, as has been the condition of human beings since ancient Athens.

14
Salvaging Sunk Costs

Joshua Heter

After the numerous trials and tribulations he faced in Season One, Jimmy is dejected. He confesses to Kim that not only does he want to turn down a new, potentially promising job offer from Davis and Main, he wants to quit the law entirely. Kim—perhaps unsurprisingly—is none too pleased at the suggestion.

> KIM: It's a great opportunity, and you're walking away from it?! Look, shouldn't you at least try the job before you say no?
>
> JIMMY: And waste everyone's time, including my own? Kim, I appreciate your concern, but it's not for me. I don't want it!
>
> KIM: Jimmy, do you remember how long you studied for that bar [exam]? How hard you worked? All that effort—you're just going to toss it away?
>
> JIMMY: That's the sunk cost fallacy, the fallacy of sunk costs. It's what gamblers do. They throw good money after bad, thinking they can turn their luck around. It's like, "I've already spent this much money or time or whatever; I've gotta keep going!" ("Switch")

Though Jimmy has both the ability and the tendency to spin a dubious yet persuasive argument out of thin air, he isn't doing that here. The sunk cost fallacy is something that has received a fair amount of attention not only from philosophers but from economists and psychologists as well, and Jimmy's explanation of it here isn't all that bad. The sunk cost fallacy is a specific type of flaw or error in reasoning that occurs when you make a cost-benefit calculation about the rationality of some potential future action, but in so doing, you factor in previously invested resources which cannot be recovered.

It does seem as if Kim has a point. Jimmy spent years earning his law degree, it took him three attempts to pass the bar exam, and he's toiled endlessly at the job, first as a public defender, then as solo practitioner. If he were to walk away from the law now, all of that would have been for naught. Surely, one might think, the rational thing to do would be to continue practicing the law so that those investments do not go unrealized.

But of course, if Jimmy really doesn't enjoy practicing the law, if continuing as a lawyer really would make his life worse, then all of those "sunk costs," the time, money, and effort that led to this point in his career as a lawyer, are irrelevant. He cannot recoup any of those investments, so why should they be a factor in his current or future decision making? So it would seem, they shouldn't, and factoring them into future decisions would be to commit the fallacy of sunk costs. Jimmy's analogy of relentless gamblers seems apt: when deciding whether it is rational to place the next bet, losses from previous bets should be immaterial.

So at least initially, it does seem as if it would be a waste of all his previously invested time and effort for Jimmy to just abandon the law. Yet, it also seems as if taking those sunk costs into account moving forward would be to reason fallaciously. This tension raises two important questions. Is it *ever* rational to take sunk costs into account when deciding whether or not to pursue some present or future action? Put differently, is factoring sunk costs into a future-looking decision always fallacious? If the answer to this question is no, if it is at least *possible* to rationally consider sunk costs in ones forward-looking decision making, we can then revisit Jimmy's case here in particular: is it rational for him to take his sunk costs into account when determining whether or not to continue working as lawyer?

Sunk Costs All Around

The sunk cost fallacy is an issue that appears in *Better Call Saul* with some regularity. In Season Five, Kim attempts to persuade Kevin, Paige, and the rest of the Mesa Verde Bank team to move their proposed call center site to resolve the conflict between the bank and Mr. Acker who is currently living on the site. To this suggestion, Paige objects: "Are you saying that we eat three weeks, and what, eat the cost of the land we already own?!" ("Namaste"). This seems to be a textbook example of the sunk cost fallacy. Whatever the *present* course of action is in the best interest of Mesa Verde moving forward, the resources they've already spent (and importantly, *cannot recoup*) should make no difference in that determination. And, to factor in those expenses to their current decision would be to commit the fallacy of sunk costs.

In Season Three, after Jimmy questions why Kim would stick by his side despite his current, self-inflicted troubles, Kim simply responds "Let's just call it the fallacy of sunk costs." The perhaps tongue-in-cheek implication is that she isn't sticking by Jimmy because it's a smart bet for her moving forward, but because she has already invested so much in their relationship and doesn't want to see all that investment go to waste, thereby committing the fallacy of sunk costs ("Sunk Costs"). You could argue that Jimmy himself commits the fallacy just a few episodes later when, while trying to convince Kim that they should keep their shared office space despite the fact that he's had his law license suspended and has no use for an office, he argues: "We didn't go through all this just to give up everything after one day [of suspension]!" ("Off Brand").

The writers of *Better Call Saul* haven't overpopulated Albuquerque with a disproportionately high number of poor reasoners with an unusual predisposition to factor in sunk costs to their decisions when they shouldn't. The tendency to cling to sunk costs is fairly common, as Howard Garland points out. It's difficult to admit defeat and move on. It makes us psychologically uncomfortable to walk away from previously invested resources *whether or not* they are at all relevant to current or future decision making. Because of this, thinking carefully about sunk costs should be important to us in a way that goes well beyond how the issue affects the characters in our favorite television show. The broad question at hand: whether or not it's ever rational to factor sunk costs into future decision making is as relevant to you and me as it is to Kim and Jimmy.

Varieties of Costs and Benefits

In essence, we're attempting to determine whether or not the sunk cost fallacy (as here described) really is a fallacy in every single case. Let's assume for the sake of argument that in every case, whether or not the decision in question is a rational decision is entirely a function of costs and benefits; in every case, a course of action is rational to pursue if and only if the benefits of pursuing the action outweigh the costs of pursuing the action. This is an oversimplified picture at least in part because it does not take into account the probability of success or failure. If you make a decision to pursue some action with a ninety-nine percent chance of failure and with a benefit of success that only modestly outweighs the cost of pursuing the action, then pursuing the action may be irrational even in the unlikely instance in which it turns out to be successful. Nevertheless, for the purposes of our argument here, the oversimplified picture will do.

With this in mind, it's important to point out just how many different *types* of costs and benefits there might be for any possible course of action. In Season Three, Jimmy has scammed his elderly former client Irene into settling the Sandpiper class action lawsuit so that he will be paid his $1.16 million share of the lawyers' fees without a. having to wait for it and b. risking the small chance of losing out on the settlement entirely ("Fall"). However, after seeing the toll his scam has taken on Irene, he decides to reverse his course of action, re-scamming her so that she'll change her in mind about settling the lawsuit ("Lantern").

A superficial reading of this decision might lead us to think that Jimmy is being irrational because the relevant costs and benefits to him are primarily (if not entirely) financial. If he walks away after his initial scam, Jimmy has $1.16 million in hand. He can invest that money and generally use it to improve his position in life. However, his decision to reverse his course of action, scamming Irene into *not* settling the lawsuit forces him to go without the $1.16 million at least for a long while and risk not getting it at all.

If we calculate the costs and benefits with this superficial analysis, it seems just obvious that the rational thing for Jimmy to have done is maintain his initial course of action, collect his share of the settlement, and move on to his next venture. But of course, the costs and benefits that are relevant to Jimmy in this instance are not entirely financial. At the very least, we can identify three additional relevant types of costs that are important to him: psychological, social, and moral costs.

If Jimmy maintains his original scam and keeps the money, he will incur a psychological cost in the form of guilt. It's one thing to scam a greedy bar patron; that's something Jimmy just does for fun. Scamming a sweet older lady like Irene, on the other hand, is something that even Slippin' Jimmy can't live with. He also risks incurring the social cost of alienating friends and loved ones. Kim is amused by if not attracted to Jimmy's penchant for scamming, but that has its limits. She might not want to be with a man who is willing to take advantage of the truly innocent and vulnerable. And of course, if

Jimmy were to maintain his original scam, he would incur a moral cost. Doing despicable things like scamming (and truly harming) the innocent and vulnerable erodes a person's character; it's corrosive to the soul. Jimmy knows that there are some scams that he wants no part of because of the type of person it will make him. We might think of *Better Call Saul* as the story of Jimmy ultimately losing this battle—the battle of maintaining his character and stopping himself from becoming the person he doesn't want to be. But, at this point in his story, he's more than willing to still put up a fight.

When we take these factors into consideration, Jimmy's decision to reverse his course of action by re-scamming (or unscamming) Irene and walking away from the money (at least for the time being) seems much more rational. Having $1.16 million in hand is surely a significant benefit, but it may not be worth the cost of potentially losing Kim, his psychological well-being, or his soul.

There's an interesting question here about how we do cost-benefit calculations when there's such a wide variety of types of costs and benefits to consider. What does not seem to be questionable is the fact that we make such calculations. Presumably, you had to expend certain resources in order to obtain this book (thanks, by the way). Those resources (such as your labor or your property) are a very different types of things than the enjoyment you receive by owning and reading the book. Yet, you were able to make the decision that (in all likelihood) the benefit of the enjoyment that you will get out of owning and reading this book will outweigh the costs of the resources you had to spend to obtain it.

Rationally Considered Sunk Costs

Ultimately, the question we want to consider is whether it's ever rational to take sunk costs into consideration when making a forward-looking decision. And, we can now say that that debate rests on two important assumptions: the rationality of any decision is reducible to a cost-benefit calculation, and when making such calculations–at least in a number of cases–there will be a variety of costs and benefits that should be considered.

Now, the point is this. There is a case to be made that there are at least some instances in which it *is* rational to take (so-called) sunk costs into account because in such instances, taking those costs into consideration *in conjunction with additional, relevant factors* will ultimately result in benefits that outweigh the costs of performing the action in question overall. The sunk costs should not be factored into the cost-benefit calculation themselves. However, ignoring them altogether is a mistake in a number of cases, because reflecting on sunk costs can allow a subject to appropriately gauge the scope of the types of costs and benefits that are relevant to help them achieve the goals which are most important. That is, without reflecting on sunk costs, you may make the mistake of doing your cost-benefit calculation only in regard to a specific goal as opposed to maximizing your benefits and minimizing your costs *all things considered*. Let's consider a number of different (types of) examples.

Habit Formation

Suppose Jimmy has purchased a ticket to see *The Magic Flute* (An example like this is given by Nozick, p. 22). Between the time Jimmy has made his costly purchase and the start of the show, he realizes that he doesn't actually care much for the opera. He would much rather spend the night at home watching old movies with Kim. Unfortunately for Jimmy, his ticket is non-refundable, and on the night of the show, it's too late to for him to sell it. Jimmy doesn't want to let the money he has spent on his ticket just go to waste, even though he recognizes it as a sunk cost.

In deliberating whether or not to attend the opera or stay home with Kim, if Jimmy were to take the cost of his ticket into account, would he be making a rational mistake? Would he be committing a fallacy? Not necessarily. If the only concern for Jimmy is maximizing his enjoyment for the evening, then Jimmy should cut his losses and stay home with Kim. Again, the money he has spent on his opera ticket cannot be recouped whether or not he attends the opera. So, relative to the goal of achieving a maximally enjoyable evening, that cost is irrelevant (and, if Jimmy were to count the cost of his ticket as a variable in that cost-benefit calculation, he would be committing a fallacy).

However, it is not the case that Jimmy should simply ignore his sunk costs as this is arguably an insufficient accounting of the relevant costs and benefits that will result from Jimmy's decision on how to spend his evening. There may be additional costs and benefits that Jimmy may want to consider in deciding whether or not to attend the opera as opposed to staying home with Kim.

Especially early in his career as a lawyer, frugality is extremely important to Jimmy. Yet, like even the best of us, he is susceptible to failing to live up to his own standards in this regard. If at some point he realizes that he has taken on the habit of making impulsive, irresponsible purchases (such as a costly opera ticket), he may have to put some work into remedying that bad habit. Perhaps in this particular case, if Jimmy forces himself to suffer through the performance at the opera (knowing full well that he could be enjoying himself more at home), the decision to purchase his ticket will weigh on him, and he'll begin to take his purchases more seriously. Thus, by taking his sunk costs into account in this decision, he will be less likely to make similarly lamentable decisions in the future; he'll be less likely to take on sunk costs at all from here on out. This is to say that in the long run, he will be better off because forcing himself to stew at the opera will likely help him form more responsible purchasing habits. Thus, taking his sunk costs into account in this instance, in this manner is rational because doing so brings about a maximal benefit in the long run.

Regret Avoidance

In Season Three, Jimmy suggests that he and Kim should keep their shared office, even though he's temporarily lost his law license, and Kim has only one large client that doesn't typically make use of her workspace. "We didn't go through all this just to give up everything after one day [of suspension]!" Jimmy argues ("Off Brand"). It's painful for Jimmy to think of all of the time, money, and effort they have put into finding their office and making it their own. But, whether or not it's ultimately beneficial for them to keep the office, those sunk costs seem to be irrelevant. To be sure, they are irrelevant directly to Jimmy and Kim's business and financial interests, and it would be fallacious for them to add those sunk costs into the cost-benefit calculation of maximizing their financial interests moving forward. However, the sum total of Jimmy and Kim's interests (the costs and benefits that matter to them) are not reducible to their businesses or finances.

If moving on from their shared office will result in a great deal of regret about having put in so much effort to secure their office, then that mental and emotional toll could—in principle—be so great that it outweighs the financial benefits that would come from breaking their lease and moving forward without their office, a point explained by Thomas Kelly. That is, it could be that giving up their office after putting in so much to obtain it will weigh on them psychologically so much that it might be worth keeping it, even if doing so is a net negative to them financially.

The obvious response to this line of reasoning is that Jimmy and Kim should simply get over it! They should recognize that in regard to their demonstrable (perhaps "objective") costs and benefits (their finances and their actual utilization of office space moving forward), abandoning their office is the rational decision because doing so will maximize the benefits and reduce the costs of those very important factors. However, this response fails to appreciate that Jimmy and Kim (just like the rest of us) simply do not have a perfect, infallible control over their own psychological states. No one (or hardly anyone) can simply choose what they do and do not care about; no one can just will themselves to stop regretting some previous course of action. If Jimmy and Kim can just "get over it," and realize that moving on from their office arrangement is the rational thing to do relative to maximizing their best possible financial situation, then perhaps they should. However, if they cannot, and if the rationality of their decision is to maximize their benefits and minimize their costs all things considered, then the rational thing for them to do all things considered could very well be to keep their office.

Signaling to One's Opponents

Finally, recall also that in Season Five, Kim attempts to persuade Kevin, Paige, and the rest of the Mesa Verde Bank team to move their proposed call center site. To this suggestion, Paige objects: "Are you saying that we eat three weeks, and what, eat the cost of the land we already own?" ("Namaste"). Despite Paige's protestations, what benefit could there possibly be in taking the bank's sunk costs into consideration moving forward? Whatever the best place for their call center is now, the costs they have already incurred and cannot recoup are irrelevant relative to the goal of them picking the best site.

However, there may very well be a reason for taking their sunk costs into consideration in circumstances such as these. It's important for the leaders of a business (or anyone participating in a competitive activity) to bear in mind the ways in which they are being perceived by their competitors. Failing to do so in a variety of circumstances will result in diminished benefits and increased costs. Certainly, relative to the narrow goal of finding the most advantageous spot for this particular call center site, Mesa Verde's sunk costs are immaterial. However, this is only one of a number of business decisions the bank will make over the course of its life. There may be a benefit to Mesa Verde in signaling to their business competitors that they are willing to "stick to their guns" so to speak and that—in regard to future business dealings—it will be a fruitless exercise to try to wait them out, to wait for them to change course, even at the expense of increasing costs and minimizing benefits in regard to this one particular business deal. If Mesa Verde garners the reputation that they aren't willing to "eat" their sunk costs so easily, that could drastically increase their costs all around in future business dealings.

Admittedly, in taking this course of action, they are signaling to opponents that they are in some sense potentially willing to act irrationally (or appear to be irrational) relative to their immediate goal of finding the best site for their call center. But, if doing so in this and similar cases increases benefits that outweigh costs for the sum total of their business dealings overall, then it is the rational course of action.

Career Calculations

While this may not be an exhaustive list, it seems that we have at least three types of cases in which it may be rational to take sunk costs into consideration when making forward-looking decisions: cases in which we are concerned with habit formation, regret avoidance, or signaling to our opponents. Again, the sunk costs are not a relevant variable in the cost-benefit calculations themselves, but reflecting on them can inform us about which goals those calculations are best aimed. Should any one of these examples hold up to scrutiny, then the sunk cost fallacy (again, as here described) may be a fallacy typically, but it is not a fallacy in every case.

Consider again our original example in which Jimmy considers abandoning his law practice (in the face of Kim's disapproval). Is it rational for Jimmy to take his so-called sunk costs (the time, money, and effort he put into becoming a lawyer) into account when deciding on whether or not to continue practicing the law? Plausibly, the answer is yes. Let's be reminded that the more narrow question at hand is whether or not Jimmy should take his sunk costs into consideration in regard to his future-looking decision of whether to remain working as a lawyer. The question is *not* whether those sunk costs—in this particular case—make it rational for Jimmy to continue as a lawyer. There could be sunk costs that are relevant (such as costs important to habit formation, regret avoidance, or signaling to one's opponents) in the sense that they should inform Jimmy's cost/benefit calculation even if the calculation ultimately says that the rational thing for Jimmy to do is to quit the law.

The example Jimmy originally cites in explaining the sunk cost fallacy to Kim—the relentless gambler who doesn't know when to quit—is relatively straightforward. Relative to the fairly simplistic goal of walking away from the card table with the maximum amount of money, any amount a gambler has already lost is irrelevant to whether or not he should place another bet, and factoring that amount into the decision to continue to bet is to make an irrational mistake and to commit the sunk cost *fallacy*. However, in a decision as complex as continuing a career he has spent years preparing for, Jimmy should carefully consider a wide range of factors, even some costs which may reasonably be described as sunk.

15
Saul's Bullshit's Not All Good, Man.

JOSHUA LUCZAK

Saul bullshits. In fact, he's a master of it. He's a bullshit artist. But while his bullshit is entertaining and sometimes brings about a worthy end, it's not all good. In fact, it's often harmful. People who behave like Saul and spread bullshit everywhere are causing all of us to live less desirable lives.

According to a common and widely endorsed view, often attributed to Harry Frankfurt, bullshit is communication that does not show a proper concern for the truth. Naturally then, bullshitters are individuals who communicate in ways that do not show a proper concern for the truth. Bullshit is often distinguished from lying by noting that liars properly care about the truth. Liars care about what is true, so that they can intentionally deceive others about it. According to what James Mahon calls the traditional definition of lying, liars make statements they believe to be false with the intention that others believe them to be true.

Bullshitters do not properly care about the truth. They typically care more about other things, and they speak from a place that is motivated by that. If saying true things just so happens to coincide with what they believe to be true or with what they want to communicate, then they will speak the truth—but not because they are genuinely aiming or care to speak the truth. Similarly, they may, like the liar, say false things, but, unlike the liar, not because they are genuinely aiming or care to speak falsely. Speaking falsely just so happens to coincide with what the bullshitter wants to communicate.

Unscrupulous used car salespeople are often thought to be good examples of bullshitters. They typically do not care about saying true or false things, they just care about saying whatever they need to say to make a sale. Saul is a bullshitter *and* a liar. Sometimes he says things that he believes to be false with the intention that others believe them to be true, but, on other occasions, he, like some used car salespeople, doesn't care all that much about what is true or false. Sometimes, all he cares about is winning.

Some Bullshit

Let's begin by looking at an instance of Saul's bullshit, and see why it is bullshit. Well, it's actually Jimmy's bullshit—but potayto, potahto. In particular, we'll look at the bullshit he offers up to the panel who are deciding on whether to reinstate him as a lawyer after his license to practice law was suspended ("Winner").

Prior to his hearing, Jimmy engages in a collection of schemes designed to win favor with members of the panel who will decide on whether he can return to practicing law (for instance, "anonymously" paying for a library built in Chuck's honor, and feigning sorrow at Chuck's grave). It seems pretty clear from his attitude and behavior away from others that none of these things are being done sincerely. All of them are aimed at getting others to think that he is genuinely sad and sorry about Chuck's death. This, he thinks, on Kim's advice, is key to getting his suspension lifted. When Jimmy later "goes off script" in his hearing and describes himself, Chuck, and his relationship with him, the viewer, and Kim, are led to believe that Jimmy is no longer trying to con the panel. Instead, everyone is led to believe that Jimmy is finally opening up, and speaking from the heart. He says:

> Look, my brother loved me, in his own way. Loved me as a brother, but . . . he did not love me as a lawyer. Big part of the reason I became a lawyer was . . . Chuck. He was the most brilliant man I ever knew. An incredible lawyer. And he knew exactly who he was. Exactly. And I wanted to make him proud. And, believe me, he was a hard man to make proud. Like climbing Everest without supplies. But if you were one of the few who reached the peak, made him proud even for a moment. . . wow. What a feeling. He let you know it. But if you weren't one of those people . . . He was always polite enough to everyone, but he sure didn't suffer fools, y'know? He was judgmental. He was difficult. Knew how to get under your skin. And he could be a real son-of-a-bitch. Chuck was the one who was "always right." Always. And, honestly, he usually was. So, y'know, a guy like me . . . did lousy in school, lacked ambition, always cut corners . . . For me to live up to somebody like Charles McGill . . . heh, c'mon. Look at me. I'll never

be as moral as him. Never be as smart. Never as respected. I'll never be as good as Chuck. But I can try. I can try. And if you allow me to be a lawyer again, I'll do everything I can to be worthy of the name "McGill." And if you decide I'm not a lawyer, then . . . y'know what? Doesn't change anything. I'm still going to be the best man I can be. Look, I'm lucky. I got this letter. I never wrote a letter to him. Never got a chance to say all the things I should've. I gotta believe, somehow, he knows . . . I'm sorry. That's. . . That'll have to do it for me. I—Thank you.

As we learn when Jimmy is talking to Kim shortly after the hearing, all of these seemingly heart-felt, soul-bearing words were merely another, but impromptu, play in getting the panel to vote in favor of lifting his suspension. Interestingly, and importantly though, what helps make Jimmy's speech so compelling, and trick Kim, the panel, and presumably many viewers into thinking that he was speaking sincerely, was its truth. Everything that Jimmy said about himself, his brother, and their relationship, is true. But, as his actions, words, and attitude before, but especially after the hearing make clear, Jimmy was not speaking with a proper concern for the truth. He did not say what he did because he really cared about the truth, or about expressing how he may really feel deep down inside. Rather, he said what he did because he thought that this is what the panel wanted to hear, and what he needed to say in order for them to lift his suspension. Since Jimmy cared so much about "winning", and so little, if at all, about speaking truthfully, it seems most appropriate to describe his speech, despite its truth, as pure and utter bullshit.

Harmful Bullshit

Okay, so we just looked at an instance of Jimmy's bullshit. Now let's talk about some significant ways in which bullshit is harmful. As we will see, it's often harmful because it undermines the epistemic demands imposed on people by what they care about. It's often harmful because it undermines the epistemic demands imposed on people by the social roles they occupy. And it's often harmful because it contributes to a broad and general corrosion of epistemic trust.

While it might seem straightforward that the bullshit Jimmy spreads in this hearing and elsewhere is harmful, it is not the case that all instances of bullshit are harmful. Sometimes, we suspend speaking with a proper concern for the truth because we're engaged in acts of communication that have other important, and morally decent, goals. Wholesome jokes are

a good example. Sometimes telling a joke requires us to suspend
speaking with a proper concern for the truth in order for it to
function as a joke. Nothing is obviously wrong with such a practice, especially when everyone participating in the joke knows
what's going on. Other times we suspend communicating in
ways that display a proper concern for the truth because we are
trying to achieve some morally valuable goal. Scott Kimbrough
notes, for example, that sometimes we not only tolerate but
encourage children to issue bullshit apologies when they have
wronged someone to foster good moral development. The
thought is that through repetitive modeling of good behavior
children learn how they ought treat people they have wronged.
While they do not mean what they say now, they are more likely
to issue sincere apologies in the future by engaging in such a
practice. Since, on the basis of cases like these, it is not always
true that bullshit is harmful, it's important that we carefully
spell out the ways Jimmy (and Saul's) bullshit here, and elsewhere, is indeed harmful.

Jimmy and Saul's bullshit is often harmful because it undermines the epistemic demands imposed on others by what they
care about. If we care about anything, then we care about holding and acquiring true beliefs about the things we care about.
Holding and acquiring true beliefs about the things we care
about means that we are better able to show proper care for the
things we care about. So, we have a responsibility to conscientiously acquire and hold beliefs about the things we care about.
While the conscientious acquisition and retention of beliefs
about the things we care about does not guarantee their truth, it
does appear to be the best we can intentionally do to have and
hold all and only true beliefs about the things we care about.
Jimmy, for example, has a goldfish that he comes to care about
("Chicanery" and "Off Brand"). Since he cares about this goldfish, he ought to hold and acquire true beliefs about it. He ought
to know, say, how much food it needs, what temperature its water
should be kept at, and whether it needs a bubbler, etc. Knowing
these things will enable him to show proper care for his goldfish.

Now, if someone bullshits us, then we either identify that
they are bullshitting us or we do not. If we do not recognize that
they are bullshitting us, and we trust them, then it is more
likely that we will come to hold false or imprecise beliefs than
if they spoke with a proper concern for the truth. Naturally
then, if bullshitters are speaking about matters that concern
things we care about, then, in these circumstances, it's more
likely that we will come to hold false or imprecise beliefs about
the things we care about.

But holding false or imprecise beliefs about the things we care about means that we will be less able to take proper care of the things we care about. This is bad for us, and it undermines the epistemic responsibility we have towards those things we care about in virtue of our caring. It's bad for us because if we are less able to take proper care of the things we care about, and the desirability of our lives is at least partially determined by how well those things flourish, then our being less able to take proper care of the things we care about will diminish the desirability of our lives. But, now, if, on the other hand, we identify that someone is bullshitting us, and we respect ourselves, then this will corrode our trust in them as a source of knowledge—especially if they bullshit us about matters that concern things we care about.

But then, if instances of bullshit corrode our trust in them, then we will have fewer sources of information available to us. And if we have fewer sources of information available to us, then we will have fewer sources in which we can pull facts from. This seems to straightforwardly make it more challenging for us to conscientiously acquire and hold beliefs about the things we care about, and so makes it more challenging for us to show proper care for the things we care about. This result is also bad for us since the desirability of our lives will be diminished in virtue of it being more challenging for us to take proper care of the things we care about.

Since, for example, Kim cares about Jimmy, and the desirability of her life is at least in part determined by how well Jimmy is doing, it's important that she know facts about Jimmy so that she can show proper care for him. It is important, for example, that she conscientiously acquire and hold beliefs about Jimmy's mental state and how he's dealing with Chuck's death so that she can act in ways that display a proper concern for him. But then Jimmy's courtroom bullshit, at the very least, makes it more challenging for her to achieve this. Since Kim was clearly taken in by this bullshit, she may, if she ever trusts Jimmy again to speak sincerely about his mental state and feelings about Chuck, fall victim to it again in the future, and so once more come to hold false or imprecise beliefs about Jimmy. If, on the other hand, she does not trust him to properly speak the truth about these things, then she may not believe what he says, even when he is speaking sincerely. Either way, his bullshit makes her worse off, and so, she is harmed by it.

We all find ourselves in situations like Kim's from time to time, and so all of us experience the harms that come from bullshit that undermines fulfilling the epistemic demands that apply to us, given the things we care about. Sure, Jimmy offered up a pretty compelling pile of bullshit in this case, but that it was so compelling doesn't mean that cases that aren't so compelling are not harmful. When we are trying to conscientiously acquire and hold beliefs about the things we care about we may come to rely on information we get from people and places that cough up compelling piles of bullshit. If what they say is false or imprecise, then we will be harmed. If what they say just so happens to be true, then we may, in that instance, be no worse off, but that's only because we got lucky. Relying on them is risky, even if we don't know it. If the people and places we rely on serve up detectable (and so not compelling) bullshit, then, provided we respect ourselves, we should distrust what they say. But then we have fewer sources of information to pull facts from. So bullshit, regardless of how compelling it is, makes us worse off. It is harmful.

Now, while some of our epistemic demands arise because we care about certain things, others spring from other sources. For example, some of our epistemic demands spring, not from the things we care about, but from the social roles we occupy. Many of us, for example, are required, from time to time, to serve as jurists. As citizens of societies with justice systems that populate juries with citizens, we have a responsibility, when our number is called, to be good jurors. If we are a jurist in a litigation case, then we have an obligation to reach a decision conscientiously, regardless of whether or not we care about the case. Here, our epistemic demand springs not from what we care about personally, but from the importance of the role we occupy.

Now think about the panel members who will decide on whether Jimmy's suspension should be lifted, and suppose that these people are not personally invested in the case. These people have a responsibility, given their role within the New Mexico Bar Association, to reach a decision conscientiously about Jimmy's future as a lawyer. Since it seems clear that sincerity is at least one of the criteria they are using to determine whether Jimmy can return to practicing law, and since they are treating truthful discussions of Chuck that appear sincere as evidence of genuine sincerity (which seems entirely reasonable), Jimmy's bullshit undermines their ability to reach a just and appropriate decision. It undermines their ability to do their job properly. So, Jimmy's bullshit renders them worse off. As holders of an important social role, they are harmed by it.

While many of us will not be in this particular kind of situation, we will, however, be in many situations like this, given the many social roles we occupy throughout our lives. That is, we will often be in situations in which our ability to perform our social roles well will depend, in part, on others displaying a proper regard for the truth. If people bullshit us in these contexts, then we will not be able to properly uphold the responsibilities our social roles impose on us, and so not be able to perform our roles well. So bullshit, in these contexts, damages our social roles. What's more, if the desirability of our lives are at least in part determined by our ability to perform our social roles well, then bullshit in these contexts also harms us personally.

Jimmy and Saul's bullshit corrodes epistemic trust. Since so much of our knowledge comes from other people, we depend on them caring that they have knowledge, and on them showing, through what they communicate, that they have a proper concern for the truth. But then, if people spread bullshit, like Jimmy and Saul do, day in and day out, and we become aware of it, then epistemic trust has been broken. If breaks in trust happen in numbers that are great enough, or from sources we depend heavily on, or are about matters that matter greatly, then this corrosion could have consequences that extend beyond these numbers, or sources, or matters. Bullshit could lead to a much greater and more general corrosion of epistemic trust than it does in a small number of cases.

If instances of bullshit lead us to generally distrust others since it may render us unable to distinguish between those we can trust to speak with a proper concern for the truth and those we cannot, then the consequences of bullshit extend much further than isolated cases. So then, at the very least, in addition to the specific harms individuals are subjected to with respect to bullshit, they are also at risk of bearing the consequences that come from a much broader corrosion of epistemic trust. At worst, if Jimmy and Saul's bullshit, or frankly anyone's bullshit, plays a meaningful role in a genuine and general corrosion of epistemic trust, then it would be some very harmful bullshit indeed.

16

Better Call Saul Because Chuck's Condition Is Real

AMBER E. GEORGE

Whether we're living with an illness, disability, or other health malady, we have good reason to care about how individuals are represented on screen.

As the global population of people living with health conditions grows, it's no surprise that one of television's most popular shows, *Better Call Saul*, chose to feature a character with a health condition. Chuck McGill, Jimmy "Saul" McGill's older brother, has an uncommon medical condition that causes him to have an allergy to electricity.

The show's creator, Vince Gilligan, refers to Chuck's condition as electromagnetic hypersensitivity (EHS), leaving the audience skeptical that such a state exists, both physically and psychologically.

Let's define 'health' as an existential sense of profound harmony. A person's mental, physical, and spiritual well-being are inextricably linked. 'Illness' is an uncomfortable, intrusive experience that makes performing daily tasks difficult. 'Disability' encompasses not only health and illness but also social exclusion and stigma.

Given these definitions of health, illness, and disability, Chuck seems to encounter moments where he has health, illness, and disability through his experiences with EHS. EHS describes how a person feels after being exposed to electromagnetic fields (EMFs) emitted by electronic devices such as wi-fi routers, microwave ovens, computers, and cell phones (Gareth Cook, "The Nocebo Effect").

While technology has improved our lives, Chuck's concerns about potential health hazards from EMF emissions are not unfounded. Despite its prevalence, especially in industries that require a high level of radiation exposure, EHS is not a medically recognized condition. There is currently no scientific or medical evidence linking EMF exposure to EHS symptoms.

Chuck McGill Is Who He Is

The brilliant actor, Michael McKean, plays Charles "Chuck" Lindbergh McGill, Jr. as a partner at the prestigious law firm Hamlin, Hamlin, and McGill (HHM). Chuck appears to have type-A personality traits such as "operating at a more urgent pace, demonstrating higher levels of impatience, having a more competitive nature, getting upset easily, and associating self-worth with achievement," to quote psychologist Elizabeth Scott. When we first meet Chuck, he appears quite satisfied with his hermit-like lifestyle. Although he has what most would consider a pitiful existence, he appears in good health so long as he avoids electricity. Jimmy is a devoted caregiver for Chuck, going by his house daily to deliver groceries and his mail and newspaper, while following his "rules" to minimize electrical exposure.

Jimmy's character arc is revealed in flashbacks throughout the first season, beginning with his not-so-humble beginnings as a con man known as "Slippin' Jimmy" to his loftier goals of attending college. Chuck chastises his younger brother's dubious con artist behavior. Chuck's animosity toward Jimmy grows even stronger after he becomes an attorney, as he tells his brother during a fight, "Slippin' Jimmy with a law degree is like a chimp with a machine gun."

Chuck uses deceptive, underhanded tactics to keep Jimmy from working at HHM and eventually gets him disbarred. Chuck seems unhappy that Jimmy got so far by being dishonest while acting honorably has benefited Chuck so little. Personality clashes, sibling rivalry, and familial dysfunction have exacerbated the rift between the brothers. Furthermore, the McGill parents' preference for Jimmy over Chuck is revealed in Season Two.

Several early sequences in the series show what occurs when Chuck comes into contact with electricity. These encounters shed light on Chuck and Jimmy's relationship and how the general public, law enforcement, and medical community perceive EHS. After they discovered he had been stealing his neighbor's newspaper for several days in a row, Chuck was tased by the police. Audiences witness the symptoms, including dizziness, musculoskeletal pain, difficulty concentrating, skin redness and tingling, fatigue, nausea, and headaches. Jimmy finds Chuck unconscious, surrounded by electrical machines and flashing lights at the hospital. "All these lights, you might as well throw him in a microwave," Jimmy says" as he frantically fights security to turn off all the electricity in the room.

When Chuck regains consciousness, he tells Dr. Cruz that he has a "condition" in relation to electromagnetic fields that began two years ago. The doctor dupes Chuck by secretly turning on a machine at the foot of the bed without his knowledge or consent, to which Chuck pays no attention. This raises valuable questions about the issue of autonomy and consent in medicine. Once outside the room, the doctor advises Jimmy to have his brother committed for psychiatric treatment. As Chuck's next of kin, Jimmy ultimately refuses to institutionalize him.

Chuck returns home wrapped in his aluminum "space blanket," protecting him from electromagnetic waves. At this point, viewers may be left wondering about Chuck's level of agency and self-awareness. He is unaware that people have debated whether he is mentally fit to continue living a semi-independent life at home. Furthermore, nobody has presented this fact to him directly, so that he could make an informed decision based on facts. Is Chuck mentally competent? Is he aware of what's going on around him? What is real and what is imagined for Chuck?

Reality?—That's So Meta

A central focus in metaphysics is the question, "What's real?" In medical science, what's real is often defined using scientific concepts and laws to explain how things work. Philosophers frequently go beyond the metaphysics of medicine to study ontology, which entails understanding what health, disease, and illness mean and determining what causes them. Philosophers also mix metaphysical and epistemological concerns to answer the questions, "What do we know?" "And how do we know?" Some philosophers spend their entire careers discussing realism versus antirealism. This difference affects how diseases are recognized, diagnosed, and managed. Within this realm of inquiry, one might ask, "If EHS is real, then how could we test for it?" And, "If EHS is not real, what does that mean for people who have symptoms similar to EHS?"

Someone who believes that medical science can explain everything can be called a realist. A realist might propose finding a measurable biomarker (a misfiring brain chemical or gene expression) responsible for the condition within the body to diagnose EHS. They might then recommend that everyone who has this marker for EHS has EHS. Realists may argue that one cannot exist without the other. This actual factor for EHS has yet to be determined by science, but let's assume scientists are looking for it. Realists typically hold that "universals—abstractions of objects and events—are separate from the mind cognizing them" (James Marcum, "Philosophy of Medicine").

Even if there's no discernible diagnosable component to EHS, we could argue that whatever is happening to Chuck is life-altering and, depending on who you ask, disabling. He is sometimes unable to perform daily tasks (such as retrieving the newspaper from outside or purchasing groceries), and he is also shamed, shunned, and perceived as "abnormal." Realists may only discuss EHS when there is a discernible way of identifying it through a diagnosis. Anti-realists, on the other hand, may take a more phenomenological stance, arguing that no disease marker or condition is required. This is because brain chemistry or gene expression is a clinical construct that is difficult to replicate. When this construct changes, often due to technological advances, one's understanding of the disease changes. Thus, anti-realists may be less comfortable solidifying any concrete conclusions about diagnosing EHS due to the changing nature of reality.

Who's Gonna Put the Phenomenology into Medicine?

The phenomenology of medicine is a philosophical discipline that investigates health conditions through the patient's subjective experience. A patient's phenomenology or lived experience (first-person perspective) can enhance medical sciences (third-person perspective) and healthcare personnel's (second-person perspectives) ability to treat a patient.

Understanding a person's life story, feelings, and overall subjective experience of illness require a first-person perspective. Medicine has favored third- and second-person viewpoints without fully considering the patient's subjective experience. This privileging of objectivity to the detriment of subjectivity has long historical roots in philosophy, dating back to the mind-body problem and beyond.

René Descartes was the first to discuss the relationship between thought and consciousness in the mind, which is distinct from the brain as part of the physical body. Descartes believes that because the mind and body are distinct, they exist as separate entities. The Cartesian view of the mind and body has caused schisms in medical science. The separation of mind and body, or Cartesian dualism, runs through medicine like a "geological fault," with most disciplines falling on one side or the other (Mattsson and Mattsson 2002).

Conditions that solely affect the mind are frequently referred to psychiatry, whereas those involving the brain are addressed by neurology. This makes us wonder about conditions that involve both the brain and the mind, because isolating neurology and psychiatry into their respective silos leaves people without specialized care. Furthermore, advancements in neuroscience "make it increasingly difficult to draw a precise line between neurological disorders (considered to be 'structural brain disorders') and psychiatric disorders (considered to be 'functional brain disorders')" (Thibaut 2018). While this conversation regarding medical treatment is informative, it leaves us wondering which discipline of medicine can help Chuck. This analysis implies that medical science can help Chuck but not fully understand him. What is missing are the social, cultural, existential, and psychological influences that contribute to his condition.

When a condition emerges as a disease with no known cause, it's referred to in scientific literature as "idiopathic environmental intolerance (IEI)" (Eberle 2017). Some research questions whether IEIs like EHS are delusional disorders, to which the overwhelming majority responds that they are "overvalued ideas," "preoccupations," that are "unreasonable," and likely stem from "cultural beliefs" (Hausteiner et al.) rather than actual disease pathology. This dismissal is common among patients with psychosomatic conditions. People, for example, hesitated to accept Chronic Fatigue Syndrome (CFS) and fibromyalgia as "real" medical conditions. They were thought to be created by the imaginations of some mentally "disturbed" people, labeled "crazy" for "overreacting" to something no one could see, hear, or taste, such as electromagnetic frequencies. This illustrates the bias in health analysis that favors second- and third-person identification.

In a situation such as Chuck's, illness can only be defined inasmuch as it can be quantified and measured. The ability to obtain an official medical diagnosis could mean the difference between saving someone's life through treatment or allowing them to die alone. It should not matter whether someone is experiencing an easily definable illness or an ambiguous situation. There are instances where people become ill for no apparent medical reason, such as when they get dizzy, faint, or vomit upon seeing blood. Even though we cannot find a scientific explanation for how these illnesses originated, we nonetheless recognize them as real conditions that can potentially change people's lives.

Whether EHS is real or not, it is something that Chuck and countless others experience. Adopting a stance that incorporates both medical science and one's direct experience of life as it manifests in subjective reality is likely to provide more assistance to those in need. As a result, we consider both objective and subjective aspects of existence without favoritism.

Thinking Himself In and Out of Wellness

The belief that people can think themselves into wellness is a common cultural trope in Western culture. People believe that a positive mindset coupled with an ambitious attitude can help them recuperate faster. Chuck appears eager to use this method to alleviate his symptoms. As early as the "Bingo" episode during season one, Chuck is ready to "go back to work, to feel useful again." Jimmy comes home to find Chuck standing outside for two minute increments for conscious "exposure treatment." During the "Pimento" episode, Chuck and Jimmy are outside, sitting on a park bench (under an electrical transformer), barefoot on the grass, continuing his exposure therapy. When he learns that EHS is likely psychosomatic after his breakdown in court, he seeks help from Dr. Cruz. By Season Three, his regular sessions with Dr. Cruz enabled him to get groceries and go about his daily life without accommodations such as the "space blanket." Chuck unknowingly tolerates electromagnetic fields while preoccupied by work, making his best effort to consciously, and perhaps even unconsciously, think himself into being healthy.

While you can think yourself into wellness, you must wonder whether it's possible to think yourself into illness. The blackouts, anxiety, and dizziness seem to manifest Chuck's subconscious mind rather than a physical condition. His physical symptoms may be an attempt to disguise his emotional distress and inner turmoil. Chuck's method for dealing with stress may have caused him to develop a condition that justifies his isolation from social interaction. His subconscious chose this state over the possibility of future heartbreak or social rejection. When bodies and minds are distraught, they can experience a dissociative response as an extreme way of coping with distress. In this case, Chuck's conscious mind becomes uncontrollably separated from reality. Humans express their unhappiness in various ways, such as crying, complaining, self-medicating with substances, or, in Chuck's case, having an extreme reaction to electricity.

If Chuck's symptoms arise in his subconscious, how they manifest is determined by what else lives there. He was a workaholic and an overachiever before developing EHS, yet he was always tormented by gnawing insecurities, perfectionism, and the perception that his parents did not love him. Perhaps his working-class parents were unsure what to do with his brilliance, so they concentrated their attention on their innately charismatic son, Jimmy, with whom they could relate. This is especially evident in Season Two, when we learn that their father and mother favor Jimmy over Chuck.

While Chuck's intellect and determination were admirable, his arrogance and other personality quirks made it difficult for him to gain acceptance. Furthermore, type A personality traits have negative consequences, such as increased stress, harming your health. According to Elizabeth Scott, people with type A personality traits are more likely to develop stress-related health problems and social isolation. As neurologist Suzanne O'Sullivan, M.D., states, "I have found myself astounded by the degree of disability that can arise as a result of psychosomatic illness. I have come to realize that these disabilities can serve a fundamental purpose. They happen for a reason. When words are not available, our bodies sometimes speak for us—and we have to listen."

Chuck may have developed EHS to deal with his obsessions, eccentricities, and pressures from his incessant perfectionism. Furthermore, the breakdown of his marriage to Rebecca Bois, the only woman he had ever loved, may have been the biggest blow to his fragile sense of self. It should have been a wake-up call for him to re-evaluate his life and priorities. However, his pride would not allow him to slow down. Instead, as a way of dealing with his hurt, his subconscious mind created a new outlet—EHS. It allowed him to become a recluse, take a break from work, and force Jimmy to help him for a change. Instead of allowing him to reassess his life, it kept him in limbo for two years while his resentment of his brother reached a boiling point.

Dr. Michael Witthöft of Johannes Gutenberg University Mainz argues that sensationalized (scientifically unfounded) media reports about harmful substances, can cause EHS symptoms in susceptible persons. According to Witthöft, the "nocebo" effect is "the mere anticipation of potential injury may actually trigger pain or disorders." This is the opposite of the analgesic effects we know can be associated with exposure to placebos." An example of this occurs during his second hospitalization in the episode "Klick," when Dr. Cruz checks for brain damage using a CT scan after Chuck falls. There was no mention of whether Chuck had consented to the scan that left him in a stress-induced coma. Just as the study suggests, the "nocebo" effect allowed Chuck's body and mind to work together to put him into a self-induced coma to avoid EHS symptoms.

Please Help Chuck. He's in Crisis

Chuck's subconscious was teeming with memories, heartbreak, and a slew of other emotions and life experiences that shaped his experiences with health, illness, and disability. Additionally, our culture, society, and relationships all play a role in responding to adversity. Perhaps he could have been spared from the madness that pushed him to take his own life if he had understood his condition. If his illness was intended to treat loneliness or dampen unattainable standards, perhaps treating that loneliness and disappointment would have made his condition disappear.

Chuck, Jimmy, or Dr. Cruz could have used all available resources to pinpoint the trauma that triggered his extreme sensitivity to electricity and then address it from there. One of the most heartbreaking scenes was when he calls Dr. Cruz to cancel his upcoming appointment, claims that he will see her next week, and promptly disconnects his phone. He could have said something like, "Please help me, I'm in a crisis," but his pride gets in the way. Chuck's experience demonstrates how adopting a whole person perspective toward a person's responses to health, illness, and disability is crucial for life and death matters.

Medically unexplained conditions can have serious existential consequences for those who experience them. Perhaps it was his existential anxiety about the fragility of life and his inability to live an authentic life (before or after his leave of absence from HHM) that made him vulnerable to taking his own life during season three. Despite making critical inroads towards improving his condition, he broke with HMM and his brother. Instead of continuing to help himself, he blamed the outside world for his problems, as shown in the Season Three finale "Lantern" during the final confrontation between brothers. After his confrontation with Jimmy, he relapsed into a frenzied hunt for active electrical wires, indicating he went to a very dark, and dangerous mental place. Michael McKean, the actor who plays him, describes this scene as "a man looking for a way out, and he had to settle for that way out" (Matt Patches interview). The episode ends with Chuck methodically kicking a gas lantern until it falls over and sets the house ablaze.

Jimmy is stoical when he learns of Chuck's death in the episode "Smoke." He was astonishingly emotionless while reading the obituary and attending the funeral. Jimmy responds almost gleefully when Howard, Chuck's former HHM co-partner, shares that he believes Chuck intentionally sparked the fire and firing him may have contributed. It's unfair to blame Jimmy or Howard for Chuck's taking his own life, but there may have been a point when both of their actions contributed to Chuck's relapse. Whether real or imagined, Chuck's embodied way of being in the world was thwarted by his condition. As a result, he finds himself in a state of "alien being (being my-self, but not me)" that causes him to spiral into despair (Svenaeus 2013). We know that tens of millions of people experience anxiety, depression, and death by suicide due to living with conditions, whether mental, physical, or a combination of the two. The hope is that for the person experiencing such despair will only be in it for a short time. And that with the right social supports, they can break free from this state of "alien being."

Unfortunately, when Chuck's health condition was essential to the show's plot, his persona was often presented as frantic, with images emphasizing his unpredictable and "crazy" nature. It does not help that Michael McKean, who plays the character said, "This strange, kind of psycho-physical problem this man seems to have, it's been intriguing to research . . . Part of the fun is finding out what it is or learning what it is along with us" (Megan Friedman).

Accurately portraying this character should not have been left up to guesswork or mystery. Audiences are then free to reject or ridicule him as a result. Chuck might have received more support and felt better about himself if he had not been portrayed as "crazy." No shortage of research proves that Western culture is saturated with disparaging representations and a lack of critical insight, along with empathy, that encourage people to "other" those with health conditions (Rose et al.). Positive media representations can boost self-esteem, motivation to seek help, and adherence to treatment or drug schedules, ultimately improving well-being (Stuart 2006).

The show's creators could have portrayed Chuck's condition more positively by tackling the stigma, discrimination, and sneering that people with health issues frequently face. The show's creators could have dispelled misconceptions rather than escalating the drama, bias, and confusion surrounding his condition. Instead, they chose to showcase his mania, and eventual demise without regard for the ramifications. Exposure to information surrounding another person taking their own life, or to sensationalized depictions of dying, can be a risk factor for others struggling with their own mental health (Scalvini 2020). Since portrayals of self-harm and suicide can be such a powerful trigger among susceptible people, the media industry must consider the consequences of their creative choices (Wang and Bohanna).

Perhaps the show's creators could have communicated with the psychiatric consumer/survivor/ex-patient (c/s/x) movement that actively addresses human rights violations from the healthcare industry. Participants in this cause emphasize their right to express their experiences using their own words. People like Chuck, who do not fit into fundamental clinical classifications and experiences, could have found solace within this movement as they make room for first-person narratives in medical, intellectual, and creative arenas.

To avoid perpetuating harmful representations, this movement discourages media from speaking on behalf of people with health conditions. Controlling how people with health conditions are portrayed and exploited in the media is critical to destigmatizing their experiences and encouraging others to seek treatment. Using first-person narratives about Chuck's experiences could have given a more accurate and relatable picture of him and prevented the romanticization of someone taking their life on screen.

V

See, that's your problem— thinking the ends justify the means

17
Is Morality for Suckers?

ABE WITONSKY

In the first episode of Season Two, Jimmy McGill and Mike Ehrmantraut have the following conversation:

> **JIMMY:** Did I have one million, six hundred thousand dollars on my desk, in cash? No one on God's green Earth knew we had it. We could have split it fifty-fifty . . . Why didn't we?
>
> **Mike:** I remember you saying something about doing the right thing.
>
> **Jimmy:** Yeah, well, I know what stopped me, and you know what, it's never stopping me again ("Switch").

Although Jimmy doesn't explain exactly what it was that stopped him from taking the money, a reasonable assumption is that it was his *conscience*—that is, a guiding belief about what is moral and immoral. At the time Jimmy decides not to take the money, he had been trying to honor an agreement with his brother Chuck to turn his life around and live honestly. So his conscience was likely telling him that either breaking his agreement or stealing money is immoral. Why does Jimmy resolve never to listen to it again?

Jimmy may think that acting immorally is in his best interest, if he doesn't get caught. He knows that morality, with its rules such as don't lie, don't cheat, don't steal, restricts him from doing whatever he wants. For example, morality says that he shouldn't steal money, no matter how much he may want to. (To say that it's immoral to steal money is not to say that it's *always* immoral to steal money. For example, it may be morally acceptable to steal money to save someone's life.) Since Jimmy thinks that morality puts constraints on him, he reasons that immorality, which lacks these constraints, can be better for him.

179

The idea that immorality can be in a person's best interest is one that Plato explores in his dialogue the *Republic*. According to a character named Glaucon, most people think the best life is the immoral life. To support this, Glaucon tells a mythical story about a shepherd named Gyges who finds a ring that gives him the power to be invisible. With this power, Gyges realizes he can do immoral acts with impunity. So he seduces the queen, kills the king, and takes over the kingdom. Glaucon contends that most people, including so-called "just" people who always follow the moral rules, would act just as immorally as Gyges does, if they had his ring and would not get caught. This suggests to Glaucon that most people want to act immorally, but realize that they can never feel secure in a world where everyone can do whatever they want. But if they could get away with being immoral, as Gyges did, they would.

Jimmy and Gyges

Jimmy seems to think about morality a lot like Gyges does. They both think immorality pays as long as you don't get caught. Jimmy has a long history of taking advantage of people and enjoying it. In the very first episode of the series, he tells the story of how he got his nickname *Slippin' Jimmy*; he would stage "slip and fall" accidents to make quick money. He proudly says that when he was known by this name, he "was the man" and "everyone wanted to be" his friend ("Uno"). We see him as a young man having fun with his friend Marco conning a stranger into giving him a lot of money for a fake Rolex ("Hero"). We see him reunite with Marco when he's older to scam people out of money after he finds out that his brother had been working to undermine his legal career ("Marco").

As a young child, Jimmy steals money from his own father's till ("Inflatable"), and we see one reason why he enjoys taking advantage of people. It bothers him to see his father, a person he loves, being a pushover. By taking money from the till, he feels good about being a "wolf," and not a "sheep" like his father, whom he sees as a chump for having a strong work ethic and a kind personality.

Jimmy doesn't have a ring that can make him invisible, but he is a master deceiver with an amazing ability to hide his real feelings and motives. Consider the final episode of Season Four, where, in an attempt get his law license reinstated, Jimmy makes an impassioned speech before a panel of lawyers of the New Mexico State bar ("Winner"). His speech moves both the members of the panel as well as his girlfriend, Kim. When Jimmy and Kim walk out of the hearing, he says to her, "Did you see those suckers?" It's at this moment Kim realizes that she had been duped by Jimmy's words and that his real intentions were invisible to her. As Jimmy excitedly describes the highlights of his deceptive speech, he brings up the movie *The Matrix*, and says, "I was invincible. I could dodge bullets, baby." He could even have said, *I felt like Gyges with his magic ring*, reveling in his ability to get what he wants by lying.

Jimmy doesn't always choose immoral behavior. In fact, he does good deeds for his brother, his romantic partner, and many of the people he works with. Jimmy also does moral acts when doing so hurts his reputation, or even threatens his life. For example, he intentionally makes himself appear dishonest in front of Irene and her friends, because he realizes that this is the only way to get them to like her again after he had manipulated them to distrust her ("Lantern"). He risks his own well-being to convince Tuco, a ruthless drug kingpin, not to kill two skateboarders because he feels responsible for their situation ("Mijo").

Jimmy believes that doing moral acts can sometimes be desirable because of their *usefulness*—they can be used to get things he wants. When Jimmy acts morally, other people like him, and he feels less guilty about things he has done. These are pleasant outcomes for him. But does he get pleasure from doing the moral acts themselves? It causes him a lot of pain to follow his conscience and refrain from taking the 1.6 million dollars. And he finds it unpleasant to put himself down so Irene's friends like her again. Jimmy seems to agree with Gyges, that acting morally is not pleasant in itself. Glaucon believes that most people think the way Gyges does, that morality is not pleasant in itself. He challenges Socrates, another character in the *Republic*, to show that morality is pleasant in itself as well as desirable for its usefulness.

Because Jimmy thinks about morality much like Gyges does, he is not going to like what Plato has to say in the *Republic*. According to Plato, the reason a person deliberately acts immorally and doesn't always find moral behavior pleasant in itself is that he has an unhealthy mind.

Jimmy on Plato's Couch

Plato believes that having a healthy mind is pleasant and that having an unhealthy mind is unpleasant. Plato also believes that when a person's mind is healthy, and only then, she will always try to act morally and also be able to enjoy life's best pleasures. To understand Plato's view, we first need to look at his view of human psychology, in particular what he believes a healthy mind is.

Plato believes that the human mind has a structure with three parts: the *appetitive* part, the *spirited* part, and the *rational* part. Plato believes that the mind has parts because a person sometimes wants opposite things. For example, a person might want to drink something because they are thirsty, but at the same time not want to drink something because she is going to have surgery and shouldn't drink.

Each of these three parts can be thought of as drives which seek different types of pleasures. The appetitive part seeks things such as food, drink, sex, and money to buy these things. The spirited part seeks the pleasures of *honor*—the pleasures of being liked, appreciated or respected. The rational part seeks the pleasures of knowledge and learning, and doing what is in one's overall good. There are different personality types depending on which part of the person's mind *rules*. The person prefers and seeks the pleasure of that part of the mind that rules. For example, if the appetitive part rules in a person, she will seek appetitive pleasures over pleasures of honor or knowledge. However, if the rational part rules, she will be a lover of wisdom—a philosopher—someone who will seek the pleasures of contemplation over appetitive and spirited pleasures.

When each of the three parts of the mind does what it's supposed to, then the parts of the mind are in harmony, and the mind is healthy. Plato thinks this occurs only when the rational part rules since it is the only part of the mind that exercises foresight on behalf of the mind as a whole. A person with this type of mind will be able to do what she believes is in her best interest. As a consequence, she will have self-control.

In contrast, when a person has a mind that doesn't have the rational part in control, she will have an unhealthy mind because it is not thinking about what is good for the mind as a whole. Such a person will not always be able to do what she believes is in her best interest and may sometimes deliberately choose to do what she knows is not for her overall good. Take a woman who loves to eat and who has a mind that is ruled by the appetitive part. She will eat even when she knows it's not good for her to eat. When a person with a mind out of harmony does something that is not good for herself, for example, eat food when she shouldn't, she doesn't believe that it's good for her to eat. Rather, the part of her mind which rules her behavior will seek pleasures, independently of whether they are good or not for the mind as a whole. The desires of this ruling part will win out over any other competing desires, including the desire to do what is in her best interest.

What part of the mind would Plato say rules in Jimmy? Although Jimmy is clearly very articulate and clever, he does not seem to have a mind with the rational part in charge. To say that the rational part rules is not to say that the person is more intelligent or better at identifying the overall good than other personality types. You can have a person who is very intelligent and calculating, such as Jimmy, but not ruled by his rational part. And you can have a person who isn't very intelligent, but who is ruled by his rational part.

Jimmy is not a person who takes joy in knowledge for its own sake. For example, we never see him reading a book or thinking about abstract issues. Jimmy's mind seems to be ruled by the appetitive and spirited parts. When Jimmy is with his friend Marco, his appetitive part appears to rule, for he seems driven by partying and devising scams to get money to support this lifestyle. When he is with his brother or girlfriend, he seems more motivated to develop or maintain relationships, and his spirited part seems more in control. To Plato, this means that Jimmy has an unhealthy mind, and therefore lacks self-control.

Jimmy sometimes does things that are not in his best interest because his rational part is not in control. When he is calling numbers for bingo at the local senior center and starts thinking about how his brother had been sabotaging his career, he is extremely upset by these thoughts. This betrayal by his brother causes his spirited part to feel dishonored, as he believes that he is not getting the respect and love from his brother that he thinks he deserves. But instead of keeping his feelings to himself, he begins to ruminate aloud about what he did to contribute to Chuck's displeasure with him. He announces to everyone in the room not only that he had gotten arrested, but that his crime was defecating through the sunroof of a rival's car, not realizing that there were two kids sitting in the backseat ("Marco"). His frustration with Chuck is understandable, but the confession is unwise, since he is trying to gain the trust of the seniors. Ruled in this moment by his spirited part, he does something that he knows is not for his overall good. In contrast, if Jimmy were ruled by his rational part, he would be able to contain his upset feelings because sharing them in this setting is not in his best interest.

Plato's Defense of Morality

Jimmy might acknowledge that his mind is not ruled by his rational part, and thus he can't always do what he knows he ought to do for his overall good. But he might ask Plato what this has to do with morality. When we think about morality, we typically think about how we should treat others, not just ourselves. So why would a person with a mind in harmony, with the rational part in control, necessarily always try to be moral? Without an answer to this question, Plato will not have shown that people with healthy minds will always act morally. Plato scholars propose different answers to this question.

One answer is that a person whose mind is ruled by the rational part will not do immoral things because this sort of behavior will interfere with their enjoyment of the rational pleasures of contemplation. So if Jimmy's mind were ruled by his rational part, he might spend his time enjoying books like the *Republic*, instead of wasting it trying to con people.

A problem with this answer is that even if the rational part of Jimmy's mind were to rule and he were to focus his energies on the pleasures of this part, he might still choose to do immoral things to support these desires. For example, he might steal money so that he can purchase the newest translation of the *Republic*.

A second answer to why a person with a mind in harmony always acts morally is because of a deep psychological need to be unified or connected with others. This requires that the person consider what is good for others when deciding what to do. Plato doesn't explain why we have such a need. But one idea that comes out of Eastern religions is that at some deep level we are actually connected to others. We're only under an illusion when we think we are separate individuals with separate selves and separate desires. When we let go of this illusion of separateness, we see that our happiness is related to others doing well.

To be happy, a person needs their relationships with others to be in harmony, and acting morally contributes to harmonious relationships. When Jimmy acts immorally, such as conning a stranger out of money, he disregards what is good for that person. He is then not in harmony with the person he is taking advantage of, and this hinders his own happiness.

This answer offers an explanation for why people with healthy minds will act morally towards people they want to be connected with. But is it true that people have a need to be unified with *all* of humanity? It's questionable that Jimmy, or most people, have a need to be unified with everyone, especially unsympathetic strangers, such as Ken, the obnoxious businessman whom Jimmy and Kim trick into buying an expensive bottle of tequila ("Switch").

Let's Make a Deal

Suppose we convince Jimmy that a mind in harmony with the rational part in control will always act morally, and this state is pleasant in itself. He may still prefer to have his own mind and act immorally. He may believe that the pleasures he experiences with his unhealthy mind are better than those he would experience with a mind ruled by the rational part. If Jimmy were to meet Plato, he might say the following:

> I know my mind is out of harmony because my rational part is not in control. And I know that it's unpleasant not to be able to always get myself to do what is for my overall good. I also know that if my mind were in harmony, I would act morally and experience the pleasures of acting morally, as well as the pleasures of contemplation. But so what? I get so much pleasure from the scheming and scamming, that it's worth it to me to have a mind out of harmony and to be able to act immorally.

We get a sense that this is how Jimmy may think when we watch him try to work out a deal with Chuck. Jimmy is trying to prevent Kim from getting punished for his airing a Sandpiper commercial without approval from partners at Davis and Main.

JIMMY: What did I do that was so wrong?

CHUCK: You broke the rules. You turned Kim into your accessory. You embarrassed Howard, who inexplicably vouched for you with Cliff-Main. You made Cliff and his partners look like schmucks . . . You're like an alcoholic, who refuses to admit he has got a problem . . . Life is not one big game of *Let's Make a Deal*.

JIMMY: Yes it is! I'm Monty Hall. What's behind Door Number Two? ("Gloves Off")

Jimmy can't imagine a more enjoyable life than his, where he is the mastermind of any game. If Plato is going to convince Jimmy that acting immorally is not in his best interest, he needs to give him a reason to believe that the pleasures enjoyed by the rational part are the best pleasures. This is no easy thing to do. But Plato tries.

Plato believes that the rational part of the mind is immortal. Thus its pleasures, in particular the pleasures of contemplation of the eternal truths, will remain constant and can be enjoyed forever. In contrast, the appetitive and spirited pleasures are fleeting and will not last forever. They are pleasures that always have to be replenished, and they require the body, which will stop functioning when the person dies. (Plato gives two other reasons why the rational pleasures are the best, but he thinks that the reason that has to do with the immortality of the rational part of the soul is his best reason.)

There's a major problem with Plato's best reason. The idea that our rational part is immortal is questionable and difficult to prove. Even if our rational mind is immortal, Plato at most would only show that the rational pleasures are the longest lasting (because they go on for eternity), not necessarily the best. Pleasures can also be measured in terms of their intensity. The thrill of conning a stranger might be far more intense for Jimmy than the feeling he might get by being unified with a stranger or reading the *Republic*, no matter how much longer this latter feeling lasts.

Plato's view has similarities to how some religions think about the relation between morality and happiness. Some religions say that while immorality may pay in this life if one is not caught, this life is only a short period of a person's existence. When a person's body dies, the person's soul will continue to exist and will eventually get what he deserves, in the afterlife from God, or through karma. So when we consider a person's happiness from the perspective of eternity, it's not in a person's self-interest to be immoral. This answer explains why acting morally is good for its usefulness (a person can get rewarded if she was virtuous), but it doesn't explain why acting morally is pleasant in itself.

Jimmy may never agree with Plato that the rational pleasures are the best and curl up with the *Republic*. But after he finds himself in Omaha with a life that is stressful, lonely and with little purpose, he may finally admit that immorality does not pay. Perhaps he will then try out the life of moral behavior, listening to his conscience once again.

Plato, of course, would bet this new behavior wouldn't last very long, as Jimmy lacks the kind of mind needed for self-control. That's okay, though. Jimmy's immoral life makes for better TV.[1]

---

[1] This essay would not have been possible without the amazing editorial assistance of Sammy Whitman.

18
Dissenting Opinions

CALLIE K. PHILLIPS

—If this isn't using our powers for good, I don't know what is.
—*We're not doing that.*
—But, Kim, we can do it. It'll work.
—*I am not scamming my client.*

—"Magic Man"

When we first meet Kim Wexler in *Better Call Saul* we see someone who appears to offer a moral counterbalance to Jimmy McGill. She encourages him to stay within the boundaries of the law and to stop committing trademark infringement to spite Howard from HHM, for example.

With each season we get to know Kim better, and gradually we see that often Kim's objections to Jimmy's lies and scams are really more practical than moral. She worries about him losing his law license, landing in jail, or even getting himself killed. Perhaps it's not so much a difference in morals between them but a difference in how much risk each is willing to tolerate. By the end of Season Five, we're left wondering whether Kim's moral beliefs really differ much from Jimmy's after all.

However, there are a number of occasions across the seasons of the show where there does seem to be a real conflict between Kim's and Jimmy's moral beliefs. Deep and seemingly irresolvable disagreement with others about moral matters is something we all experience in our lives. It may be a paradigmatic disagreement over whether abortion is morally permissible, or a disagreement over whether it's always wrong to lie to a client.

Cases of moral disagreement are especially troubling when the person who disagrees with us is someone whom we take to be just as informed about the issue, or just as smart and just as open-minded. Are we justified in maintaining the same confidence in our belief after learning of our disagreement with someone just as capable of reasoning about the matter and just as informed? Should we suspend judgment about what the right view is? The same questions arise when the disagreement concerns nonmoral beliefs, such as whether some action poses too much risk to one's career.

Peer Disagreement

Suppose Kim and Jimmy go out to eat at a restaurant. They both agree that a twenty percent tip is appropriate for their server and look at the bill. Kim says the server is owed $6.25. Jimmy says the server is owed $5.25. And let us suppose that when it comes to claims turning on simple math (in this case how much the server is owed) Kim and Jimmy are epistemic peers. Two people are epistemic peers with respect to some question like how much the server is owed if they are each just as likely to be right.

Being just as likely to be right about something is often a matter of overall intelligence, relevant background knowledge on the subject, how much time you spend thinking about it, whether you come your conclusion hastily while facing distractions, how much evidence you consider, biases or prejudices, and open-mindedness. Depending on the question, some of these things will be more relevant than others. How should Kim and Jimmy respond when they discover that they disagree about how much to tip the server?

Suppose also that Jimmy and Kim *believe* that they are epistemic peers with respect to this question of how much to tip the server. Since they think that they're both just as likely to be right but came to different conclusions about what a twenty-percent tip is in this case, it seems obvious that one of them must be mistaken. They should probably both take a moment to recalculate in hopes that they get the same answer the second time around. But before they do that, what should each do about their belief in light of the fact that they both believe that they are epistemic peers, and yet somehow ended up with different beliefs about how much the server is owed?

One plausible answer to this question is that they should suspend judgement about how much to tip the server. After all, if each thinks the other is just as likely as they are to have done the math correctly, then they shouldn't be confident that they weren't the one to make the mistake. Call this the *conciliatory view*.

Another possible answer is that Kim and Jimmy should each remain *steadfast* in their original belief about how much to tip the server. If that's the case, it might seem bizarre for them to then go on to each recalculate how much they think the server is owed, but we can suppose that their choice to recalculate is motivated by the fact that they need to come to a decision about how much to tip or that it is just something that they agreed to do expecting that the other will come to see that they were mistaken after recalculating. Remaining steadfast in your beliefs after learning of your disagreement with an epistemic peer often coincides with conciliatory *actions* whether it's recalculating the tip or some kind of compromise.

For example, when Jimmy tells Kim they should start their own practice together, Kim disagrees. She thinks it would be a bad idea. While both remain steadfast in their beliefs about whether they should start a law practice together, learning of their disagreement with one another does lead to a compromise in their course of action. Kim proposes that they go in on an office space together yet form their own separate law practice and Jimmy is satisfied with this plan.

How can the steadfast view be motivated? It's hard to see how we could defend the steadfast view if both parties recognize that the person disagreeing with them is their epistemic peer, that they are just as likely to be right. But there may be some wiggle room once we appreciate that even if two people are just as likely to be right about something (in the tip case it's simple math), human beings are fallible. It doesn't mean one or the other won't make a mistake on any particular occasion.

Two world-class chess players who are just as likely to win a game of chess don't always come to a draw in a game with each other. Sometimes one makes a critical mistake. When Kim and Jimmy disagree on how much to tip the server perhaps each is justified in thinking that on *that* particular occasion they are not the one who is mistaken, even though they think in general they are both just as likely to calculate a tip correctly. Jimmy can say to himself, "I know that I was focused and careful when doing my calculation, so it's got to be Kim who is mistaken." Of course, Kim could reason in the same way to justify remaining steadfast in her belief.

Whether remaining steadfast in one's belief is rational depends on whether it's really rational for Kim and Jimmy to reason in that way. For one thing, we should all readily admit that we've often made mistakes even when we're focused and careful. With this in mind, you might think you should at least be less confident in your belief upon learning that a peer disagrees with you, even if knowing that you've been careful and focused gives you some grounds for not suspending judgement on the question at hand.

Moral Disagreement

Of course, many of our disagreements are more difficult to resolve than a difference over calculating the tip. We often have disagreements about morality. Throughout the show Kim and Jimmy have a number of disagreements about what kinds of actions are morally permissible. For example, Jimmy feels morally justified in committing trademark infringement with a billboard advertisement to spite Howard at HHM ("Hero"). Kim, on the other hand, doesn't think it's the right thing to do. To Jimmy she says, "you're better than this," shortly before walking out of the nail salon when Jimmy is unwilling to concede that he was doing something wrong, morally as well as legally.

Moral disagreements seem different from the example of the disagreement over how much to tip the server once they agree on twenty percent. It seems perfectly rational for Kim to remain steadfast in her conviction that Jimmy has done something wrong when he put up that billboard advertisement. The same goes for Jimmy if we assume that he genuinely believes that his actions were morally justified. Think about a moral belief you have. Maybe you think late-term abortions are never permissible or that we have a moral right to decent healthcare. Many of us would not feel any pressure to give up a sincerely held moral belief on learning that someone disagreed with us. Perhaps we have a duty to hear out arguments that might change our mind about the issue upon learning about a disagreement with our epistemic peers, but nonetheless it seems that we are entitled to be steadfast in our belief and maintain our confidence in the correctness of the position.

Why does it seem as if different responses are rational when it comes to moral as opposed to a nonmoral disagreement? One possible explanation is that we are much less likely to view these disagreements as disagreements with epistemic peers. Another possible explanation is that with most nonmoral questions there is a fact of the matter about what the correct thing is to believe, and that this is not the case when it comes to moral questions. Let's start by considering the last possibility first.

Empirical questions such as whether the Earth is flat or round, or whether the tree on my lawn is an elm, are the kinds of questions that have answers independently of what people think about the matter. Sometimes people argue that moral questions, such as whether it is morally permissible for people to eat meat, are not like these empirical questions. Perhaps we talk as if there are moral facts when there simply are none, or maybe moral facts are relative to societies or individuals. If the latter is true, it may be morally permissible for me to steal a car yet morally impermissible for you to steal a car. This is not the claim that we have different views on whether it's morally permissible to steal cars; it's the claim that there's really no objective fact of the matter; there are only the truths relative to individuals or groups.

These kind of views on which there is no fact of the matter about questions of morality have some initial appeal. Indeed, some philosophers have argued that the fact that moral disagreements are so intractable provides reason to think there must be no fact of the matter about moral questions. Regardless, we do tend to assume it's *possible* to truly disagree with someone on a moral issue. The assumption that it's possible presupposes that there is some fact of the matter to disagree about. If what's true for me simply isn't true for you, it makes no sense to debate the issue. There's no question of what the rational response to moral disagreements is on these views if there is no fact of the matter when it comes to moral questions.

Moreover, these "no fact of the matter" views come with serious costs that should make us doubt whether they could be correct. For example, these views seem to imply that we don't have moral grounds for saying that someone is unequivocally incorrect if they believe slavery is morally permissible or that it's okay to kick puppies just because you feel like it. So let's assume there's generally a fact of the matter about moral questions, that moral disagreement is possible, and move on to the other possible explanation I suggested for why it's rational to remain steadfast in our *moral* beliefs in the face of disagreement but perhaps not in cases like the disagreement about how much to tip the server.

For it to be rationally required that you suspend judgement or lower your confidence in a belief upon learning an epistemic peer disagrees with you, you need to be able to judge that the person is your epistemic peer on the question *independently* of the question you are disagreeing about. To judge that someone is your epistemic peer on a question is to judge them to be just as likely to be right about that kind of question. And moral beliefs are often closely linked with other moral beliefs so that if you disagree on one moral belief, you will likely disagree on many others. As a result, it's rare that you will judge someone to be your epistemic peer in cases where you do find yourself disagreeing with someone on a moral issue. Consider the question of whether it's morally permissible for a lawyer to lie to their client to get them to take a plea deal that's in their best interest. Whether you think it's morally permissible or not is closely related to the question of whether you think in general the means justifies the ends, whether it's okay to do something we would normally consider wrong if it's what would lead to the greatest happiness for all parties involved. It's also linked to questions of when it's morally permissible to break the law or violate professional obligations. Chuck, Jimmy's brother, clearly thinks Jimmy gets the answer wrong to all kinds of closely related moral questions and so isn't going to view Jimmy as his epistemic peer on the question of whether it's morally permissible for a lawyer to lie to their client to get them to take a plea deal that's in their best interest. If it's usually the case that we don't judge someone who disagrees with us on a moral question to be our epistemic peer because we think they're mistaken about lots of other moral questions (and so not just as likely to be right about the question at hand), then it's usually rational to remain steadfast in your moral beliefs even when people disagree with you.

The Evolution of Kim

One reason Kim is such an interesting character is that her substantive moral disagreements with Jimmy don't keep her from forming the connection with him that she does, something that you might think suggests she does view Jimmy as an epistemic peer with respect to many moral questions, at least if sharing moral values is an important part of romantic compatibility. But perhaps more interesting than that is the question of whether she really has the kind of foundational moral disagreements with Jimmy we took her to have at the outset at all.

Many of us took her to be a kind of moral counterbalance early in the show, but perhaps this was a mistake. Maybe it was risk aversion and discomfort with parting from professional and social norms that kept her from openly embracing moral beliefs more like Jimmy's. At least, that's a tempting line of thought when we see her growing willingness to lie and scam. Finally, we discover in "Something Unforgiveable" that Kim may be even more willing to defy the law and end Howard's career for a cause than Jimmy. After Jimmy says, "Kim, you wouldn't be okay with it, not in the cold light of day," Kim looks him in the eye and says, "Wouldn't I?" In a scene that left many with goosebumps, viewers were left wondering if Kim was shedding the last vestiges of a shell that had disguised her real moral beliefs.

One competing explanation of Kim's evolution in the show is that her moral beliefs that bear on scamming and deception have changed as a result of her moral disagreements with Jimmy. Apart from what we think the epistemically rational response to disagreement is, it is a well-documented psychological phenomenon that people generally *do* lower their confidence in their beliefs on learning someone disagrees with them. So there's reason to think that spending a lot of time with someone you frequently disagree with on moral matters could lower your confidence in many of your moral beliefs, maybe even to such an extent that they your system of moral beliefs is gradually transformed.

Lowering your confidence in certain beliefs affects the actions you think are morally justified and the choices you make as a result. But that climactic scene where Kim responds to Jim's incredulity at her willingness to sabotage Howard's career for a greater good with, "Wouldn't I?" shows that the value Kim had put on professional integrity and honesty early on are gone, along with her unwillingness to treat Howard or anyone else as a means to an end. We see that she's prepared to take scamming even further than Jimmy. No amount of conciliation in the face of disagreement with Jimmy could explain that change.

An important piece of this puzzle is Kim's growing appetite for scamming. We see Kim take greater and more elaborate risks, and it's evident she finds a successful scam deeply thrilling and invigorating. Each time she needs to go further to get the same high. One question here is whether Kim is experiencing a kind of weakness of will, intentionally doing something despite believing that she shouldn't do it. For the most part, she does not say much that would indicate that she's doing something that she thinks she shouldn't except in a scene from "Magic Man."

Kim is frustrated with a pro bono client who doesn't want to take the deal she recommends, a deal that will likely provide a better outcome for the client than not taking it and having the case go to a jury trial. Jimmy shows up and tries to talk Kim into a scam that would scare the client into taking the deal. He says, "If this isn't using our powers for good, I don't know what is." Kim puts her foot down and replies, "I am not scamming my client," clearly frustrated with Jimmy's insistence. But she ends up taking Jimmy's suggestion. As a result, her client is scared into taking the deal she recommended, what she thinks is clearly in his and his family's best interest.

Once she's alone again, we see that Kim is upset despite getting the outcome she wanted for her client. The viewer is left with the impression that she's angry with herself for compromising her moral and professional integrity by lying to her client at Jimmy's urging. Notably this isn't a case where Kim appears to be thrilled by the successful scam.

Kim, like many of us, may have found herself going down a path where actions she found thrilling were things that she could find a plausible-sounding moral justification for. We might feel good about scamming someone wealthy and powerful by supposing the deception is morally justified if it's for the sake of helping those who are less fortunate in life (and maybe if it's just relatively harmless). In a situation where someone who is not wealthy and powerful has trusted you to be honest with them, a scam in that circumstance might feel entirely different, even if we can rationalize it using the same moral principles. In some cases, this might reflect a tension in our moral beliefs that we may not have appreciated. In other cases, we might realize that we have been deceiving ourselves about what we truly believe about the moral permissibility of scamming, for example.

It's difficult to say what might be going on in Kim's case given that she eventually becomes more and more willing to scam, even when it comes with more risks to herself and her professional standing. This happens alongside her growing commitment to her pro bono work and disillusionment with her work for Mesa Verde, a bank that's working to expand profits and makes no discernable positive impact on the world. Is she growing into an admirable Robin Hood character who takes from the "haves" to give to the "have-nots"? Or is she falling into the trap that so many of us do, deluding ourselves into thinking we are acting from a pure sense of moral duty when we are really motivated by something else less noble. Maybe it's the thrill of scamming, defying some norm, or taking a risk and coming out unscathed. Ultimately, while it's tempting to view these possibilities as mutually exclusive, they need not be. Kim might be both an admirable Robin Hood character *and* self-deluded about her motivations for acting as she does. She might even be deluded about her reasons for holding certain moral beliefs.

We've been assuming in our discussion thus far that people believe what they do based on their best judgments about what the evidence supports, and that insofar as people make mistakes, it's because they've misjudged the evidence or made some error in reasoning. But plausibly in some cases we believe something because it serves our own self-interest to believe it. Or at least, the fact that the belief is in our own self-interest, that it can help us feel justified in taking actions we otherwise couldn't feel justified in taking, can cause us to misjudge the evidence for that belief.

Reflecting on these ideas highlights a perhaps cynical reason for why we might remain steadfast in our moral beliefs in the face of disagreement (whether or not we think remaining steadfast is a rational response to moral disagreement): it's in our self-interest to hang on to that belief. That self-interest in holding a belief shouldn't always be viewed in a negative light. Our moral values (in Jimmy's case perhaps the lack thereof) shape our identity and our self-narratives in ways that ultimately give our lives meaning and purpose.

In the absence of clear moral experts, the scientists of the moral domain to whom we should generally defer and who can prove conclusively that some moral belief is correct, it is easier to let self-interested reasons for belief lead us to be more committed to those beliefs than we otherwise would be if we could achieve a neutral perspective free of the influence of self-interest or the need to create a cohesive and meaningful understanding of our selves and life stories.

19
Can We Blame Jimmy for Being Jimmy?

DANIEL CARR

Is it Jimmy's fault that Jimmy is Jimmy? It's very tempting to say that, despite being endearing, and occasionally quite compassionate, Jimmy *is a bad person*, and *it's Jimmy's fault* that he's a bad person.

But according to the philosopher Thomas Nagel, we might be wrong to judge Jimmy as a bad person. In a provocative essay called "Moral Luck," Nagel seriously calls into question the notion of categorizing some people as bad. Nagel tries to show that too many things *beyond our control* influence how we get morally assessed. When factors beyond our control end up determining whether we count as a morally good or a morally bad person, Nagel calls this "moral luck." His idea is that moral luck is everywhere, and this undermines our ability to reasonably blame people for bad behavior or credit them for good behavior.

I think that factors beyond Jimmy's control do influence how people assess whether Jimmy is a good person or a bad person. However, applying some wisdom from the poker world, I believe that Nagel's argument is not as powerful as it looks. There's still room for blaming and crediting people for living a bad life or a good life.

One of the most entertaining aspects of *Better Call Saul* is watching Jimmy, by hook or crook, get himself out of sticky circumstances, much like a professional poker player who's able to turn a long-term profit regardless of what cards he or she is dealt. Factors beyond Jimmy's control may have pushed Jimmy in the direction of corruption, but Jimmy's simply too resourceful to be considered a victim. *Better Call Saul* is a cautionary tale about gradual but *unnecessary* moral decline of very likeable characters who make a series of bad decisions.

To answer Nagel's challenge of moral luck, instead of abandoning moral judgment altogether, we can refocus our moral assessments of people on the gradual acquisition of virtue and vice through free decisions. Jimmy is responsible for what he made of himself over his lifetime of free decisions, and so we can fairly assess Jimmy to be a bad, even if an often well-meaning, person.

The Case for Moral Luck

Immanuel Kant warned against letting matters of chance influence how we assess people's decisions; when an attempted murder, revolution, or rescue succeeds or fails, what counts *morally* is the decision that was made (including the motivation), not which outcome occurs. Thomas Nagel might be interpreted as saying that the public frequently ignores that Kantian principle by fixating on outcomes. This occurs all the time in the legal realm. What type of criminal you are (and therefore which sentence you face), such as "murderer" or "attempted murderer," may depend on a silly chain of events such as bird randomly flying in front of a bullet, or whether the nearest passerby was an ER doctor or a *drunk* ER doctor. The difference that the bird or bottle makes on your life might be a decade of jail time.

However, Nagel is doing something more ambitious than telling us to pay more attention to Kant's prohibition relying on outcomes when morally assessing people. Instead, he's claiming that *all* the main factors that produce our behavior are out of our control. In which case, whenever someone gets classified as a good person, they're simply lucky, and whenever a person gets classified as a bad person, they're simply unlucky. Furthermore, anybody doing the labeling of people as "good" or "bad" is being irrational because people are the wrong kind of thing to praise or blame for what they are like.

Nagel has in mind four major factors that he believes are beyond our control and that lead to us being called good or bad people. It's easy to react too quickly to each factor, and to think that none of these factors by itself makes you good or bad. The force of his argument comes when we realize that he intends us to take all of these factors *collectively* as explaining whether we consider someone good or bad.

The first factor is constitutive luck. Our personalities, preferences, and misbehavior risk factors (such as high testosterone), are just facts about who we are that we have no control over. Many of the people we call bad were simply born, with no fault of their own, with problematic constitutions. Other people have a natural leg up on life, with constitutions that are conducive to thriving and being helpful to others. Beyond birth, we have positive or negative childhood experiences that we can take no credit for that further shape our dispositions. For example, by genetics and childhood trauma, I could have anger management issues that lead to me being violent.

The second factor is circumstantial luck. We face many opportunities and problems that affect how our life turns out. Nagel gives us the poignant example of a German businessman who moves to Argentina prior to the rise of the Nazis. Had the businessman not had the opportunity to go to Argentina, he probably would have become a Nazi or Nazi sympathizer himself, because that is what most people in Germany did at the time. So, supposing that his affairs in Argentina end up relatively friendly, the man might get to be called a "good" person, even though he was not circumstantially far from being a Nazi. The example is suggestive of the natural question: how can we be certain that we would not have become Nazis too if we lived in 1930s Germany?

The third factor is the mechanistic happenings of the universe that cause our behavior to happen. This is a little bit different than the opportunities and difficulties from the second factor. Now we're not just considering whether the distributions of opportunities and problems is favorable or unfavorable for becoming a good person; instead, the issue here is the deterministic clockwork of the universe. The laws of physics and the past state of the universe lead directly to us behaving one way or another. If our behavior boils down to biochemistry in the brain, which boils down to physics, then it would seem that our behavior is predetermined and thus not controlled.

This brings up the classic debate of whether free will is compatible with "determinism," which is the idea that all events in the universe are completely determined by the laws of physics and the particular facts about the distribution of matter and energy in the universe. The compatibilist (who thinks that determinism is compatible with free will) may say that we're free if we do what we wish to do without being coerced. However, if we're in a clockwork universe, this strikes me as only an illusion of control because we never could have wished to have done otherwise, because our wishes themselves are predetermined. Similarly, Nagel is operating under the assumption that the clockwork nature of the universe (if this is indeed how the universe works), undermines our ability to be responsible for our decisions. Note that many scientists now believe that the best way to interpret our best scientific theories allows for genuine chance, meaning that the world is not deterministic. Nagel might be able to modify his argument to account to deal with randomness. For instance, he could say that adding randomness to the behavior of particles can only diminish our control of our behavior, not enhance it.

The fourth, and final, factor that contributes to whether we get considered a good person or bad person also has to do with cause and effect. We frequently make decisions based on incomplete information and then, as a result some opaque network of cause and effect, various outcomes occur. Afterwards, it's a matter of luck whether the choices we made end up with good results. If the outcome is morally significant, but the outcome is uncertain, then our moral status seems to be a matter of luck. Consider a reckless driver who never hits anyone. This driver predicted that they would not hit a pedestrian (otherwise why would they drive this way?) and then they turned out to be right. Nobody likes drivers like that, but our strongest judgments against such people are reserved only for when they hit someone. If outcomes are not morally relevant, as Kant would have us believe, then a reckless driver should feel equally guilty for their conduct whether or not they hit someone, and we should judge them the same either way. Yet, we tend to think that a person should feel particularly guilty if a bad result occurs from their recklessness. Hence, unpredictable outcomes play a critical role in how we assess the goodness or badness of others.

Now consider these four types of luck *in conjunction*. Once we consider a person's constitution, their opportunities and problems, the deterministic cause and effect of the universe, and the inability to predict whether your actions will bring about good or bad, there's little or nothing left that adds to the explanation of how it comes about that the person gets called "good" or "bad."

One quick clarification: even if Nagel is right that we have no basis for calling people good or bad, we still might be justified in saying that people have traits that are negative or positive. The point is that we can't rationally blame or credit people for being the way they are. Humans are simply the wrong kind of thing to be morally responsible for their actions.

Jimmy's Unlucky Life

Can we rationally blame or credit Jimmy for being Jimmy? I'm going to temporarily adopt the position that Jimmy lacked control over his life. My goal is to view *Better Call Saul* through Nagel's eyes.

The people closest to Jimmy give us some commentary on Jimmy's character. Chuck tells Kim, "My brother is not a bad person. He has a good heart. It's just . . . he can't help himself" ("Rebecca"). If Chuck is right that Jimmy's penchant to con people is compulsive, then it is out of Jimmy's control. Kim thinks that Jimmy's flawed character is the result of Chuck's failures as a brother. She defends Jimmy to Chuck, saying, "I know Jimmy's not perfect. And I know he cuts corners. But you're the one who made him this way . . . I feel sorry for him" ("Nailed"). If Jimmy's problematic character is the result of a lifetime of being dismissed by his brother, then Jimmy is not responsible for being the way he is. In fact, we should feel bad for him because he was unlucky to have such a brother.

While *Better Call Saul* doesn't tell us much about Jimmy's childhood, we're given two indicators of when Jimmy began his predilection of conning people. First, in a late-night heart-to-heart between Kim and Chuck, Chuck explains that his father had to sell the corner store because of all the money Jimmy, who was a child a time, stole from the store ("Rebecca"). Second, in the opening scene of "Inflatable," we get to see the formative experience of nine-year-old Jimmy that presumably precipitated his practice of stealing from his unsuspecting father. Jimmy is assisting his father at the shop when a man comes in asking for help. The man claims to have a sick child and car trouble. Jimmy realizes that the man is trying to con his father, but his father ignores Jimmy's pleas not to be taken advantage of. After handing the con artist some cash, Jimmy's father goes to the back of the store to find a spark plug for the man's supposedly non-starting car. While Jimmy's father is away, the con artist, who apparently has plenty of cash, buys two cartons of cigarettes from Jimmy and tells Jimmy that there are two types of people in the world: sheep and wolves. Jimmy then pockets the payment instead of putting it into the cash register, and the con artist departs.

Now suppose that the con artist had gone to a different shop instead. Perhaps, Jimmy would never have become a thief if not for the interaction with the con man. It was beyond Jimmy's control—you might say a matter of bad luck—that Jimmy had this formative experience. If the difference between being a thief and not being a thief is a chance encounter during childhood, then it's hard to blame someone for being a thief.

Jimmy's opportunities and problems seem to show the sorts of luck Nagel warned us about. A series of opportunities and obstacles made Jimmy realize that he wanted to stop playing by the rules. After Nacho suggests stealing from the

Kettlemans, who had themselves ripped off the county for 1.6 million, Jimmy tries to warn the Kettlemans, causing the Kettlemans to flee into the wilderness. When Jimmy finds the Kettlemans and tries to convince them to take the plea deal that their lawyer, Kim, had secured, Jimmy and Mrs. Kettleman fight over a bag. In the struggle, the bag rips open, revealing bundles of cash ("Nacho"). To help Kim's reputation at the firm, Jimmy secretly hires Mike Ehrmantraut to steal the cash and return it to the county in order to force the Kettlemans to take the plea deal ("Bingo").

Afterwards, Jimmy reflects to Mike on having missed the opportunity to keep the 1.6 million in cash. Jimmy says, "When I close my eyes, I can still see the money. It is burned into retinas like I was staring into the sun . . . Why didn't we take it? What stopped us?" Mike says, "I remember you saying something about doing the right thing." Jimmy replies, "I don't even know what that means . . . I know what stopped me. And it is never stopping me again!" ("Marco"). This is when Jimmy decides to return to the con artist ways of his past. If Nacho had never presented the opportunity to rip off the Kettlemans, then Jimmy would never have seen the money, and Jimmy may have continued to work for good at his new law office of Davis and Main.

The fourth type of moral luck Nagel discussed, luck in predicting outcomes, is ubiquitous in "Better Call Saul." Perhaps the most poignant example is Jimmy's experience with the "Chicago sun-roof," which Jimmy tells us was a popular prank, or means of revenge, in Chicago. As recounted by an unraveling Jimmy to a stunned bingo audience, a drunk Jimmy defecated through the sun roof of a personal enemy's car, not knowing that there were children in the car ("Marco"). Jimmy then faced life-altering sex-offender charges, but was rescued legally by Chuck, who then gave Jimmy a new life working in the mailroom at Hamlin, Hamlin, and McGill. Here, we see an unlucky outcome (children being in the car) and a potentially lucky outcome (an opportunity for a clean life). Jimmy feels like a victim of the whole situation; his whole life direction, including moving to Albuquerque and becoming a lawyer, stemmed from the bad luck of there having been children in the car. None of Jimmy's moral mistakes in Albuquerque would have occurred if there had not been children in the car in Chicago.

Jimmy's life was full of factors beyond his control that led to him doing all the bad things that we would like to blame him for. If Nagel's right, then we should consider Jimmy a victim of being thought poorly of. If Nagel is wrong, then Jimmy is a rational agent that we can appropriately praise or blame for his various deeds.

Should We Bet on Skill or Luck?

In poker, after all the cards are dealt, you have the opportunity to bet more money to try to win more from your opponent or to get your opponent to give up and fold. However, there are situations where you think that you probably have the best cards, but you still should not bet any more money. This happens when all the worse cards your opponent has will fold if you bet (so you get no value from betting) but all the better cards your opponent has will call or even reraise, which is a disaster for you. Consider this chart:

	My opponent's cards are worse	My opponent's cards are better
Bet More Money	Opponent folds; no benefit for me	Opponent calls or raises; I lose more
Don't Bet More	No extra benefit or harm	No extra benefit or harm

The chart shows that, in the language of game theory, a branch of mathematics, the strategy of *not* betting more money "weakly dominates" the strategy of betting more money, which means that it is *never worse* but is *sometimes better* to decline to bet money in this situation. In other words, you should not bet in this situation, even though you probably have better cards than your opponent.

We face a choice when pressed with the claim that our moral choices are beyond our control. Perhaps we find the moral luck argument somewhat convincing, but we aren't sure. Should we set up our attitudes, behaviors, and legal systems to follow Nagel, or should we continue to think and act as if moral choices are at least partially under our control? Consider two competing theses. Let the "Fatalist Thesis" be that our moral choices are beyond our control. Let the "Freedom Thesis" be that our moral choices are sufficiently under our control that it is worth trying to control our choices so that we can become better people. To wager on a thesis is to adopt it as a way of looking at the world.

	Fatalism Thesis True	Freedom Thesis True
Wager on Fatalism	No extra benefit or harm	Small or massive moral failure
Wager on Freedom	No extra benefit or harm	Small or massive moral benefit

The contents of the chart need some explaining. I said that there is "no extra benefit or harm" to wager on fatalism if fatalism is true. You might think that we might feel less guilty or judgmental, so the chart should show some benefits. However, if fatalism is true, then you were going to feel less guilty or less judgmental anyway, so there is no net benefit. Likewise, you might think that wagering on freedom has some harms or benefits even if we are not free, but that is a logical mistake.

If we're not free, and we act and think as if we are free, that was inevitable, so we shouldn't include any benefits or harms in that spot in the wagering chart. Another thing to notice in the chart is that I left it open whether we can make a big difference by trying to be better people, or just a small difference. It is possible to be pessimistic about the degree to which people can change but still think we should try. Or, perhaps, we could be very optimistic and think that significant moral change is possible. In summary, betting on freedom is never worse, but is sometimes better, than betting on fatalism. This leads me to my argument for rejecting a Nagel-like denial of human moral responsibility:

Premise 1: We have to (consciously or unconsciously) wager on freedom or wager on the fatalism.

Premise 2: Wagering on the freedom weakly dominates wagering on fatalism.

Premise 3: If wagering on freedom weakly dominates wagering on fatalism, then we should wager on freedom.

Conclusion: We should wager on freedom.

Suppose that I've convinced you that we should at least try to be better people, just in case it works, then how do we go about actually becoming better? We might need to think about rules, duties, and consequences to know what decision is best in a given situation, so it is worthwhile to study ethical theories like Utilitarianism, Kant's deontology, or perhaps religious rules. However, the most relevant branch of ethics for this discussion is "virtue theory."

Virtue theory is about becoming the kind of person that tends to do the right thing. You do this by building positive habits. We can do the right behavior over and over again, in a variety of situations, so that it becomes instinctive and automatic. Also, we can find people that are really good moral examples and we can try to copy them as much as possible.

Virtue theory tells us that it matters how our character changes over time. We might start out with lots of vices. For example, Jimmy's genetics, childhood experience, ability to guess what other people are thinking, and gift of the gab may have made him into a naturally dishonest and manipulative person. In poker, you have to learn how to play good and bad cards wisely. Despite the heavy element of chance, if you build the habit of making smart decisions over and over. You may be dealt bad cards sometimes, but you can still make the most of them (or at least avoid disasters). Dispositionally, Jimmy was dealt mostly bad cards. He is naturally inclined to cheat the system.

However, Jimmy is incredibly resourceful and hard working. Howard even has the nickname "Charlie Hustle" for Jimmy because of his work ethic. Furthermore, Jimmy's ability to manipulate others shows that he has the skills necessary to manipulate himself into becoming a better person. He can get other people to change their behavior, so it is not a stretch to think that he could get himself to change his own behavior. With this in mind, consider my final argument:

Premise 1: Nobody prevented Jimmy from becoming a good person.

Premise 2: Jimmy has the internal traits necessary to change for the better.

Premise 3: If nobody prevented Jimmy from becoming a good person and Jimmy has the internal traits necessary to change for the better, then Jimmy's moral decline was unnecessary.

Conclusion: Jimmy's moral decline was unnecessary.

Better Call Saul is a parable about likeable characters in progressive, but unnecessary, moral decline. It displays how someone with "a good heart" can end up making terrible choices, and then rationalize these choices. While *Better Call Saul* does humanize people who make bad choices, I don't think that the appropriate lesson is that being a "bad person" is a mere matter of luck. Just in case there is enough meaningful freedom in the world that gives us long-term control over our character, we should bet on freedom. The way to bet on freedom is to try to gain the skills to habitually make the best decisions with whichever cards we are dealt. If we believe in freedom, then we should believe that people have the genuine ability to change over time—even if only slightly—and therefore there's room to credit people for becoming better and blame people for becoming worse.

Over a long series of decisions, Jimmy decided to return to the con-artist ways of his youth, and we can rightly criticize him for this because it was not inevitable that Jimmy turned out the way that he did.

20
Why Is Breaking Skateboarders' Legs Wrong?

J. SPENCER ATKINS

Philosophers aren't just interested in identifying what actions are wrong; they're interested in what *makes* an action right or wrong. They want to understand what we might call the wrong-making feature of an action. Any action that has such a feature is *morally wrong*.

But what feature of snapping skateboarders' legs in the desert *explains* why this action is morally wrong ("Mijo")? Why is embezzling 1.6 million dollars from Bernalillo County("Hero") or lying about the war hero Fudge Talbot ("Fifi") wrong? These things immediately strike us as wrong, but why? Philosophers give more explanations than there are Mesa Verde branches.

Different Moral Theories

First, consequentialists argue that outcomes are what matter for morality. It's morally right to cause a good outcome like saving a man dangling from a billboard; it's morally wrong to cause a bad outcome like forgetting Chuck's copy of *Albuquerque Journal*. But what makes some outcomes better than others?

John Stuart Mill promoted a moral theory called utilitarianism. He argued that "actions are right in proportion as they tend to promote happiness; wrong as they tend to produce the reverse of happiness" (*Utilitarianism*, p. 7). Good outcomes increase happiness, and bad outcomes decrease happiness. By the term "happiness," Mill had in mind pleasure. Thus, according to Mill's utilitarianism, we must always act so that we cause *the most* pleasure.

There are many kinds of consequentialism, so let's briefly distinguish utilitarianism from consequentialism. Utilitarianism is one type of consequentialism. Utilitarians like Mill argue that the best outcomes are those that cause the most happiness. However, some consequentialists argue that values other than happiness create the best outcomes, like preference satisfaction or well-being. What utilitarianism and all other forms of consequentialism have in common is that the outcome is the wrong-making feature of an action.

Breaking someone's legs hurts them. Embezzling money from the county treasury harms the community. Though lying can produce good outcomes sometimes, lying about Fudge nearly cost Captain Bauer his job. Since pleasure is preferable to pain, the better outcome is not to break the skateboarders' legs, or embezzle the money, or lie. Those actions are wrong *because* they undermine happiness and cause pain. More specifically, those actions are wrong because of the bad outcomes they produce.

In contrast to consequentialists, deontologists think moral rules are the most important value. Immanuel Kant formulates the categorical imperative, that is, the rule that we must always follow: "Act only according to that maxim whereby you can at the same time will that it should become universal law" (*Groundwork of the Metaphysics of Morals*, p. 35). A maxim is an individualized principle that dictates our actions. Kant thinks we should only act on maxims that everyone could adopt. For example, suppose Jimmy promises Clifford Main that he will not make a commercial for Davis and Main but then does so anyway. Jimmy could have formulated the following maxim: "*When it is in my interest, I will break my promise, to do what I want.*"

According to Kant, we should not act on maxims that would involve a contradiction. Imagine that everyone adopts Jimmy's maxim. Everyone would break their promise when it is in their interest. If everyone would just break their promise when it is in their interest, then why make promises at all? Jimmy's maxim undermines promise-making itself. There's simply no point to making a promise, and this internal contradiction makes Jimmy's maxim morally wrong.

Not all morally bad maxims involve a straightforward contradiction. Kant also thinks that if a fully rational person would not want to live in a world where everyone acts on some maxim, then it's not a rule; it's wrong. Consider the following maxim that Jimmy and Kim could use: "*When it is in our interest, Kim and I will lie, and become Viktor and Giselle St. Clair.*" Would any fully rational agent want to live in a world where everyone would lie about their identity—like Jimmy and Kim do—when it's beneficial to them? While it might make for a much more interesting world, any fully rational person would not want to. But if a rational person *would* want to live in a world where everyone acts on some maxim—say, *when the rent is due, I, Jimmy McGill, will pay Mrs. Nguyen*—then it *is* a rule that we must follow, so long as there is no contradiction.

Any maxim that says I ought to break skateboarders' legs or embezzle money or lie about Fudge, fails to be a moral rule. Would fully rational agents want to live in a world where it's okay to do those things? No way! These examples illustrate maxims that cannot become universal laws—such actions violate the categorical imperative and, therefore, are morally wrong. Tuco Salamanca, Craig Kettleman, and Jimmy McGill each break a rule, so that's what *explains* their wrongdoing, according to deontologists.

Finally, in contrast to deontologists and consequentialists, contractualists think that there are implicit contracts between reasonable people. T.M. Scanlon argues: "An act is wrong if its performance under the circumstances would be disallowed by any set of principles for the general regulation of behavior that no one could reasonably reject as a basis for informed, unforced, general agreement" (*What We Owe to Each Other*, p. 153).

According to Scanlon, reasonable people can reject some principles. Consider a principle that says that the penalty for calling Tuco's abuelita a "biznatch" is death ("Mijo"). The two skateboarders can reasonably reject this principle—it's wrong to then kill them. But not every principle can be rejected. There is, therefore, a set of moral principles that no one would reject. Such principles function as a kind of contract between everyone, since everyone *would* consent to those principles. Performing an action that deviates from the principles that everyone would agree to makes that action wrong.

According to contractualists, these principles form binding contracts, which generate moral obligations. For example, there's an implicit contract between Tuco and the skateboarders, Craig and Bernalillo Country, and Jimmy and Captain Bauer. The skateboarders, as I've alluded to, can reject a leg-breaking principle. The citizens of Bernalillo County should reject an embezzlement principle, and Captain Bauer wouldn't consent to Saul's lie. Breaking legs, embezzling, and lying all violate moral contracts. Those things are wrong *because* we would reject the terms of such contracts.

Consequentialism, deontology, and contractualism each identify different moral values: outcomes, moral rules, and contracts, respectively. According to these views, if we cause a bad outcome or break a rule or violate a contract, we've done something wrong. Chuck McGill, Jimmy McGill, and Mike Ehrmantraut show us that fixating on a single moral value is problematic. *Better Call Saul* is chockfull of characters who adopt these moral values—outcomes, rules, and contracts—and we'll see that solely adopting any of them is more trouble than a squat-cobbler fetish film.

There may be deontologists, consequentialists, and contractualists who reject what Chuck, Jimmy, and Mike do. Those moral theories, some proponents could argue, categorize their actions as morally wrong.

Deontology, consequentialism, and contractualism each prioritize a single moral value—outcomes, rules, and contracts. My point is not that Chuck, Jimmy, and Mike show that these moral theories are false. I'm instead saying that, in practice, when we make a single moral value our prerogative (as the moral theories demand), we can end up doing the wrong thing, mistaking it for the right thing. If I believe that only outcomes matter, for instance, I may be tempted to hurt someone in order to benefit more people. But this seems wrong. *Better Call Saul* shows us that, to live a moral life, we must combine several different moral values.

Chuck McGill: Deontologist

Chuck McGill loves the law (and the moral rule of the categorical imperative). He keeps the law close, like the mylar lining in his jacket. Chuck also *knows* the law. Throughout the show, we see he knows more than all his colleagues. Chuck respects the law and the rules. Following the rules is its own reward, according to Chuck: "The price of excellence is eternal vigilance." His love of the law starkly contrasts with how he views his brother, Jimmy McGill.

To see how Chuck appeals to the rules, consider why he despises his brother. Chuck justifies his contempt of Jimmy by appealing to higher moral standards (though we know that he is also jealous of his brother). Despite Jimmy's constant care, Chuck thinks Jimmy only acts for his own self-interest. Jimmy doesn't value procedure (or any set of moral rules in general), and this explains some of Chuck's contempt. In a flashback in Season Two, Jimmy has dinner with Chuck and his wife Rebecca. Chuck says to Rebecca later, "My brother is not a bad person. He has a good heart. It's just . . . he can't help himself. And everyone's left picking up the pieces." Jimmy likes to bend the rules, and Chuck can't help but hate that ("Rebecca").

Chuck *really* doesn't like Jimmy practicing the law: "Slippin' Jimmy with a law degree is like a chimp with a machine gun." Chuck says that "the law is *sacred*," and Jimmy, in Chuck's eyes, fails to appreciate that. Chuck thinks that Jimmy's degree—from University of American Samoa—undermines the integrity and prestige of the legal profession.

But the most important thing about Chuck is that he will not break the rules even when it benefits him. When given the opportunity to coerce Jimmy out of his bar license, Chuck refuses even if it means Jimmy quits practicing law. (This probably would have been the best outcome for everyone. Had Chuck taken Jimmy's deal, perhaps he would have prevented many of the events in *Breaking Bad*, but I digress.) The point here is that Chuck follows the rules even when it is in his own individual interest not to.

Consider two problems with Chuck's loyalty to the rules. First, his commitment blinds him to his relationship with Jimmy. He mistreats Jimmy merely because he thinks Jimmy taints the law. He's not appreciative of Jimmy's visits, and he even *expects* the supplies. Chuck, moreover, holds grudges against Jimmy. Consider Chuck's testimony at Jimmy's bar trial:

> Jimmy will never change, ever since he was nine, always the same. Couldn't keep his hands out of the cash drawer. 'But not our Jimmy, couldn't be precious Jimmy!' Stealing [our parents] blind!

Chuck's commitment to the moral rules forces him to hold a nearly lifelong grudge. Chuck can't forgive Jimmy. Because of his commitment to a single moral value—rules—Chuck loses out on his relationship with his brother. Chuck fails to find value in other meaningful things: forgiveness, loyalty, friendship between brothers. He lives a sad life because of his inordinate concern for the rules.

Secondly, following the rules often precludes us from the best outcomes. Sometimes we should break the rules to do the right thing. French philosopher, Benjamin Constant thought so. He argued that we ought to lie to a "murderer at the door" ("On Political Reactions," p. 425). Consider a "murderer at the door" case inspired by *Better Call Saul*:

> Suppose the Salamanca family puts a hit out on Chuck McGill. Salamanca hitmen, Nacho and Tuco, don't know where Chuck lives, so they go from door to door asking whether Chuck lives in the house. Ernesto happens to be delivering ice, mylar, and propane gas when he hears a knock. Tuco and Nacho ask him whether Chuck lives at this residence, but, as they raise the question, Nacho receives an

urgent phone call. Ernesto forms the belief that if he lies and says that Chuck doesn't live at this address, then Tuco and Nacho will leave quickly. But if he tells the truth, they will certainly kill Chuck.

Should Ernesto lie to Tuco and Nacho? I sure think so! But if actions are wrong in virtue of the fact that they break the moral rules (we already saw that you can't universalize maxims about lying), then Ernesto should tell the truth. Lying to Tuco and Nacho would be wrong. But getting the best outcome means lying to Tuco and Nacho. So perhaps Chuck—as I've been arguing above—is wrong: the rules aren't the only moral value. Outcomes matter too. Consequentialists will argue that *only* outcomes matter; Ernesto should, therefore, lie. But is this right?

Jimmy McGill and the Consequences

Unlike his brother Chuck, Jimmy McGill cares about outcomes. He bends the rules when it's in his interest. Jimmy loves to scam, especially when it means getting a free bottle of Zafiro Añejo, selling a worthless coin, or intimidating three skateboarders at a piñata store. Sometimes Jimmy bends the rules to help other people. Jimmy often justifies his behavior—bad or good—by identifying outcomes.

Consider Jimmy's case against Sandpiper Crossing. Jimmy lies about having to use the bathroom at the Sandpiper Crossing facility so he can write up a demand letter. Jimmy later solicits the elderly with bingo nights and "dog-and-pony-show" bus visits: "Wait, a doggone, $24 for a side of biscuits?! That doesn't sound right!" And he goes over Clifford Main's head to produce and air his own commercial—"Who stole my nest egg!?" In an attempt to get fired, he refuses to flush the toilet (not to mention those god-awful, retro suits) . . . *gross*! He justifies his reckless behavior by calling attention to *all* the new clients against Sandpiper Crossing; according to Jimmy, the outcomes justify his actions. To Jimmy, the means are subordinate to the ends: it's okay to bend the rules, so long as you have a good outcome.

Think about the other intricate lies and scams that Jimmy pulls off. To get his bodyguard, Huell Babineaux, out of legal trouble, Jimmy impersonates Pastor Blaise Hansford and convinces the DA's office that his congregation's "keener on Huell than butter on a biscuit!"[1] He pays two dopey skateboarders to

---

[1] Help us get our Huell out of trouble! Call Pastor Hansford at 318-426-9662 with your testimonial or visit <www.freewill-baptistchurch.com> to make a donation to Huell's legal defense!

jump in front of Betsy Kettleman's car. He fakes saving a man dangling from a billboard. Jimmy later convinces the police that Daniel Wormald (a.k.a. "Pryce") is a fetish-film superstar by making him record *Hoboken Squat Cobbler*. All these actions cause good outcomes for Jimmy or his loved ones.

Jimmy's reckless pursuit of beneficial outcomes has three problems. The first problem is that someone must decide what counts as a good outcome. In every case, Jimmy gets to decide the best outcomes: persuading more plaintiffs against Sandpiper Crossing, rescuing Huell from jail, or getting a shot of Zafiro Añejo for Kim. But lying and scamming strike us as morally wrong (after all we would not want to be scammed), so Jimmy shouldn't get to decide what the best outcomes are. Outcomes do matter, but we need a standard of evaluation that is independent of Jimmy's whims.

Chuck brings up a second problem: "That's your problem, Jimmy . . . thinking the ends justify the means." Chuck thinks that how we get an outcome—whether we must lie or steal or hurt someone—matters for morality. Jimmy often does not see this. He thinks that so long as the outcome is good, it does not matter how we get there.

Lastly, by always trying to make things better, Jimmy sabotages his own commitments. Bernard Williams argues that consequentialism divorces us from integrity. Having integrity, for Williams, means we make decisions that are consistent with our deepest commitments (*Utilitarianism: For and Against*). Suppose (falsely) that Daniel Wormald has a deep commitment against the fetish film industry. When Jimmy confronts him about making the squat-cobbler movie, Daniel is faced with a choice: make the movie to avoid jail time or don't make the movie and go to jail with integrity. A consequentialist would advise Daniel to make the movie despite his commitment against fetish movies. It is safe to say that Jimmy is committed to Chuck and Kim. Jimmy's reckless pursuit of good outcomes often strains his relationships: Kim reprimands him for the squat-cobbler debacle, and Chuck believes he is untrustworthy. Jimmy can't have integrity because he won't act consistently with his own commitments.

Chuck and Jimmy McGill show us that morality is more than just rules and more than just outcomes. Let us turn now to contractualism. Perhaps contracts—making and sticking to agreements—is a viable candidate for the sole moral value.

Contracts by Mike Ehrmantraut

Mike Ehrmantraut follows the terms of an agreement. For instance, Mike *always* makes Jimmy get his parking card stamped. From everything we know about Mike, he does this because he is holding up his end of the bargain with the city of Albuquerque: he has accepted a job, and one condition of this job is to ensure that everyone pay to park. Agreements and consent matter to Mike. So, following Scanlon and other contractualists, we might think morality is based on a series of contracts.

When Jimmy asks Mike to steal the Kettlemans' money, Mike takes the money to the DA's office, even when he could have kept it. Mike justifies his behavior saying, "I was hired to do a job. I did it. That's as far as it goes." After beating up and intimidating two gun-toting thugs, Mike asks the dorky pill-peddler, Daniel Wormald, "Now that I'm doing the job alone, I get the full 1500. We agree upon that?"

Consider another example. Nacho hires Mike to kill Tuco Salamanca. Mike, however, doesn't like to kill people (though we see him kill blabber-mouthed, German engineer, Werner Ziegler). So instead of killing Tuco, Mike sets him up to be arrested. Later, after Hector Salamanca pays up, Mike gives Nacho half of the money since Mike only completed part of their contract.

Eventually, Gus Fring hires Mike as a "security consultant." Even though Mike's supposed to let his money roll in, he insists on completing the job by, for instance, sneaking into facilities and stealing employees' ID badges. When Lydia Rodarte-Quayle calls Fring to complain about Mike, Fring, knowing how Mike is, "suggests she give the man a badge." Mike always completes tasks he agrees to do, even *fake* ones. These cases show that Mike sticks to contracts.

The problem is that Mike's *contracts* strike us as deeply immoral. Breaking and entering, protecting dangerous drug-dealers, and intentionally setting up Tuco are all generally wrong. Even though Mike and his associates have made an agreement, those agreements are themselves morally problematic. Contracts, Mike Ehrmantraut's life shows us, can obligate us to do immoral actions.

Scanlon and other contractualists may argue, as we saw above, that the principles Mike follows are reasonably rejectable. Tuco Salamanca would reasonably reject a principle that says someone can frame him for assault. The Kettleman family could reject a principle that states Mike can enter their house without their consent. I think this is correct. But the broader point is that Mike fixates on contracts and acts on the basis of those contracts. Yet, in virtue of doing so, often does the *wrong* thing. He does not think about whether his contracts cause bad outcomes—such as his agreement to provoke Tuco Salamanca—or whether they violate any moral rules—like when he agrees to kill Werner Ziegler. Mike's choices show us that focusing exclusively on contracts can lead to morally problematic behavior. Like Chuck and Jimmy, Mike ought to adopt a wider scope of what's morally valuable.

Tallying the Score

Though philosophers may theorize about morality and argue that only one moral value matters, *Better Call Saul* reveals that this is not right. Sole commitment to any one moral value—outcomes, or rules, or contracts—leaves us as bad as Ernesto after messing up Chuck's grocery list . . . yet again! Prioritizing one value over the others leads to broken relationships, bent rules, and dirty contracts. When we see the lives of people who follow a single moral value, we see a life of unhappiness and struggle. Fixating on a single moral value, *Better Call Saul* demonstrates, leads to confusion about morality. If this is right, then no moral theory that we have seen here is totally correct. They all get something right, but each individually fail to tell the entire story of morality.

Jimmy is right to value the outcomes of his actions, but he shouldn't break his promises. Mike should only uphold his contracts that do not hurt other people. It's good for Chuck to follow the moral rules but not at the expense of his relationship with Jimmy. To live a moral life, we need to value outcomes, rules, and contracts—along with many other things!

Moral theories tell us to prioritize a single moral value. That value, according to the moral theories examined here, is a trump card against any other consideration. I have argued against this picture of morality, much like Jimmy arguing with Rich Schweikart about Sandpiper Crossing. Consequentialism, deontology, and contractualism each have *something* to teach us about the moral life, but alone they do not give us the whole picture. The characters of *Better Call Saul* show us that we must adopt a plurality of moral values, "if we are to play our cards right," our moral cards, that is.

VI

Never make the same mistake twice

21
Finding the Good in Nacho

JAMES ROCHA

No one wants to make a racist TV show about the drug trade. But if you're filming a show with drug dealers in New Mexico, you may want to realistically include some Latinx characters working for the Mexican Cartel. Nonetheless, if you want to avoid racist depictions, then you need to make sure these characters don't all end up looking like Tuco Salamanca.

You could provide some balance by placing some of these Latinx characters on the other side of the law, such as DEA agent Steven Gomez. You could even have some of these characters be main characters, such as a cunning but ultimately ruthless drug and fried chicken czar like Gus Fring. But what you're really going to want to create is a morally complex main character who is unabashedly in the middle of things, and yet remains morally redeemable.

It's quite possible that Ignacio "Nacho" Varga from *Better Call Saul* is that character. Nacho is not just a good person (he's a drug dealer and he can be ruthless), but he also isn't simply a bad person: Nacho loves his father and shows concerns about violence. Nacho challenges moral theories that require us to develop a fully moral character before we can be considered good. Instead, Nacho is quite often a bad person in one moment, a good person in another moment, and a person whose morality is nearly impossible to determine in many other moments. Nacho shows the complications that lie within moral life.

Nacho's moral complexity doesn't indicate that there's no such thing as right and wrong. Moral complexity doesn't imply that everything is morally gray. Rather, Nacho shows us that most of us engage in right and wrong actions at different times throughout our lives; no one is perfect, just as no one is perfectly bad. Moral assessment is very difficult, and we should work hard to determine how to morally judge other people. Because people are complex and are not very morally consistent, it makes more sense to assess morality in individual choices and not in overall character. Sometimes a largely bad person makes a morally praiseworthy choice, just as a generally good person can sometimes make an immoral choice. Even once we acknowledge this level of personal complexity, there can still be moral complexity in a given choice. We must remember that judging each particular moral choice can be as much of a pain as driving around in a yellow hummer with red flames on the side.

Immanuel Kant may help us analyze Nacho's complexity. Kant maintained that morality derives from rationality. In this way, Kant argued that when someone is acting immorally, it's precisely because their action cannot be rationally justified. Kant is criticized, unfairly I think, for holding that morality must be black and white, where there are always right and wrong answers. I don't say this representation is unfair because Kant *doesn't* think that. He absolutely thinks that: moral actions are the rational ones and the immoral ones are irrational. In fact, I also believe that morality has right and wrong answers (it is wrong to murder people; it is right for lawyers to provide their clients with quality representation).

The criticism of Kant is unfair because it assumes that if you believe that morality has right and wrong answers, then you must also believe that morality is simple, but actually nothing could be further from the truth. Chemistry also has right and wrong answers, but that doesn't mean everyone gets an A in Chem.

According to Kant, morality has right and wrong answers, but some of the questions at stake are very complex. Nacho gives evidence of some of that complexity in at least two ways. While Nacho seems like an immoral drug dealer in many parts of the show, Nacho also seems like a morally driven son when it comes to his father, Manuel Varga. In the first complicated matter, Kant may be suspicious of Nacho's morals since Nacho's morality is closely connected to his loyalty to his dad. But you could argue that his relationship with Manuel shows Nacho to be a morally good son. As an additional complication, Nacho's normally a bad man, so it's unclear whether he should count as a good person in certain limited moments. Is it possible to be morally good just in certain situations? Kant would think so, and Nacho will show us why Kant is right.

Before examining Nacho as a good son, it's worth discussing Nacho's various attempts to kill members of the Salamanca family. In "Gloves Off," Nacho asks Mike Ehrmantraut to kill Tuco Salamanca. Then, Nacho attempts to kill Hector Salamanca ("Lantern"). To complete the trifecta, Nacho assists with the attempted assassination of Lalo Salamanca. Nacho doesn't seem to like the Salamancas, and I want to give him partial credit for this viewpoint because it is right to side against this group of cruel drug dealers ("Something Unforgivable").

It's only partial credit because we are not here to praise attempted murder. Nacho's actions against the Salamancas are, indeed, seriously immoral. And, we should keep in mind that Nacho is not a good person: he is a drug dealer, and his immorality is well established just by thinking of all the lives his profession is destroying. Nacho also wanted to rip off the Kettlemans ("Mijo") and he did steal the baseball cards from Daniel Wormald ("Switch"). I'm not arguing that Nacho is a good man, but that even a bad man can sometimes be good.

While Nacho is a bad, bad man, the attempted murders of the Salamancas tell us something important about who he is beyond these transgressions. At no point are we given the impression that he wishes to kill any of the Salamancas for his own personal profit. Besides Lalo, where there was pressure from Gus Fring to assist with the killing, Nacho is consistently acting out of concern that the Salamancas are out of control and dangerous. In fact, they are: the Salamancas create the risk that their drug trade will destroy lives in various directions that no one will be able to limit.

In his efforts to kill the Salamancas, Nacho is doing undeniably bad things. Yet, we see that Nacho thinks through the situation and is an active reasoner, which Kant believes is key to becoming a good person. For Kant, we learn what morality requires by reasoning out what we should do in the situations in which we find ourselves. Nacho indeed views the world around him in a complex fashion that acknowledges how, even in the drug trade, some people are even more destructive than the standard chaos created by the drug trade itself. Nacho is thinking through the moral problems around him, which is a necessary step to becoming a good moral agent. Although these attempted murders at least let us see that Nacho is an active reasoner and does want to limit the woes that surround him, they do not show him being moral since his choices to attempt murder are immoral. We will want to discuss these attempted murders in more detail later, but we will first need to discuss Nacho's relationship with his father to give us more context for his motivations to try to kill Tuco and Hector Salamanca.

Nacho shows signs of being a good person with his concern
for his father, Manuel Varga, but we need to analyze Nacho's
actions here. Kant is well known for his suspicion about our
moral deeds done for the ones we love. After all, if duty requires
you to do the right thing, then it should be completely irrelevant whom you save or help—you should do the right thing
because it's right, not because of whom it benefits or protects.
If you only do the right thing when doing it favors you or your
loved ones, then you aren't really motivated by duty. Thus, it is
worrisome that Nacho's best traits only come out when he's
concerned about his father.

It's easy to get confused about what Kant's point is when he
is skeptical of moral deeds done for loved ones. Kant gives an
example of a shopkeeper who is honest because his reputation
for honesty brings him more customers, which ends up making
the shopkeeper more profit (*Groundwork*, p. 53). The shopkeeper
is honest, but his motivation for honesty could come from multiple sources: perhaps he is honest because it makes him money or
perhaps he is honest because honesty is morally right. It's hard
to tell what drives the shopkeeper's honesty.

And that is Kant's whole point: the shopkeeper case is use-
less to a philosopher writing a book about morality because we
can't tell why they are being honest. Further, Kant does not
believe that we can use the results of the shopkeeper being
honest to help us judge if what they did was moral. For Kant,
morality only lies in what you intend, not what you accomplish.
Kant suggests that we should look for a case where someone is
doing the right thing even though everything in their life moti-
vates them not to do it.

Consider when Jimmy McGill has a public fight with Erin
Brill where he confesses that he tricked and manipulated Irene
Landry, his elderly client from the Sandpiper Crossing case.
That confession, which Jimmy is sharing with everyone in the
home, is going to destroy Jimmy's chances to ever work in elder
law again. Jimmy is sabotaging his future legal career.
Everything in Jimmy's self-interest suggests Jimmy should not
help Irene, but moral duty requires that he make up for
destroying Irene's friendships. Kant's point is not that Jimmy,
in helping Irene, is a better moral person than the truly honest
shopkeeper. Kant's point is that Jimmy is a more useful example for figuring out what duty truly requires since we can tell
that in that moment Jimmy is motivated solely by duty, as his
self-interest suggests that he not confess.

Kant recognizes that a case like Nacho's is very difficult
because Nacho could be motivated just to help his father, but

he also could be motivated to help an innocent man being coerced into the drug business. I would like to think it is the latter. And I believe that Nacho's attempted murders, which are not in themselves morally permissible, suggest that Nacho is at least thinking about the rampant destruction that the Salamancas are carrying out against innocent people. But we do have to be careful in these cases: by the time Nacho is trying to kill Hector Salamanca, Nacho's father is involved as Hector was using Manuel Varga's business, putting Nacho's father at risk. Perhaps we should then start with the first attempted murder against Tuco Salamanca.

When Nacho wants to kill Tuco, Tuco had not involved Nacho's father in the drug business ("Gloves Off"). Long ago, Tuco had developed his own drug addiction. Then, due to Tuco's infamous (false) confidence in his own ability to detect when people are lying to him, Tuco decided their connection, Dog Paulsen was lying to him, and Tuco immediately shot Dog and accidentally hit Nacho, who was behind Dog. But Nacho points out that when Tuco is using drugs, he is "loco," and Tuco is using again ("Gloves Off"). Further, Nacho is con- cerned that Tuco may find out that Nacho is selling pre- scription drugs independently.

Although it doesn't involve his father, this situation too pro- vides a tough case for moral appraisal since Nacho is concerned about his own well-being. But Nacho is a smart person and he clearly convinces Mike to help him, surely because Mike can see that Tuco as a drug user is definitely dangerous to everyone around, innocent people included. While Nacho may be con- cerned about his own independent ventures, there's also no reason Tuco would ever find out about them. As Nacho explains Tuco's strange reliance on a fake lie-detector test, Nacho clearly does not believe that Tuco can accurately detect lies. Instead, Tuco's failure to be rational is worsened not only by his drug use, but also by Tuco's false confidence that he can detect dishonesty or disloyalty by staring at people. While Nacho is worried for himself, it is clear that a reckless Tuco could harm anyone.

And again, no credit goes to Nacho for potentially having good reasons for wanting to kill Tuco. Killing people is of course a horrible thing to do. But it gives us some insight into the complexity that lies within Nacho's head. While Nacho may be worried that he may one day get killed by a drug-abusing Tuco, he is likely more worried that Tuco, using drugs and having irrational false confidence in himself, could hurt just about anyone, and it would not be right no matter whom Tuco endangers. But, again, this case is not ideal as there is definitely a lot of self-interest involved, but I suspect that Nacho is not merely acting from self-interest and also has moral concerns.

In Nacho's third attempt on a Salamanca's life, we again don't get a great case for moral analysis. Nacho must help Gus try to kill Lalo because at this point, Gus is threatening Nacho's father ("50% Off" and "Something Unforgivable"). Of course, we do get a general sense that Nacho is as concerned about Lalo as he was about his prior Salamanca bosses. Yet, we cannot give him credit for being part of an attempted murder plot, as this act is a deplorable thing, and we cannot give him credit for doing what he must do. Or at least, similar to what Kant points out with his example of the shopkeeper, it's very hard to philosophically analyze an action someone is forced to do since they didn't make a free choice, so we don't know if they are doing it for any reason other than the one we know for sure (they are being forced).

In spite of all of this, we do get a sense that Nacho is thinking morally in "Wexler v. Goodman" when Nacho confronts Mike for working for Gus. Nacho sits in judgment of Mike, as Nacho himself is being coerced into working for Gus, since Gus has a gun to Nacho's father's head. This position is interesting because Nacho takes the morally superior position, even though they are both in the drug game, and, technically, they both work for Gus. At the very least, it makes you wonder how much Nacho feels pressured into his life, constantly having to work for morally problematic people, while wishing he could escape.

We're given compelling evidence that Nacho wishes he could escape the drug game. When Nacho tells his father (incorrectly, given what happens later) that his father is no longer in danger, Manuel asks his son when it will be over for Nacho. Nacho claims he is working on it ("Breathe"). It is a very authentic moment. Thanks to Michael Mando's incredible acting as Nacho, we truly *feel* his yearning to be out of the drug game in that moment. We similarly *feel* his frustration when Jimmy/Saul tells Nacho that he, Jimmy, doesn't want to be involved in Lalo's war, and Nacho resignedly and tiredly responds that what he wants is irrelevant ("The Guy for This"). Nacho too wants to be out of the drug game, but you don't simply exit the drug game.

Indeed, this point is very important for Kant, as we judge people based on what they plan to do, not just on what they accomplish or achieve. Nacho deserves moral credit for *trying* to get out of the drug game, if he is genuinely trying and if it is, due to factors out of his control, impossible for him to accomplish his goal. And we buy that Nacho is determined to get out, but we also buy that he cannot do so. Mando's acting is selling Nacho's committed motivation to get out, and Kant would give Nacho credit for that, even if a consequentialist (a moral philosopher who believes you should be judged on what you accomplish, not just what you intend) would not.

And this is why Kant allows room for giving positive moral assessment for people who are generally bad agents. Nacho is in the drug game, and so he is a bad mother-(shutting my mouth here). Nacho deserves moral blame for all of the bad things he does in the drug game. But now that Nacho is in the drug game, he is entirely trapped in bad behavior. Even if he's completely motivated to get out, it is not necessarily possible for him to do so. At least it is not *practically* possible if we include within what's practically possible that he can only truly exit the drug game if he can do so in a way that is safe for him and his loved ones. While some moral theories would judge Nacho's entire life as a moral failure, Kant would want to give nuance to our moral analysis and blame him for entering the drug game, while also finding ways to praise him for trying to minimize the damage and to earnestly attempt to get out.

Whenever we morally assess others, we walk a fine line because we do not know their lives as well as they do. And if it is possible to isolate the good from a whole lot of bad, as Kant encourages, then we must be careful to look for positive intentions even for a person who exhibits a plethora of immoral intentions. Nacho shows us why this approach is absolutely necessary as people we could dismiss as entirely bad can often still have good in them.

As much as I want to put Nacho in that morally complex category, I must admit that I have struggled to find a clear-cut example where Nacho acted morally. In most of these cases he was either interested in protecting himself or protecting his family. And it is at least possible that he was *only* interested in self-preservation and the preservation of his loved ones. Yet, there is one example that I believe rescues my quest to find the good Nacho.

In "Something Unforgivable," Nacho has a quick phone call with the assassins Gus is paying to murder Lalo. Lalo's compound includes numerous people who are only *technically* in the drug game, as they work for a notorious drug dealer. They are cooks, cleaners, and people whom Nacho points out have never hurt anybody. Maybe they are not entirely innocent as they work for Lalo, after all. But Nacho sees the humanity in them and cannot stomach seeing them hurt. He argues with the assassin on the phone that these mostly innocent people should be spared.

Of course, Gus's assassin ignores Nacho and hangs up on him. And Nacho is no novice: he knew that would be the result. He knew his plea would fall on deaf ears. Further, Nacho's plea could upset the assassin or, even worse, Gus. In this quick phone call, Nacho is risking everything to take a small chance to save people he hardly knows. And Nacho takes this risk with little hope of success, but he had to do it because it was the right thing to do. Sure, he could have done more. Sure, he could have taken even greater risks by warning everyone. That could have saved the people there, but it would have ensured Gus would kill Nacho and his father. That much risk may not have been practically feasible for Nacho, and so he took the greatest risk he felt he could take in this circumstance. And even though he was still risking everything and only had a tiny chance of saving these mostly innocent people, Nacho took that chance. And that's Nacho doing the morally right thing for no other reason than it was the right thing to do.

In the end, Nacho gives *Better Call Saul* a morally complex Latinx character who teaches us about ordinary morality's constant complexity, especially when examined through a Kantian perspective. I'm not saying Nacho is a hero. He isn't. I'm not saying Nacho isn't a bad man. He is. But Kant allows us to understand that Nacho can be a generally bad man, who still deserves our respect as he is at least trying to do the right thing, *sometimes*.

22
Breaking Bad Promises

F.E. GUERRA-PUJOL

> You can be on one side of the law or the other, but if you make a deal with somebody, you keep your word.
>
> —MIKE EHRMANTRAUT

The proposition that "promises ought to be kept" is quite possibly one of the most important normative ideals or value judgments in daily life. But what about illegal or immoral promises, promises that are wrongful or "bad" in some legal or moral sense? What moral obligations, if any, do illicit promises generate? May we break our "bad" promises, or must we keep them?

These paradoxical philosophical questions are posed time and time again in *Better Call Saul*, beginning with the episode "Uno"—the series premiere—when our hero Jimmy McGill, with the help of two teenage accomplices, orchestrates a phony vehicle-pedestrian accident in order for Jimmy, a small-time struggling Albuquerque attorney, to lure a prospective client.

Jimmy's accomplices, the Lindholm twins, agree to help him stage a traffic accident in exchange for $2,000. The moral dilemma here, however, is this: had this elaborate but illicit scheme worked according to plan (spoiler alert: it does not!), wouldn't Jimmy have been morally obligated to keep his promise to pay the twins the promised $2,000? On the one hand, we have a general moral obligation to keep our promises, but at the same time, wasn't Jimmy's promise part of a well-intentioned but illicit scheme? If so, how can the Lindholm twins have a moral claim to their promised payoff?

As it happens, Jimmy McGill's/Saul Goodman's entire persona—beginning with his conman's past as Slippin' Jimmy in

Cicero, Illinois—is a living embodiment of this moral paradox. Back in Cicero, for example, Jimmy's closest friend was Marco Pasternak, a fellow con artist. Together, they would run an elaborate scam in which they duped unsuspecting marks into buying fake Rolex watches ("Hero" and "Marco"). The victim of the con thinks he's buying a genuine Rolex off of a dead man, but the mark must also know that what he's doing is wrong, since he's buying the watch with the dead man's own money! Either way, is the sucker of this serpentine swindle morally entitled to get 'his' money back? Do Jimmy or Marco have a moral obligation to make their 'victim' whole?

It's no exaggeration to say that most of the relationships in *Better Call Saul* are explicitly premised on illicit promises, beginning with Craig and Betsy Kettelman.

The Kettleman Conspiracy

Craig Kettleman, a thieving county treasurer, has been accused of embezzling 1.6 million in taxpayer dollars from Bernalillo County. With the help of his wife Betsy, who is fully aware of her husband's crime, the Kettlemans decide to keep their ill-gotten gains and soon go into hiding, and at one point, they offer Jimmy McGill the sum of $30,000 to keep their hiding spot a secret ("Hero").

The criminal conspiracy between Craig and Betsy Kettleman, not to mention their bribing of Jimmy, once again generates a difficult moral dilemma: should Jimmy keep his promise to stay quiet? After all, he has accepted their money, and we have a moral duty to keep our promises. But at the same time, lawyers have an ethical duty to avoid assisting a client—even a prospective one—in conduct that the lawyer knows to be criminal. (Model Rule 1.2 of the American Bar Association's Model Rules of Professional Conduct prohibits a lawyer from counseling or assisting a client in conduct the lawyer knows is criminal or fraudulent.)

But Jimmy McGill is not the only character in *Better Call Saul* who's a party to an ongoing illicit agreement. As it happens, most of the characters in this popular spin-off series, just like many of the characters in *Breaking Bad*, end up making promises that are either illicit or illegal, or both. In fact, aside from the title character Saul/Jimmy, we could argue that the character who exemplifies this moral paradox the most is the retired ex-dirty-cop Michael "Mike" Ehrmantraut, my favorite character in both *Breaking Bad* and *Better Call Saul*.

The Tuco Salamanca Conspiracy

Season Two of *Better Call Saul* features a contract for a hit. The parties to this illegal agreement are Ignacio "Nacho" Varga and Mike Ehrmantraut, who conspire against Nacho's boss, the drug lord Tuco Salamanca. Nacho works for Tuco, helping him run his illegal drug operations in Albuquerque, and is one of Tuco's most trusted men. But Tuco repeatedly violates the number one rule of the drug trade—don't get high off your own supply. (This admonition also appears in the 1997 hip-hop track "Ten Crack Commandments" on disc two of The Notorious B.I.G.'s final studio album *Life after Death*. I thank my wife Sydjia de la Guerra for bringing this classic song to my attention). Nacho hires Mike, whom he trusts from their multifarious previous dealings, to assassinate Tuco. Or as Nacho himself so eloquently puts it in "Amarillo," "There's a guy. And I need him to go away." Mike then formulates a fail-proof assassination plan—the use of a discreet and expert sniper—and he offers to be that sniper in exchange for $50,000.

Although this contract is an illegal one—and no doubt immoral too—Mike, a man of his word, refuses to accept the full fifty-thousand-dollar payment when he is unable to follow through on his original assassination plan. Specifically, when Mike modifies the plan—instead of killing Tuco, he decides to stage an altercation with him in order to get Tuco arrested for assault with a deadly weapon, which carries a mandatory prison sentence of five to ten years—Mike reduces his original fee down to twenty-five thousand ("Gloves Off"). Furthermore, when Mike's illicit plot backfires altogether, Mike gives Nacho a full refund (!), returning the 25k to Nacho in its entirety ("Bali Ha'i"). That Mike would feel obligated to return money paid based on an illegal promise is the most striking and morally salient aspect of this entire ordeal, for Mike feels morally compelled to return his payment because, despite his best efforts and through no fault of his own, he failed to uphold his part of the original deal with Nacho. But his dealings with Nacho are not Mike's only illicit agreement; at that point in the series Mike has yet to meet the enigmatic Gustavo Fring.

La Conspiración Pollos Hermanos

Among other things, Season Three of *Better Call Saul* reconstructs the origins of the long-lasting illicit partnership between ex-dirty-cop Mike Ehrmantraut and the owner of the Los Pollos Hermanos fast-food chain, Gustavo "Gus" Fring, who uses his business as a front to operate an illegal drug cartel. After Mike's attempt to assassinate Hector Salamanca is mysteriously thwarted at the end of Season Two, Mike eventually discovers in Season Three that it is Gustavo Fring who has been tracking him all along and who had foiled his attempt on Hector's life ("Sunk Costs"). Although Gus has his own nefarious reasons for wanting to keep Hector Salamanca alive, he allows Mike to interfere with Hector's drug-smuggling operations, and with this informal arrangement in place, Gus and Mike develop an uneasy truce: Gus agrees to stop tracking Mike's whereabouts, while Mike agrees to leave Hector Salamanca alone.

Subsequently, this loose arrangement develops into a fullblown and mutually beneficial criminal partnership when Gus arranges for Mike to be hired by Madrigal Electromotive as a "security consultant" ("Slip" and "Fall"). Mike needs a steady source of employment in order to launder a large amount of money that he had previously stolen from one of Hector Salamanca's trucks—ill-gotten gains that Mike wants to leave to his family—while Gus needs someone as reliable and knowledgeable as Mike on his payroll to help him carry out his underworld affairs. The rest will become "*Breaking Bad* history," so to speak: Gus will compensate Mike for his illicit services; Mike will do Gus's bidding as his full-time fixer.

The Hummel Heist

Even the most minor and inconsequential of characters—such as Ira, a professional burglar and the future proprietor of Vamonos Pest—help to illustrate the problem of bad promises. In Season Four of *Better Call Saul*, Jimmy hires Ira to steal a small but valuable Hummel figurine from Neff Copiers ("Something Beautiful"). Jimmy thinks Neff's porcelain piece is worth at least four thousand dollars, and he hatches an illicit plan that involves Ira replacing Neff's piece with a knockoff, selling the original porcelain figurine at an upcoming collectors' auction, and then splitting the proceeds fifty-fifty with Jimmy, the mastermind of this little caper. Later, when Ira carries out the plan and gives Jimmy his cut from the sale, Jimmy is surprised to find out that the heist has yielded an even higher return than he expected ("Talk"). The Hummel heist also poses a fascinating philosophical question. Although Ira kept his end of this illicit bargain, was he morally compelled to?

Bad Promises, a Moral Paradox

So we've seen a wide variety of "bad" promises and illicit agreements in the series *Better Call Saul*, beginning with the staged traffic accident in the series premiere and with Jimmy McGill/Saul Goodman's conman past in Cicero, Illinois, and then continuing with several criminal conspiracies from the first four seasons of the series: the Kettlemans' illegal bribe in Season One, Nacho and Mike's hitman contract in Season Two, the formation of Gus and Mike's illicit alliance in Season Three, and Jimmy and Ira's felonious caper in Season Four.

What these multifarious examples show is that there are four possible types of illicit promises: 1. promises that are both legal and moral; 2. promises that are legal but immoral; 3. promises that are both illegal and immoral; and last but not least, 4. promises that are illegal but moral. This fourfold classification is presented in the following table below:

Table 1: Taxonomy of Illicit Promises

Illegal but Moral (the Kettlemans' bribe, which is arguably moral because the Kettlemans need Jimmy to keep quiet about their hideaway for their own safety)	**Legal but Immoral** (Mike's employment at Madrigal: although Mike is providing lawful consulting services, he is using this arrangement to launder stolen money)
Illegal and Immoral (Mike and Nacho's initial agreement to assassinate Tuco Salamanca)	**Legal and Moral** (Jimmy's legitimate representation of criminal suspects)

Illicit agreements pose a special kind of moral paradox: when may we break a "bad" promise?

On the one hand, we have a moral duty to keep our promises, but on the other hand, we also have a moral obligation to avoid harming third parties. As a result, there are two competing moral principles in direct conflict with each other whenever someone makes an illegal or immoral promise. The philosophical and jurisprudential question is: how should we resolve this moral contradiction? Alas, previous attempts to resolve this moral contradiction fall short.

Previous Solutions to the Problem of Bad Promises

To restate the problem, may we break our "bad" promises, or must we keep them? Broadly speaking, legal scholars and moral philosophers have offered two plausible but competing solutions to this question. One is to simply deny that an immoral promise is a promise. The other is to concede that an immoral promise is, in fact, a promise, but not a morally obligatory or binding one. As we'll see, however, neither solution really works.

Some theorists, such as Seana Shiffrin, define valid promises in such a way as to exclude promises to perform immoral acts. On this view of promising, a "bad" or illicit promise is not morally binding because such a commitment is not really a "promise" in the moral sense. To the point, if you don't have a right to perform X (where X is some immoral or wicked act), then a promise to do X is a defective promise, a non-promise, or a promise that is not morally binding.

The philosopher David Owens takes a different tack, reframing the act of making a promise as a transfer of authority from the promisor (the person making the promise) to the promisee (the person to whom the promise is made). Specifically, according to Owens's "simple theory of promising," whenever I make a promise to someone, what I am really doing is giving the promisee (the recipient of my promise) the authority to require me to perform my promise. On Owens's view of promising, if I lack the authority to do something immoral or illegal in the first place, then I also lack the authority or normative power to promise to do that very same immoral/illegal act in the future, or in the words of Owens: "Where the promisor has no authority to do the thing promised (for example, a promise to kill or maim), no grant of authority can be made and the promise is nugatory."

These clever reframings of the act of promising appear to solve the problem of bad promises, since promisors lack either the right to perform illegal or immoral actions (Shiffrin's solution) or the authority to do so (Owens's solution), but is a promise really a transfer of authority (Owens) or a transfer of rights (Shiffrin)? If so, how does a promise effectuate such a transfer? Or as David Hume objected long ago, how does the mere utterance of a few words change anything about the world? Alas, all such transfer theories of promising appear to be magical in nature—unable to circumvent Hume's famous objection. Worse yet, these purported solutions to the problem of bad promises suffer from a fatal flaw: they are empty. Why? Because they fail to provide any substantive criterion for determining whether you have the authority or moral right to do *X* in the first place. Owens, for example, focuses on whether you have the authority to make a promise, while Shiffrin's focus is on whether the person making the promise has a moral right to perform the promised act, but to determine whether one has the authority or moral right to perform *X* act, we need a theory to judge the moral content or moral authority of our promises. Neither Shiffrin nor Owens, however, is able to provide such a theory.

To see this objection more concretely, consider the illegal drug cartels and black markets in *Better Call Saul*. In an ideal world, it would be best if these cartels and their drug smuggling operations did not exist. But we do not live in an ideal world; markets for crystal meth and other illegal drugs exist in New Mexico and beyond, so if Hector Salamanca or Gustavo Fring—or Walter White and Jesse Pinkman—don't meet this demand, the reality is that other suppliers most likely will. Moreover, to the extent these illegal activities occur among consenting adults (to the extent these are voluntary markets), how can we say that no one has the moral authority or moral right to engage in the meth trade?

Other moral philosophers, by contrast, concede that an illicit promise is, in fact, a promise, but they—most notably James Altham and Margaret Gilbert—offer a different solution to the problem of illicit promises: they simply conclude that an immoral promise does not generate a morally binding obligation. We can, however, dispatch this purported solution with just a few words, since it borders on pure sophistry. Why? Because a promise, by definition, is something that is morally binding. So, to say that wicked promises are not morally binding because they are wicked is simply to engage in circular reasoning. Altham and Gilbert want to have their philosophical cake and eat it too!

My Saul Goodman-Inspired Solution

Does this moral paradox have a solution? I will propose a different approach, one informed by Jimmy McGill/Saul Goodman's legal training and our common law tradition. After all, common law courts—even those in American Samoa, where Jimmy McGill received his online law degree—have developed a sophisticated body of legal principles and judicial doctrines to deal with the problem of illegal bargains. See the entry for

"Legal System" under "American Samoa" in the *CIA World Factbook* (2020).

So let's turn to the law for guidance ("RICO"). Illicit agreements come in two varieties: 1. those that are immoral or *mala in se*, and (ii) those that are merely illegal or *mala prohibita*. A promise involving some form of moral turpitude—like the Kettleman's bribe or the aborted Tuco Salamanca hit—is considered *malum in se* and is totally void, while a promise in violation of a commercial statute or an economic regulation—like Madrigal's ghost hire of Mike or Jimmy's staged traffic accident—is generally considered *malum prohibitum* and is thus treated as "voidable" by the innocent party. By way of example, contracts tainted by mistake, duress, or even fraud are all voidable at the option of the innocent party. A void contract, by contrast, does not produce any legal effects. Either way, the key to this void/voidable distinction is the gravity or quality of the harm caused by an illicit promise.

With this legal background in mind, we can now picture a continuum in which non-morally objectionable promises occupy one end of the moral spectrum, while totally immoral or *mala in se* promises fall on the other end of the moral spectrum, and so-called "voidable" promises would fall somewhere in the middle of these two extremes. In other words, just as the common law recognizes different degrees of contract validity by distinguishing between void and voidable illegal bargains, we could likewise similarly allow for different degrees of promissory duties depending on the type of harm generated by the illicit agreement.

What if we were take into account the *location* of the harm, and not just its gravity? Specifically, what if we were to ask an altogether different question about illicit promises. To the point: *who is harmed when an illicit promise is made?* By focusing on the location of the harm, we see that "bad" or illicit promises fall into one of four general categories: 1. promises that harm the promisor, the person making the promise; 2. promises that harm the promisee, the person to whom the promise is made; 3. promises that harm both parties to the illicit agreement; and 4. and promises that harm a third party.

This Saul Goodman-inspired analytic framework not only invites us to quantify the amount of harm to be caused by an illicit promise and to estimate the probability that the harm will occur; it also asks us to focus on the location of the harm. On this view, promises in which the harm is unjustified and external, such as a promise to harm a third party, should be considered void *ab initio*, a promise with no moral standing or moral force. At the same time, promises in which the harm is internal—promises in which no third party is harmed but either of the promising parties, or both of them, will be harmed—should be merely voidable. In these cases of purely internal harms, the party to be harmed could exercise a "moral veto" over the illicit promise. (In cases where both promising parties—the promisor and promise—are harmed, then either could elect to exercise this "moral veto" over the promise.)

Thus, the moral status of voidable illicit promises should depend on the location of the harm—on the wishes of the party who will be harmed if the promise is kept. An additional advantage of my Saul Goodman–inspired approach to illicit promises is that we don't need to measure the gravity of the harm to determine whether the harm caused by an illicit promise is *malum in se* or merely *malum prohibitum*.

We still need to figure out which harms should count as "unjustified" harms. If I order a chicken burrito at Los Pollos Hermanos, aren't I complicit in an unjustified external harm— the harm to the animal whose meat was used to make my burrito? If so, isn't my Pollos Hermanos order an illicit one? What about the supply contract between the Pollos Hermanos chain and the poultry supplier? My tentative reply to the second-order problem of defining harms is this: we must be careful to distinguish between the legality of illicit promises and the morality of such promises. On my theory, a promise that generates an unjustified external harm is void from a moral perspective, so even though the poultry supply contract might be legally enforceable as a matter of law, the legal status of such an arrangement does not answer the moral question—whether the killing of animals for food consumption is justified.

One of the virtues of my harm-based approach is that it compels us to question the morality of our promises, even our most prosaic and ordinary ones. If my analytic framework makes us uncomfortable, if it makes us rethink everyday practices and promises, that is a feature, not a bug.

23

Why Does Jimmy Get to Determine Chuck's Healthcare?

JAMES CLARK ROSS

Under what conditions is it morally acceptable to meddle in somebody else's affairs against their will? Paternalistic intervention is motivated by attempting to obtain another person's "best interests." But who is the interferer to decide what's best and not the person whose affairs are being interfered in?

Chuck's affairs are meddled with in *Better Call Saul*. Others believe that illness compromises Chuck's thinking to the extent that decisions about his healthcare should be made for him. Chuck disagrees. He has the mental capacity and acuity to express his will clearly: he wants to be home and continue living his life as he sees fit. So, on what grounds is any intervention justified?

Chuck is an extremely smart man. Fellow lawyers are in awe of his exceptional legal mind and intimate knowledge of the law. But, in his illness, Chuck is losing his grip on reality. He suffers from what he considers to be a medical condition that others more qualified than him, including a doctor, do not recognize.

Whereas Chuck can feel like he's thinking perfectly rationally, the opposing medical opinion is that he lacks the ability to evaluate his best interests properly. This plunges those around him, including his brother, Jimmy, into an ethical dilemma: do they override Chuck's will by committing him for psychiatric evaluation, a potentially oppressive imposition, or do they step aside to respect his agency, leaving his well-being at risk?

For Your Own Good

Paternalistic intervention is especially interesting for cases in which the subject's mental competence is dubious. A family member with dementia refuses to eat. A child spends too much time on social media. An inebriated friend wants to stay in the nightclub and sleep there alone. A struggling boxer wishes to carry on fighting. In each case, another agent—a daughter, a parent, a best friend, a trainer—acts to prevent the subject's present wishes from prevailing: they find ways to feed them, they take away their smartphone, they call a taxi and wait with them for it to arrive, they throw in the towel. "I'm doing this for your own good!" they claim. The subject can no longer be trusted to make sensible decisions: they are ill, young, drunk, or injured.

However, there are much trickier cases to consider for which we need clarification on the moral boundaries. Within these boundaries we can call our interventions ethical; outside we cannot. But where are they? Boundaries tend to be disputed in theory and blurred in practice. One candidate for such a boundary is found in rationality, which Chuck falls short of properly possessing. Should Jimmy govern Chuck's affairs to commit him for psychiatric evaluation? Yes, because Chuck's behavior is not reasonable or in line with a set of principles: it is *irrational*. He consistently fails to act with his best interests in mind (more on those later).

In a healthcare setting, patients who cannot give adequate consent are said to lack relevant mental competence ("decisional capacity"). The patient might, for example, be under a certain age or, being vulnerable, have a severe learning disability or brain injury. As such, either they cannot express their preferences at all or the ways in which they assemble their preferences are ill-formed. It is in this latter sense that Chuck's thinking is deemed to be compromised, and his consent is conferred to a guardian: namely, Jimmy, who, in the early days of their relationship, fulfils nearly all of Chuck's wishes; later, he acts against them. But is Chuck's thinking really so compromised that someone else must make decisions for him? After all, he is still an agent who expresses his will reliably and perspicuously. Good reasons are needed to ignore it.

One way to shore up the justification of the intervention can be found in Chuck's "epistemic irrationality." Though Chuck acts *willingly*, he does not act *knowledgeably*. He claims to suffer from electromagnetic hypersensitivity (EHS), symptoms of which include burning sensation on his skin, sharp pain in his bones, muscle fatigue, heart palpitations, blurred vision, tinnitus, vertigo, nausea, and shortness of breath. "For reasons unknown, my nervous system has become sensitized to certain frequencies of electromagnetic radiation." ("Alpine Shepherd Boy").

These symptoms are real for Chuck: they disable him. However, they are nonspecific, and, according to the World Health Organization (WHO), there is no scientific basis for claiming they are causally linked to electromagnetic field exposure. Notwithstanding the possibility of EHS having a basis in physical reality, Chuck's symptoms do not seem to bear a relation to the presence of electromagnetic radiation itself. In all probability, then, Chuck's EHS is in his head. In inferring the causes of his symptoms incorrectly, Chuck's beliefs lack adequate justification and are epistemically irrational.

This is demonstrated in "Alpine Shepherd Boy," by Cruz, who runs electricity through Chuck's hospital bed, and in "Chicanery" by Jimmy, who orchestrates the placement of a fully charged phone battery into Chuck's pocket. Neither action manifests Chuck's symptoms, exposing Chuck's failure to pick up on causes which are recognizable to everyone else. Furthermore, Chuck's attempts to evade society's ubiquitous electromagnetic signals are obsessive in nature, and his reactions of distress are extreme; they seem to be related to or rooted in anxiety, not physical hypersensitivity. Together, these signs lead Cruz to the conclusion that Chuck's EHS is not real but a manifestation of something deeper. Far from being in a state of rationality, he is in a state of denial. He lacks agency in virtue of being a victim of an illness which has snatched his rationality away.

In Dr. Lara Cruz's opinion, therefore, Chuck should be committed for psychiatric evaluation. His EHS equates to a *psychological* illness, not one of physical origins. Without dealing with the real causes, Chuck will continue to pose a danger to himself and to other members of society, whom he inconveniences by requesting the absence of nearby electrically powered devices—not an easy feat in the twenty-first century.

> Coleman lanterns indoors? A camp stove? He could burn his house down, or the entire neighbourhood. And then you're looking at a commitment of ten to twenty years. What if he just hurts himself in a household accident? How does he call for help? You have the power to help your brother. Truly help him. Ignoring this won't make it go away.

Chuck's behavior wasn't always so irrational. Before the onset of his illness, when Chuck had HHM as his focus, he was formidable and unproblematic. Then his decision-making became unpredictable, his character vindictive and vengeful.

Over the course of *Better Call Saul* we witness clues as to how Chuck's mental health deteriorated. His symptoms worsen in moments when he doubts his esteem; for when he is practising law again—in his element; succeeding—Chuck shakes many of them off. Was his divorce a significant cause of his condition's development? Regardless of the condition's exact set of causes, we are left mulling over Chuck's right to control his medical treatment.

Irrationality Is Normal

In Albert Camus's *The Plague*, the onset of Father Paneloux's life-threatening illness becomes a supreme test of his faith. Paneloux repeatedly turns down the landlady's attempts to obtain medical attention for him, choosing to embrace God's divine will instead. For Paneloux, it is important that he succumbs to this illness before God. And while we may think the landlady was wrong not to intervene, this devoutly lived life is his, not hers, after all.

We ought to be sensitive to people's wishes and claims to agency. Danger lurks where we too willingly hand over control of their lives to family, friends, and healthcare workers. How do we even prove that someone has deviated so far from rationality that they are mentally ill? Their loss of rationality may only be a lapse from which they swiftly recover. We are on tricky territory on which we must tread carefully. We tried to secure the territory by calling to the concept of rationality, but there is further trouble ahead, for human beings—all of us—are curious creatures who motivate their actions in the weirdest and most wonderful of ways, confounding the moral boundaries once more. But maybe we can look to the content of our motivations to explain how alarming some behaviors are.

As any philosopher knows, defining rationality is no simple task. There's no simple formula to divide rational from irrational behavior. Somebody like Chuck is sharp and intelligent and often adamant about not wanting or needing help and he's logical and lucid in arguing as such. In "Fall," Howard even claims that Chuck *still* has the best legal mind he has ever known. It will be a challenge for any professional or friend to convincingly demonstrate his irrationality, even with the most qualified assessments available.

A common-sense approach is to expose someone's irrationality from the sheer absurdity of their decision-making. In Chuck's case, he's a recluse who's losing friends, money, and status and is depriving himself of a range of everyday and professional experiences he used to value. To claim he is in his right mind is to beg the question since he clearly has little intention of maintaining these states of affairs, which previously made him happy.

But however absurd somebody's decision-making appears to us, in practice, they can always provide reasons for their actions and, in turn, define their best interests differently to how we define them. In this sense, many of Chuck's actions are at least *minimally* rational, that is, he can lay out reasons that, to him, make perfect sense. Of course, he's wearing a space blanket: it shields him from electromagnetic radiation. Smashing the house to bits? Obviously, he needs to find the cause of his electricity meter still running.

Chuck is hardly alone. We, too, apparently do irrational things that do not seem to be in our best interests all the time, and our affairs are not meddled with. We are victims of bad habits, bias, and ignorance. We are *wilful* in our actions, also. For example, I follow my favorite sports team to misery, being well prepared for the sadness of inevitable loss well in advance. Following the team, on the whole, gives me more stress than joy, but I do not expect to be committed for psychiatric evaluation for it! Why not apply the same leniency to Chuck? The risks associated with how he lives his life are mostly his to take, are they not?

Pursuing this thought further, Sharon Street believes that we can form reasons on the backs of "evaluative attitudes," amongst a combination of other things, and that it does not follow that we are being incoherent. She argues that our motivational structures are best understood as being complex. In one of her examples, Street explains how it's not implausible for an anorexic woman to have coherent reasons to starve herself to death, as bad as that sounds. The woman does not value having a supermodel's figure because it is an intrinsically valuable state of being. Rather, like anyone else, she is sustained by "utterly typical human goals and values": in this case, to be loved, to be beautiful, to feel in control of her life, and so forth. And she can be so clearheaded about and impassioned by this goal to the extent that she is willing to die in a doomed pursuit of it. Arguably, then, her motivations are rational.

Although this case is exceptional in nature, we might suspect that something similar is happening in Chuck. Attitudes matter, and Chuck has negative attitudes towards electromagnetic radiation, about which he is internally consistent. The lesson here is that the "deeper" causes for Chuck's peculiar preferences, as alluded to by Cruz, may be at their roots evaluative, but that does not rule out the coherence he maintains in holding them. There's no bright line between rational and irrational preferences, which complicates the matter of justifying intervention.

We might be tempted to call behavior irrational in case the subject presents little aversion to pain or loss in their decision-making, as Chuck does. Chuck's physical health is at stake, as is his mental health. He neglects proper care of his medical and financial affairs. His career has stalled. He has few relationships. But many philosophers warn against such a view. In a particularly interesting case study, Diana T. Meyers explores the claim that some women *choose* to undergo female genital mutilation (FGM). On first impression, their choice is absurd. But, by their autonomy, these women seemingly fashion their choices with substantive reasons for undergoing FGM, including to test their physical endurance prior to labor and to demonstrate morally appropriate fertility. As such, they can be regarded as self-determining individuals who have adopted the skill of "self-discovery." Likewise, we might also look to women who vote, on their own accord, for political parties which seek to abolish their rights—for example, right-wing populist parties with strong links to the Catholic Church (as discussed by Gwiazda)—and to elective amputation, whereby people of mental competence choose to have their healthy limbs amputated (Blom et al.)

None of these examples seem like the kinds of things we want to legitimize as rationally motivated: they are self-harming acts. At the same time, it's not clear—philosophically speaking—that the self-harming acts described are categorically different to ones we would not attempt to stop. People climb K2 in difficult conditions and navigate through the Arctic to the North Pole to feel fulfilled. They walk across fire to prove their worth to a community. They watch their lowly ranked sports team lose week upon week to feel a sense of belonging. They are not prevented. We, like Chuck, are embedded with irrational ways of thinking, albeit to varying extents. We just live with them more consonantly with respect to society's norms.

Our conclusion is not that Chuck is thinking rationally with his best interests in mind. Rather, it is that we, like him, are not as rational as we like to believe. Moreover, it is not always clear that 'irrationality' ought to be removed from our lives. To quote Friedrich Nietzsche, who thinks we have a fundamental *attitude* towards all things:

. . . from the illogical springs much that is good. The illogical is so embedded in the passions, in language, in art, in religion and, above all, in everything that imparts value to life that it cannot be taken away without irreparably injuring those beautiful things. Only men of the utmost simplicity can believe that the nature man knows can be changed into a purely logical nature. Yet were there steps affording approach to this goal, how utterly everything would be lost on the way! Even the most rational man needs nature again, from time to time, that is, his illogical fundamental relation to all things. (*Human, All Too Human*, p. 60)

Grounds for Intervention

Chuck's irrationalities are clearly not serving him well. Yet we still need to determine the grounds of an ethical intervention: something stronger than the apparent absurdity of his motivations. Unequipped with better reasons, an intervention may be oppressive.

If Chuck cannot evaluate his best interests, can somebody else do so properly? Perhaps there is scope to intervene ethically in Chuck's affairs when the aim of the intervention is to improve his *welfare*. That is to say, the best courses of action are those that increase Chuck's happiness, health, prosperity, or fortune. Perhaps Cruz has something like this in mind when she urges Jimmy to commit Chuck. In an emergency situation, other medical professionals treat Chuck with electrically powered devices despite his objections ("Klick") "I did not give you my consent. You have no right to do this!" He proclaims.

What about everyday living? For the most part, Jimmy is protective and facilitates Chuck's bizarre lifestyle, necessitating the avoidance of electricity. But for how long can he do this? Cruz maintains that Jimmy enables, not helps, Chuck by going along with his wishes. Thus, Cruz wants Jimmy to paternalistically intervene to overpower Chuck's immediate and ill-formed wishes for the sake of Chuck's welfare. There are "needs" to look after—fundamentals such as his health. "What he wants and what he needs are two very different things, Jimmy."

There are financial considerations to take account of, too. In "Uno", Jimmy and Howard debate Chuck's best interests without Chuck's being present. The topic of discussion is pay-outs from HHM to Chuck, who had not set foot in an HHM office for nearly a year by that point. Jimmy, acting as some kind of a financial guardian, thinks Chuck should receive a big pay-out. Howard disagrees with Jimmy's demands and argues that, if

Chuck were present, he would agree to being given the smaller amounts being discussed. The premises of Jimmy's beliefs here are unclear. But we know that he does not exactly shy away from money. He values having it. So should Chuck.

HOWARD: So these are Chuck's own wishes that you're conveying?

JIMMY: This is what's best him for him.

However, life goes beyond needs such as health and money. There are various other interests to look after in welfare, say, the desires we hold for meaning, harmony, community, and hope, amongst many others. To quote Christine Korsgaard:

> Unquestionably, we have some irreducibly private interests—in the satisfaction of our appetites, in food and a certain kind of sex, say. But our personal interests are not limited to *having* things. We also have interests in *doing* things and *being* things. Many of these interests cannot set us wholly against the interests of society, simply because they are unintelligible outside of society and the cultural traditions that society supports. ("Morality and the Distinctiveness of Human Action," pp. 100–01)

If we live in a society in which we care about people being able to make free choices, especially when these choices do not negatively affect others, we might want to protect preferences like Chuck's, however odd they are, as a matter of principle to render him an autonomous, self-determining individual. Like us, he has rights enshrined in law that entitle him to act in certain ways, including the right to decide the matter of his own healthcare, so long as he's deemed mentally competent.

Any intervention that breaches this right is *unjust*. But various real-life cases exemplify the moral trickiness of this kind of situation—for instance, the wearing of full-face veils, the living on the street of homeless people, and the refusal of blood transfusions and vaccinations (and, in Chuck's case, psychiatric treatment). Denying individuals from making these choices are affronts to their ways of being, and there are rights, such as freedom of conscience, to contend with. Take the example of wearing a full-face veil. Somebody might take issue with it because they think the person who wears it is not free. However, how can they know the apparently oppressed person better than the person knows themselves? This challenge was posed by Isaiah Berlin, who warned against such oppressive interventions.

> I am in a position to ignore the actual wishes of men or societies, to bully, oppress, torture them in the name, and on behalf, of their 'real' self, in the secure knowledge that whatever is the true goal of man (happiness, performance of duty, wisdom, a just society, self-fulfilment) must be identical with his freedom—the free choice of his 'true', albeit often submerged and inarticulate, self. ("Two Concepts of Liberty," pp. 24–25)

Believing we know someone else better than they do opens the door to oppression. We purport to know what the person seeks and chooses, if they were something else to what they actually are, when all we can do is second-guess their best interests.

So, how does somebody, from the outside, evaluate, aggregate, and compare all of Chuck's interests without being oppressive with an intervention? This question sits at the crux of the issue alongside the question of his mental competence (rationality), and there are no simple solutions. Jimmy and Chuck's colleagues choose to maintain Chuck's precarious lifestyle. A stalemate is broken by a doctor who calls into question the state of his welfare, paternalistically intervening on medically grounded advice. Does Chuck exhibit sufficient decisional capacity to warrant control of his healthcare? Cruz, a medical professional, believes he does not and implores Jimmy to commit him, a decision which Jimmy eventually agrees to. This pathway is spelled out in law to help protect people like Chuck. That is all there is to it, right? Yes and no. This view oversimplifies life, which, for each of us, extends greatly beyond health.

Brotherly Devotion

Throughout *Better Call Saul* we see a selfish and opportunistic Jimmy perform unethical tasks for his own benefit, increasingly with the distinct flavor of Saul. But, in a way, this description does a disservice to Jimmy, who may be spoken of in much higher terms. At least at the early stages of the show, Jimmy is devoted to protecting and empowering Chuck *unconditionally*. Jimmy evidently loves and admires his older brother, for whom he is a voluntary guardian, and yearns for his approval ("Rico").

JIMMY: Are you proud of me?

CHUCK: Hmm? Um . . . Yes.

There's no direct benefit to Jimmy from overseeing Chuck's care. He's not forced to do it. Out of brotherly love, Jimmy regularly steps in without question to fulfil Chuck's wants *and* needs. So, does Chuck return the devotion?

Here's one argument to suggest that Jimmy is not the only one who places himself in the position of devoted intervenor in this relationship. Chuck, on multiple occasions, interferes with Jimmy's affairs to force Jimmy to finally change his ways for his own good. First, Chuck gives Jimmy a new chance at life by moving him to New Mexico and finding him work at HHM. Second, Chuck keeps Jimmy out of HHM, which he does in order to help Jimmy to become his own man. "Why ride on someone else's coattails?" to quote Chuck ("Uno"). Third, Chuck has Jimmy barred from practicing law not out of spite but to teach Jimmy a lesson about his immature approach to life and encourage him to improve his conduct. "You won't wanna hear it, but this is for the best," he says ("Sunk Costs").

This line of thought is tempting to follow. However, there is a larger sense in which Chuck is not actually interested in bettering Jimmy's life paternalistically. Rather, as a prideful man, Chuck is more concerned with Jimmy no longer corrupting his image. Chuck has grievances about Jimmy to the point of deep-seated resentment. Jimmy had dirtied the family's name when their parents were still alive—for instance, by thieving from their father's store. Now, with his crooked ways, Jimmy shames the legal profession and, by extension, the M in HHM.

But, despite all of Jimmy's sins, he's devoted to Chuck's care, even in the midst of brotherly rivalry and illness, when Chuck's faculties to do so himself are tentative. By contrast, Chuck is a gatekeeper of *his own* interests: keep Jimmy away. Chuck's interventions are not paternalistic, especially towards the end of their relationship.

These differences call into question what we mean when we say "devoted". In the context of paternalistic intervention, someone is devoted to another because they genuinely want to better their interests, motivations which Chuck does not seem to possess. But perhaps I am misguided and Chuck is not, as to what Jimmy's best interests are. How, then, should we define "devotion" such that it maintains its moral essence when enacted?

Here's one way to understand it. According to Simone de Beauvoir, Chuck is not devoted to Jimmy's interests in the same way that Jimmy is devoted to Chuck's interests. To be devoted, by Beauvoir's lights, somebody must see as their end the other in possession of their own goals. Jimmy loves and cares for Chuck, making decisions which he thinks do right *by*

Chuck. He respects Chuck as his own person. Conversely, Chuck's so-called devotion to Jimmy is a "tyranny" because he imposes his will onto Jimmy. Even in the charitable case wherein Chuck wants Jimmy to be a better lawyer and a better person, these are Chuck's wishes, not Jimmy's.

> When it comes to his being, he is the only one who makes it . . . The fundamental error of devotion is that it considers the other as an object carrying an emptiness in its heart that would be possible to fill. (*What Is Existentialism?*, p. 76)

Jimmy must be set his own "departure" and have his existence willed unconditionally by Chuck to be called free. Chuck might think he knows what is best for Jimmy, like the parent does for their child in our example earlier, but Chuck's interventions, morally speaking, do not stand up to Beauvoir's scrutiny, whereas Jimmy's do. It is Jimmy's freedom that matters ethically. However, freedom is not the only function of ethics in this relationship we must consider. To say it is, is to ignore the various malpractices of Jimmy.

Jimmy is unscrupulous. He deceives, lies, scams, and bends the rules, frequently valuing the ends more than the means. In stark contrast, Chuck is a highly principled man, known for "his profound devotion to the highest ideals of the law" ("Smoke"). Still, they *both* discredit the other to the point of humiliation. By the end, their relationship is so fraught by the fact that each person sees the world so differently, devolving in dramatic and compelling fashion. This leads us to a final thought about the origins of their differences.

Jimmy was never a good egg. But, as a cause of Jimmy's transformation into the notorious Saul Goodman, perhaps Chuck can be blamed for his lack of brotherly devotion. Jimmy could never match the achievements or meet the approval of his older brother, who allowed him to do well but not well enough to be better. Chuck did not envisage a "departure" for Jimmy on Jimmy's own terms. So, Jimmy chooses to transcend his situation freely into his own chaos. Saul Goodman is the rebellion against and the paradoxical embracing of Chuck's disapproval, embodying a life of admiration for but a new turn away from his brother, the great Charles McGill.

Bibliography

Alexander, Michelle. 2012. *The New Jim Crow: Mass Incarceration in the Age of Colorblindness*. The New Press.

Altham, J.E.J. 1985. Wicked Promises. In Hacking 1985.

American Bar Association. Model Rules of Professional Conduct <www.americanbar.org/groups/professional_responsibility/publications/model_rules_of_professional_conduct>.

Annas, Julia. 1981. *An Introduction to Plato's Republic*. Oxford University Press.

Aristophanes. 1973. *Lysistrata, The Acharnians, The Clouds*. Penguin.

Aristotle. 1962. *Nicomachean Ethics*. Bobbs-Merrill.

Arkes, H.R., and C. Blumer. 1985. The Psychology of Sunk Cost. *Organizational Behavior and Human Decision Processes*.

Aurelius, Marcus. 2006. *Meditations*. Penguin.

Baker, Lynne Rudder. 2000. *Persons and Bodies: A Constitution View*. Cambridge University Press.

Baltzly, Dirk. 2018. Stoicism. *Stanford Encyclopedia of Philosophy* <https://plato.stanford.edu/entries/stoicism>.

Beauvoir, Simone de. 2020. *What Is Existentialism?* Penguin.

Bennett, William. 1989. A Response to Milton Friedman. *Wall Street Journal* (September 19th).

Bentham, Jeremy. 1970. *An Introduction to the Principles of Morals and Legislation*. The Collected Works of Jeremy Bentham. Oxford University Press.

Berlin, Isaiah. 1969a. *Four Essays on Liberty*. Oxford University Press:

———. 1969b. Two Concepts of Liberty. In Berlin 1969a.

Block, Walter, and Violet Obioha. 2012. War on Black Men: Arguments for the Legalization of Drugs. *Criminal Justice Ethics* 31:2.

Blom, Rianne M., Valeria Guglielmi, and Damiaan Denys. 2016. Elective Amputation of a 'Healthy Limb'. *CNS Spectrums* 21:5.

Bowers, Jason. n.d. Dr. Bowers's Office Hours. Plato's *Republic*. <www.youtube.com/watch?v=HhQjQ5X9E8k&list=PLRS1kQED3S-i0mSzB6To8-brb7kyHPQV1>.

Butler, Joseph. 2017. *Fifteen Sermons and Other Writings on Ethics*. Oxford University Press.

Carel, H., and D. Meacham, eds. 2013. *Phenomenology and Naturalism: Exploring the Relationship between Human Experience and Nature*. Cambridge University Press.

Centers for Disease Control and Prevention. 2021. Understanding the Opioid Overdose Epidemic <https://www.cdc.gov/opioids/basics/epidemic.html>.

Constant, Benjamin. 1988. *Constant: Political Writings*. Cambridge University Press.

Cook, Gareth. 2013. The Nocebo Effect: How We Worry Ourselves Sick. *The New Yorker* (March 29th) <www.newyorker.com/tech/annals-of-technology/the-nocebo-effect-how-we-worry-ourselves-sick>.

Crookston, Emily M., David Killoren, and Jonathan Trerise, eds. 2017. *Ethics in Politics: The Rights and Obligations of Individual Political Agents*. Routledge.

Derrida, Jacques.1989a. *Derrida and Negative Theology*. SUNY Press.

———. 1989. How to Avoid Speaking: Denials. In Derrida 1989a.

———. 1992a. *Acts of Literature*. Routledge.

———. 1992b. Before the Law. In Derrida 1992a.

De Waal, Frans. 2006. *Primates and Philosophers: How Morality Evolved*. Princeton University Press.

Dewey, John. 1922. *Human Nature and Conduct*. Holt.

Drug Policy Alliance. 2021. A Brief History of the Drug War <https://drugpolicy.org/issues/brief-history-drug-war>.

Eberle, S. 2017. An Underworld Journey: Learning to Cope with Electromagnetic Hypersensitivity. *Ecopsychology* 9:2.

Economist. 2001. How Did We Get Here? Special Report. *Economist* (July 28th).

Frankfurt, Harry G. 2009. *On Bullshit*. Princeton University Press.

French, Shannon E. 2003. *The Code of the Warrior: Exploring Warrior Values Past and Present*. Rowman and Littlefield.

Friedman, M. 2013. What's Going On with Jimmy's Brother on *Better Call Saul? Esquire*. <www.esquire.com/entertainment/tv/a32673/better-call-saul-chuck-electromagnetic-hypersensitivity>.

Friedman, Milton. 1989. An Open Letter to Bill Bennett. *The Wall Street Journal* (September 7th).

Garland, Howard. 1990. Throwing Good Money after Bad: The Effect of Sunk Costs on the Decision to Escalate Commitment to an Ongoing Project. *Journal of Applied Psychology.*

Garrett, Brian. 1998. *Personal Identity and Self-Consciousness.* Routledge.

Gilbert, Margaret P. 2011. Three Dogmas about Promising. In Sheinman 2011.

Gwiazda, Anna. 2020. Right-wing Populism and Feminist Politics: The Case of Law and Justice in Poland. *International Political Science Review.*

Habib, Allen. 2018. Promises. *The Stanford Encyclopedia of Philosophy.*

Hacking, Ian, ed. 1985. *Exercises in Analysis.* Cambridge University Press.

Hägglund, Martin. 2019. *This Life: Secular Faith and Spiritual Freedom.* Pantheon.

Hardcastle, Gary L., and George A. Reisch, eds. 2006. *Bullshit and Philosophy: Guaranteed to Get Perfect Results Every Time.* Open Court.

Hart, H.L.A. 1994. *The Concept of Law.* Oxford University Press.

Hausteiner, C., S. Bornschein, T. Zilker, P. Henningsen, and H. Forstl. 2007. Dysfunctional Cognitions in Idiopathic Environmental Intolerances (IEI): An Integrative Psychiatric Perspective. *Toxicology Letters* 171:1–2.

Hobbes, Thomas. 1985. *Leviathan.* Penguin.

Homiak, Marcia. 2019. Moral Character. *The Stanford Encyclopedia of Philosophy.* <https://plato.stanford.edu/archives/sum2019/entries/moral-character>.

Hooker, Brad. 2000. *Ideal Code, Real World: A Rule-Consequentialist Theory of Morality.* Oxford University Press.

Huemer, Michael. 2017. Devil's Advocates: On the Ethics of Unjust Legal Advocacy. In Crookston et al. 2017.

Hume, David. 2000. *A Treatise of Human Nature.* Oxford University Press.

Isocrates. 2021. Against the Sophists. <http://faculty.washington.edu/mcgarrit/COM331/againstthe-sophists.pdf>.

James, William, 2015a. *The Will to Believe, Human Immortality, and Other Essays in Popular Philosophy.* Dover.

———. 2015b. The Dilemma of Determinism. In James 2015a.

Kafka, Franz. 1978a. *Wedding Preparations in the Country and Other Stories.* Penguin.

———. 1978b. Before the Law. In Kafka 1978a.

Kaku, Michio. 2021. Why Physics Ends the Free Will Debate. Big Think <www.youtube.com/watch?v=Jint5kjoy6I>.

Kant, Immanuel. 1996 [1785]. *Groundwork of The Metaphysics of Morals in Practical Philosophy*. Cambridge University Press.

Kelly, Thomas. 2004. Sunk Costs, Rationality, and Acting for the Sake of the Past. *Noûs*. 38:1.

Kimbrough, Scott. 2006. On Letting It Slide. In Hardcastle and Reisch 2006.

Kohlberg, Lawrence. 1958. *The Development of Modes of Thinking and Choices in Years 10 to 16*. PhD Dissertation, University of Chicago.

———. 1981. *The Philosophy of Moral Development: Moral Stages and the Idea of Justice*. Harper and Row.

Korsgaard, Christine M. 2006. Morality and the Distinctiveness of Human Action. In De Waal 2006.

Latour, Bruno. 2017. *Facing Gaia: Eight Lectures on the New Climatic Regime*. Polity.

Leonhard, Chunlin. 2015. Illegal Agreements and the Lesser Evil Principle. *Catholic University Law Review* 64.

Mahon, James. 2016. The Definition of Lying and Deception. *The Stanford Encyclopedia of Philosophy*.

Marcum, James A. 2021. Philosophy of Medicine. *Internet Encyclopedia of Philosophy*. <https://iep.utm.edu/medicine>.

Mattsson, B., and M. Mattsson. 2002. The Concept of 'Psychosomatic' in General Practice: Reflections on Body Language and a Tentative Model for Understanding. *Scandinavian Journal of Primary Health Care* 20:3.

McKendry, Joe. 2019. Sears Once Sold Heroin. *The Atlantic* (March).

Meyers, Diana T. 2000. Feminism and Women's Autonomy: The Challenge of Female Genital Cutting. *Metaphilosophy* 31:5.

Midgley, Mary. 1974. The Game Game. *Philosophy* 49.

Mill, John Stuart. 1978 [1859]. *On Liberty*. Hackett.

———. 2001. *Utilitarianism*. Second edition. Hackett.

Myrvold, Wayne. 2018. Philosophical Issues in Quantum Theory. *The Stanford Encyclopedia of Philosophy* <https://plato.stanford.edu/archives/fall2018/entries/qt-issues>.

Nagel, Thomas. 1976. Moral Luck. *Proceedings of the Aristotelian Society*.

Nietzsche, Friedrich. 2011. *Human, All Too Human*. Project Gutenberg eBook.

Nozick, Robert. 1987. *The Nature of Rationality*. Princeton University Press.

Olson, Eric, and Karsten Witt. 2019. Narrative and Persistence. *Canadian Journal of Philosophy* 49.

O'Sullivan, S. 2017. When the Body Speaks. *Psychology Today* (January 3rd) <www.psychologytoday.com/us/articles/201701/when-the-body-speaks>.

Owens, David. 2006. A Simple Theory of Promising. *Philosophical Review* 115.

Patches, Matt. 2015. Michael McKean on his Better Call Saul Character. *Esquire* (February 9th) <www.esquire.com/entertainment/tv/interviews/a32671/michael-mckean-interview>.

Piaget, Jean. 1932. *The Moral Development of the Child*. Kegan Paul.

Plato. 1937. *The Dialogues of Plato*. Random House.

———. 1997. *Plato: Complete Works*. Hackett.

Robins, Lee. 1993. Vietnam Veterans' Rapid Recovery from Heroin Addiction: A Fluke or Normal Expectation? *Addiction* 88.

Rose, D., G. Thornicroft, V. Pinfold, and A. Kassam. 2007. 250 Labels Used to Stigmatise People with Mental Illness. *BMC Health Services Research* 7.

Rudd, Anthony. 2009. In Defence of Narrative. *European Journal of Philosophy* 17.

Santas, Gerasimos, ed. 2006. *The Blackwell Guide to Plato's Republic*. Blackwell.

Sartre, Jean-Paul. 1984. *Being and Nothingness: A Phenomenological Essay in Ontology*. Washington Square Press.

Scalvini, M. 2020. 13 Reasons Why: Can a TV Show about Suicide Be 'Dangerous'? What Are the Moral Obligations of a Producer? *Media, Culture, and Society* 42.

Scanlon, T.M. 2000. *What We Owe to Each Other*. Harvard University Press.

Schechtman, Marya. 1990. Personhood and Personal Identity. *Journal of Philosophy* 87.

———. 1996. *The Constitution of Selves*. Cornell University Press.

Schefczyk, Michael. n.d. John Stuart Mill: Ethics. *Internet Encyclopedia of Philosophy* <https://iep.utm.edu/mill-eth/#H3>.

Scott, Elizabeth. 2020. What It Means to Have 'Type A' Personality Traits. *Verywellmind* (July 22nd) <www.verywellmind.com/type-a-personality-traits-3145240>.

Seaman, S.R., R.P. Brettle, and S.M. Gore. 1998. Mortality from Overdose among Injecting Drug Users Recently Released from Prison: Database Linkage Study. *British Medical Journal* 316:7129.

Sheinman, Hanoch, ed. 2011. *Promises and Agreements: Philosophical Essays*. Oxford University Press.

Shoemaker, Sydney. 1963. *Self-Knowledge and Self-Identity*. Cornell University Press.

Singer, Peter. 2001. *Writings on an Ethical Life*. Ecco.

Singpurwalla, Rachel G.K. 2006. Plato's Defense of Justice in the *Republic*. In Santas 2006.

Shiffrin, Seana Valentine. 2011. Immoral, Conflicting, and Redundant Promises. In Wallace et al. 2011.

Smart, J.J.C., and Bernard William. 1973. *Utilitarianism: For and Against.* Cambridge University Press.

Smith, Adam. 2010. *The Theory of Moral Sentiments.* Penguin.

Stigler, George. 1987. *The Theory of Price.* Macmillan.

Street, Sharon. 2009. In Defense of Future Tuesday Indifference: Ideally Coherent Eccentrics and the Contingency of What Matters. *Philosophical Issues* 19:1.

Stuart, H. 2006. Media Portrayal of Mental Illness and Its Treatments: What Effect Does It Have on People with Mental Illness? *CNS Drugs* 20:2.

Svenaeus, F. 2013. Naturalistic and Phenomenological Theories of Health: Distinctions and Connections. In Carel and Meacham 2013.

Ten Elshof, Gregg A. 2009. *I Told Me So: Self-Deception and the Christian Life.* Eerdmans.

Thibaut, Florence. 2018. The Mind-Body Cartesian Dualism and Psychiatry. *Dialogues in Clinical Neuroscience,* 20.

Thornton, Mark. 1991. Alcohol Prohibition Was a Failure. *Cato Institute Policy Analysis* 157.

Wallace, R. Jay, Rahul Kumar, and Samuel Freeman, eds. 2011. *Reasons and Recognition: Essays on the Philosophy of T.M. Scanlon.* Oxford University Press.

Wang, X., and I. Bohanna. 2012. Media Guidelines for the Responsible Reporting of Suicide. *Crisis* 33:4.

Witthöft, M., and G.J. Rubin. 2013. Are Media Warnings about the Adverse Health Effects of Modern Life Self-fulfilling? An Experimental Study on Idiopathic Environmental Intolerance Attributed to Electromagnetic Fields (IEI-EMF). *Journal of Psychosomatic Research* 74:3.

World Health Organization. 2005. Electromagnetic Hypersensitivity.

Zagzebski, Linda. 2008. *On Epistemology.* Wadsworth.

The Hostile Witnesses

J. SPENCER ATKINS is currently working on a PhD at Binghamton University. He received his MA from the University of Tennessee at Knoxville. Spencer's research interests include social epistemology, ethics (especially applied and environmental ethics), and the philosophy of religion. He has published articles in *Environmental Ethics*, *Episteme*, *Logos and Episteme,* and other journals you've never heard of! Website: jspenceratkins.weeby.com. Contact: jatkins4@binghamton.edu.

THOMAS PAUL BARNES, ESQ. is a practicing attorney licensed by the State Bar of Texas. He minored in philosophy at the University of St. Thomas in Houston and earned his Juris Doctor at South Texas College of Law. Though he was at first tempted to practice criminal defense, and use a catch phrase like "Better Call Paul!", he ultimately thought better of it, focusing instead on civil litigation and transactional matters.

WALTER BARTA is a graduate student at the University of Houston, studying philosophy and rhetoric. Although he frequently considers breaking bad to pay for his student loans, Walter sucks at peddling meth, so he spends his time as "more of a humanities guy," writing philosophy in his free time.PhD

CONALL CASH earned his PhD in Romance Studies from Cornell University and is an Early Career Academic Fellow in French Studies at the University of Melbourne. His philosophical background came in handy when he discovered that the initials "JMM" on Jimmy McGill's briefcase are actually an allusion to Pascal's wager: Jansenists Make Money.

DANIEL CARR, when not chasing tornadoes or playing poker, is a PhD candidate at the University of Colorado, Boulder, focusing on virtue theory, philosophy of religion, and philosophy of science. He likes to explore philosophical questions like: what if we're all allergic to electricity?

PATRICK CLIPSHAM is a Professor of Philosophy at Winona State University in Winona, Minnesota. His teaching and research interests all pertain to various areas of ethics and moral philosophy. He hopes to someday save up enough money to become the manager of a Cinnabon in Omaha, Nebraska.

DANIEL COOK is a candidate on the Barrister Training Course at BPP University, having recently graduated from King's College London with an MA in Philosophy. His research interests encompass a wide range of topics due to his background in Law, including ethics, political philosophy, philosophy of law, contract and commercial law, criminal law, and property law. When he's not engaged in academic pursuits or playing devil's advocate, he can be found capering around a field as a rugby union referee.

BRETT COPPENGER is an Associate Professor of Philosophy at Tuskegee University and (as far as he knows) has never successfully convinced anyone that he is Kevin Costner.

DARCI DOLL is an Assistant Professor at Delta College. Early on she was interested in going into the law but her exposure to ethics classes ruined that for her. She is published in many pop culture and philosophy books including *The Ultimate Supernatural and Philosophy* (2022), *The Handmaid's Tale and Philosophy (2019)*, and *The Princess Bride and Philosophy* (2016).

LANDON FRIM is Associate Professor of Philosophy and Religious Studies at Florida Gulf Coast University. His research focuses on Spinoza, Marx, and other heretics who make people uncomfortable. But if you read his chapter on the non-existence of free will, take heart! It's not as if you could have avoided it anyway.

AMBER E. GEORGE is an Assistant Professor of Philosophy and Diversity, Equity, and Inclusion at Galen College. Dr. George is an executive board member for Critical Animal Studies (ICAS) and chief editor of *Journal for Critical Animal Studies*. With her focus on non-human animals, she's not sure how she got here, and a good magician never reveals their secrets . . . Soooo, who's up for saving the Land Crab?!

JAKOB R. GIBSON is a junior at Westminster College in Fulton, Missouri, majoring in political science and philosophy and religious studies. Having completed Ethics Training with Kim Wexler, he plans on attending law school following graduation.

TOBIAS T. GIBSON worked his way through college with Madrigal Security. He earned his PhD at Washington University in St. Louis, and is now the Dr. John Langton Professor of Legal Studies and Political Science at Westminster College, in Fulton, Missouri.

TIMOTHY J. GOLDEN is Professor of Philosophy and pre-law advisor at Walla Walla University in College Place, Washington. He's the author of *Frederick Douglass and the Philosophy of Religion: An Interpretation of Narrative, Art, and the Political* (2022). Tim earned his Juris Doctor from the Thurgood Marshall School of Law at Texas Southern University and his PhD in philosophy from the University of Memphis. He is a member of the Pennsylvania bar. He advises his pre-law students to follow Chuck's lead when it comes to law and Jimmy's lead when it comes to sibling relationships. In other words, his message to his students is: if you want to be a good lawyer, be like Chuck and if you want to be a good sibling, be like Jimmy!

F.E. GUERRA-PUJOL is an associate instructor of law at the University of Central Florida and an associate professor at the Pontifical Catholic University of Puerto Rico. He specializes in jurisprudence, legal history, and the law of ideas.

E.F. HAVEN is Philosophy Department Chair of Los Medanos College. His research orients around defining the undefinable, through postmodern philosophy and literature. He teaches course on philosophy through film and literature, philosophy of music, and postmodern humanities, among others. After graduate school he worked in a law firm, where he first understood that Kafka is closer to fact than fiction. He promises to share his secret to getting through it without ending up undercover as manager of a Cinnabon.

JOSHUA HETER is an Assistant Professor of Philosophy at Jefferson College in Hillsboro, Missouri. He is co-editor of *Westworld and Philosophy* (2019) and *The Man in the High Castle and Philosophy* (2017). Even if you aren't at all interested in sunk costs, you've already shelled out the money for this book, so you might as well read his chapter.

JOSHUA LUCZAK is an Assistant Professor of Philosophy at Singapore Management University. His primary research interests lie in philosophy of physics and philosophy of science, but he also likes to bullshit about other stuff, too.

CALLIE K. PHILLIPS is a Visiting Assistant Professor at College of Charleston. She completed her PhD at the University of Notre Dame. Like many philosophers, she's known for sharing her dissenting opinions with innocent bystanders and her general tendency to disagree with her peers. The jury is still out on whether her responses to those disagreements are rational.

SHANE J. RALSTON is a Teaching Fellow and the Dean at Wright College, Woolf University. He earned his PhD in Philosophy from the University of Ottawa, and has held posts at Mount Saint Mary's University, Western Colorado University, University of Montreal,

University of Maine, Pennsylvania State University and the American University of Malta. While his research interests include the philosophy of law, he has so far rationalized not going to law school and is instead studying ethics as a way to avoid a trip down Jimmy McGill's path of moral decline.

JAMES ROCHA is Associate Professor of Philosophy at Fresno State. One of James's main jobs is to serve as pre-law advisor. In that capacity, he has recommended numerous students to go to the University of American Samoa Law School. So far, none of them have gone there. He's currently co-editing a book on *Black Mirror*, and has published *The Ethics of Hooking Up* (2019) and *Joss Whedon, Anarchist?* (2019). Go Land Crabs!

JAMES CLARK ROSS is a PhD candidate at the University of Southampton and creator of the philosophy website *The Human Front*. His research has moved from physics to metaphysics, to metametaphysics, and now to meta-*Better Call Saul*. He is actively investigating what makes a good explanation. Demon- strably, he has no clear answers.

KRISTINA ŠEKRST is a lecturer at the University of Zagreb, an analyst who turns speculation into reality, and a philosopher who does the opposite. She is proficient in philosophy, logic, artificial intelligence, comparative linguistics, and many other words. In order to do research for this book, she devoured tons of chocolates in pajamas in front of the TV and called it science.

AMY WHITE is an Associate Professor of Philosophy at Ohio University. Dr. White spends much of her time teaching, researching, and writing about the philosophy of death and dying. However, mostly because of the spiffy uniforms and cheerful working environment, she is currently contemplating a career change into management at Cinnabon.

ABE WITONSKY is a Lecturer at Rowan University. He received his PhD from Temple University, in the city where Mike Ehrmantraut was a cop, Philadelphia. Go Eagles! During the pandemic he has been thinking about Lucretius's Symmetry Argument, and he thinks he may have a solution to it, one that assumes that personal identity is an illusion. Go Hume!

Index